SHAKESPEARE SURVEY

SHAKESPEARE SURVEY

AN ANNUAL SURVEY OF
SHAKESPEARIAN STUDY & PRODUCTION

8

EDITED BY

ALLARDYCE NICOLL

Issued under the Sponsorship of

THE UNIVERSITY OF BIRMINGHAM

THE UNIVERSITY OF MANCHESTER

THE SHAKESPEARE MEMORIAL THEATRE

THE SHAKESPEARE BIRTHPLACE TRUST

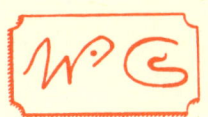

CAMBRIDGE
AT THE UNIVERSITY PRESS
1968

Published by the Syndics of the Cambridge University Press
Bentley House, 200 Euston Road, London, N.W.1
American Branch: 32 East 57th Street, New York, N.Y. 10022

Standard Book Number: 521 06421 x

Shakespeare Survey was first published in 1948. For the
first eighteen volumes it was edited by Allardyce Nicoll
under the sponsorship of the University of Birmingham,
the University of Manchester, the Royal Shakespeare
Theatre and the Shakespeare Birthplace Trust.

First published 1955
Reprinted 1968

First printed in Great Britain
at the University Printing House, Cambridge

Reprinted in Great Britain
by William Lewis (Printers) Ltd, Cardiff

PREFACE

Shakespeare's comedies have been accorded far less attention than his tragedies and history plays. There are signs, however, that the subject is one likely to be pursued more energetically in the immediate future, and towards this study the present volume of *Shakespeare Survey* presents several contributions—a survey of writings on the theme since 1900, an essay on the language of the comedies, several appreciations of individual plays, and two articles on production problems. Although more general in scope, the essay on Shakespeare's astral imagery has considerable bearing on the comedies as well as on the tragedies.

With these articles are associated others on a variety of themes. Of considerable importance is that which proves the date of *John a Kent* to be about 1589 instead of the hitherto accepted 1596; at first glance the six or seven year error may not seem of peculiar importance, but the implications of the discovery are far-reaching—possibly for an understanding of Shakespeare's career and certainly for our knowledge of early dramatic history. One of the most prominent interpreters of this early drama was Edward Alleyn, an appreciation of whose acting appeared in the last volume of *Survey*; the fact that Alleyn was active both on the theatre's stage and in the bear-garden's arena gives interest to the newly unearthed document relating to his bear-baiting interests. Another article in the last volume—'The New Way with Shakespeare's Texts'—finds a continuation here, with the study of a particular play.

For the next, the ninth, volume of *Shakespeare Survey* the central theme will be that of *Hamlet*. The tenth volume will be concerned particularly with 'The Roman Plays'.

A.N.

Contributions offered for publication in *Shakespeare Survey*, should be addressed to:
The Editor, *Shakespeare Survey*, The Shakespeare Institute (University of Birmingham),
Stratford-upon-Avon.

A*

CONTENTS

[Notes are placed at the end of each contribution. All line references are to the 'Globe' edition, and, unless for special reasons, quotations are from this text]

LIST OF PLATES

THE INTERPRETATION OF
SHAKESPEARE'S COMEDIES: 1900–1953

BY

JOHN RUSSELL BROWN

The boldest critic is apt to become modest when he writes of Shakespeare's comedies; he is afraid of taking a joke or a fancy too seriously. While the tragedies and histories seem to invite his serious attention, the comedies evade it; on the point of expounding the 'meaning' of a comedy, he hears a whisper, "But that's all one, our play is done." He may be sure that he has seen a "most rare vision", but he will prudently judge that it is "past the wit of man to say what dream it was". This modesty has often restricted criticism to praise and the expression of enjoyment.

Comparison with other comedies has encouraged this attitude. Dowden in his essay on 'Shakespeare as a Comic Dramatist' in Gayley's *Representative English Comedies*, I (1903), A. H. Thorndike in his *English Comedy* (1929), George Gordon in *Shakespearian Comedy* (1944), and many others, have dissociated Shakespeare's comedies from theories derived from Aristotle, Meredith, and Bergson; his plays are not 'corrective', and our laughter comes from a "gaiety... absolutely incompatible with contempt and indignation". Seeing that Shakespeare's comedy has no satiric meaning, many critics have presumed that it has no 'meaning' at all. In 1905, for example, Stopford Brooke wrote of *As You Like It*:

The solemn professor, the most solid moralist, will not be able to assert that Shakespeare wrote this play with a moral purpose, or from a special desire to teach mankind. He wrote it as he liked it, for his own delight.

Apparently Shakespeare's fancy flowered without any effort. T. M. Parrott in his *Shakespearean Comedy* (1949) thought that *As You Like It* was a comedy of escape, adapted from Lodge's *Rosalynde* with "little intellectual effort". John Palmer in his *Comic Characters of Shakespeare* (1946) found many "accidental" felicities, but, following Hazlitt, he believed that it is "too much to suppose all this intentional, but it very luckily falls out so". Yet critics have usually conceded that the comedies have a salutary effect. Thorndike advised his readers to "bask in the sunshine" of Shakespeare's romance and "simply watch the clouds roll by", but added that this "painless operation will fill your soul with poetry and a consciousness of duty well done". This curious moral value, like the 'gaiety' of Shakespeare's comedies, has seldom felt the touch of cold analysis. Its enduring quality is usually explained in most general terms, such as "Truth to Nature": "if we smile at the quaint forms of the hieroglyph of life", wrote Dowden, "we know that it has a deep and sacred meaning". And there the matter is apt to rest.

Some critics have gone farther, and the major successes in the study of the comedies since 1900 have been due to the belief that Shakespeare had an artistic purpose that we can try to analyse. We no longer think that the 'last plays' are the idle recreations of an old man, or that the 'dark' or 'problem' comedies are the mistakes of an irresponsible malcontent. These revaluations are so generally accepted that these two groups of comedies are usually discussed as distinct kinds of drama.

This retrospective article deals first with the interpretation of the comedies from the beginning of Shakespeare's career until *Twelfth Night*, and then considers the revaluation of the 'dark' or 'problem' comedies, leaving the 'last plays' for separate treatment in a future issue of *Shakespeare Survey*. At the outset, reference must be made to advances in our knowledge of the texts and their authority, and of the chronology of the plays, but no detailed discussion of these branches of scholarship is given here. Studies like Dover Wilson's argument for a re-writing of *A Midsummer Night's Dream* have important implications for the interpretation of the plays, but a just treatment would entail a detailed account of bibliographical and textual studies, and that is beyond the scope of this article. The omission is warrantable since F. P. Wilson has already written an account of 'Shakespeare and the "New Bibliography"' (*Studies in Retrospect*, 1945) which has been received with general assent and gratitude; Sir Walter Greg's *Editorial Problem in Shakespeare* (1942; 2nd edition 1951) has an unprecedented authority, and J. G. McManaway has reviewed 'Recent Studies in Shakespeare's Chronology' in *Shakespeare Survey*, 3 (1950).

I. The Comedies to *Twelfth Night*

A retrospective view of the study of Shakespeare's history plays or imagery reveals sustained critical and scholarly argument with progress marked by a few outstanding books. But, in the period under review, there is no clear line of development in the study of the early comedies: outstanding books have either been concerned with single plays or with specialized aspects of comedy, or else they have been followed by only a few scholars. A somewhat discursive method is needed to record what has been accomplished; there is much detailed work to report but little concerted effort.

Literary Influences

H. B. Charlton's *Shakespearian Comedy* (1938) is the most significant book on the early comedies. By tracing the evolution of Shakespeare's comedy from the forms of English, Italian and classical comedy, Charlton discovered a purpose and theme which the examination of individual plays might not have disclosed. Here Shakespeare is presented as a 'serious' comic dramatist, who sought to "elucidate the moral art of securing happiness". Charlton developed his thesis with learning and humane wisdom, and it is most unfortunate that part of his argument involves the generally unacceptable notion that *Troilus and Cressida*, *Measure for Measure* and *All's Well that Ends Well* were written before *Much Ado about Nothing*.

Literary influences have often been studied by other scholars. F. E. Schelling's *Elizabethan Drama* (1911), Thorndike's *English Comedy* (1929), and Parrott's *Shakespearean Comedy* (1949) sketch the main outlines.[1] Shakespeare's modification of the pastoral tradition was considered by Greg in his early *Pastoral Poetry and Pastoral Drama* (1906) and by E. Greenlaw in *Studies in Philology*, XIII (1916). Cornelia Coulter traced 'The Plautine Tradition in Shakespeare' in *The Journal of English and Germanic Philology*, XIX (1920), while, in his *William Shakespere's Five-Act Structure* (1947), T. W. Baldwin related one aspect of the earliest comedies to Terence and Lyly. In *Shakespeare Quarterly*, IV (1953), Northrop Frye showed how closely Shakespeare's comic characters conform to the basic types of classical and Renaissance drama. M. T. Herrick's *Comic Theory in the Sixteenth Century* (1950) will be of great use to later students in this field. At the beginning of this century, Italian influences were studied by J. W. Cunliffe and Winifred Smith in *Modern Philology*, IV (1907) and V (1908), and their lead was followed by M. J. Wolff in *Shakespeare Jahrbuch*, XLVI (1910) and O. J. Campbell in *Studies in Shakespeare, Milton and Donne* (1925), both of whom dealt specifically with the *Commedia dell'Arte*. Campbell showed that several details in *Love's Labour's Lost* and *The Two Gentlemen of Verona* might have been taken directly from the Italian, rather than through Lyly as it had been thought. In 1940 D. C. Boughner elaborated this, showing that no single literary source could account for Don Armado (*Studies in Philology*, XXXVII). Kathleen Lea's *Italian Popular Comedy* (1934) provides an admirably full basis for judging such questions. Frye's 'The Argument of Comedy' in *English Institute Essays* (1948) shows how the plots of both classical and Renaissance comedy involved not only the release of an individual but also a social reconciliation; Frye believed that this is a clue to the elusive argument or 'meaning' of Shakespeare's comedy.

In the same paper Frye stressed Shakespeare's debt to folk plays and ritual, to what he called the "drama of the green world". Traces of such a debt had already been noticed in Janet Spens's *Essay on Shakespeare's Relation to Tradition* (1916), and Thorndike had linked *As You Like It* with the Robin Hood plays (*Journal of English and Germanic Philology*, IV, 1902), but Frye made the further suggestion that the folk theme of death and revival is implicit in the forest scenes of early comedies, in the debate of winter and spring in *Love's Labour's Lost*, and in the 'renewal' of Hero. By stressing this theme in the early comedies, Frye linked them with the 'last plays', in which it is more generally recognized. Middleton Murry made a somewhat similar point in his *Shakespeare* (1936), suggesting that *The Merchant of Venice* made its appeal "to that primitive substance of the human consciousness whence folk-tales took their origin". Murry did not believe that Shakespeare consciously adopted such themes, but that he merely 'humanized' a given story.

The influence of English comedy has received comparatively little notice; Shakespeare's debt to Lyly was briefly discussed by R. W. Bond in his edition of Lyly (1902), and his debt to Greene by J. L. Tynan in *PMLA*, XXVII (1912). English romance has received its fullest treatment in E. C. Pettet's *Shakespeare and the Romance Tradition* (1949). On the analogy of characters in Sidney's *Arcadia*, Pettet argued that many of Shakespeare's young lovers are "simply pasteboard ...The tale is the thing, and Shakespeare never intended us to worry ourselves with their personalities and motives." But as early as Julia there are exceptions, and they become increasingly important; so Pettet concluded that Shakespeare had to 'reject' romance. This is a difficult position, for it implies that Shakespeare was at odds with his sources for *As You Like It* and *Twelfth Night*, and gives little reason why he should *choose* a romance theme when he really wished to 'reject' it. It seems wiser to agree with Charlton that Shakespeare was successfully developing his own kind of romance. The study of influences can only show what an artist started with; Shakespeare must be allowed to create the standards by which his own works are to be judged.

In recent years greater importance has been given to medieval influences. In a lecture delivered in 1916 Sir Israel Gollancz reminded his hearers that medieval drama was "a drama of allegory" and suggested that *The Merchant of Venice* might bear an allegorical interpretation. He developed this idea in further papers, and in 1931 A. W. Pollard gathered a group of them together in a posthumous volume called *Allegory and Mysticism in Shakespeare*. Already in the *Philological*

Quarterly, VIII (1929), J. D. Rea had suggested that the trial in *The Merchant* was indebted to the traditional Processus Belial, and later, in 'The Basis of Shakespearian Comedy' (*Essays and Studies*, III, 1950), Nevill Coghill claimed that the medieval conception of comedy as "a poem changing a sad beginning into a happy ending" was more formative for Shakespeare's comedies than the Renaissance conception concerned only with ridicule. He illustrated the medieval view from Vincent de Beauvais, Dante, and Webbe's *Discourse of English Poetry*, and proceeded to interpret *The Merchant* as an allegory or narrative 'image'. In 1951 M. C. Bradbrook's *Shakespeare and Elizabethan Poetry* claimed that "in some respects Shakespeare retained more of the medieval tradition...than the courtly poets had done".

Sources

Progress in the hunt for sources has been recorded in Sir Edmund Chambers's *William Shakespeare* (1930), in editions of individual plays, and in Selma Guttman's annotated bibliography, *The Foreign Sources of Shakespeare's Works* (1947), which covers the years 1904–40. In addition, Parrott's *Shakespearean Comedy* has brief, yet sane and fresh, accounts of the sources for each of the comedies. Fuller information is widely scattered. There have been some comprehensive studies, such as F. Sidgwick's *Sources and Analogues of A Midsummer Night's Dream* (1908), H. Conrad's study of *Twelfth Night* (*Englische Studien*, XLVI, 1912), and two studies of *The Merchant of Venice* by J. L. Cardozo and B. V. Wenger (*The Contemporary Jew* (1925) and *Shakespeare Jahrbuch*, LXV, 1929), but for the most part, each new suggestion has been the subject of a separate article. Of particular importance are: F. Brie's discussion of the relevance of Mundy's *Zelauto* to *The Merchant* (*Shakespeare Jahrbuch*, XLIX, 1913); C. T. Prouty's discussion of Beverly's *History of Ariodanto and Ieneura* and Whetstone's tale of Rinaldo and Giletta, and D. J. Gordon's of *Gli Duoi Fratelli Rivali*, as sources for *Much Ado* (*Studies in Philology*, XXXVIII–XXXIX, 1941–2); Dorothy H. Bruce's argument that *The Merry Wives* might be indebted to a tale from Riche's *Farewell to Military Profession* (*Studies in Philology*, XXXIX, 1942); and Dorothy F. Atkinson's suggestion that Wotton's *Cupid's Cautels* (1578) contained the basic plot for *The Two Gentlemen* (*Studies in Philology*, XLI, 1944). For some plays discussion of extant analogues has been curtailed by debate about conjectural lost source plays—notably *The Jew*, mentioned by Gosson, for *The Merchant* (S. A. Small offered a theoretical reconstruction in *Modern Language Review*, XXVI, 1931, but Parrott, later, rejected the whole idea), and an Italianate comedy for *The Merry Wives* (W. Vollardt discussed an Italian analogue in *Studien zur vergleichenden Literaturgeschichte*, VII, 1907, and O. J. Campbell distinguished Italianate episodes in Shakespeare's play in the University of Michigan's *Essays and Studies*, 1932).

In the early years of this century Raleigh's assumption that Shakespeare "spent no great care ...on the original choice of a theme, but took it as he found it, if it looked promising" (*Shakespeare*, 1907) would have found general acceptance, but now, as more secondary sources are discovered, this view is being superseded. C. T. Prouty's *The Sources of Much Ado* (1950) is evidence of this.[2] Despite Masefield's dissent, it has often been said that Shakespeare was interested only in Benedick and Beatrice and lighted on the Hero-Claudio story almost by accident, but, by inquiring exactly how Shakespeare's play differs from eighteen sources or analogues, Prouty has shown that his modifications of this story relate it significantly to that of

Benedick-Beatrice. So he re-interpreted the play: "Instead of romantic lovers we have two couples completely opposed to the romantic tradition. . . : for the one, love is a real emotion, for the other, a business arrangement." All critics would not agree with this analysis; one might complain that Prouty was insensitive to the charm of Claudio's verse, another that he saw the financial aspects of Claudio's match with too modern an eye, and others, with K. Neill (*Shakespeare Quarterly*, III, 1952), that he did not give due weight to the way in which Shakespeare strengthened the grounds on which Claudio believes the slander. But however these points are judged, Prouty's presentation of *Much Ado* as a carefully wrought unity may still stand: a study of sources has given a new basis for criticism.

Elizabethan Stage, Life and Thought

During the present century, critical writing on Shakespeare has been greatly enriched by an awareness of Elizabethan stage conditions, but studies devoted to particular problems of the comedies have been disappointing. G. P. Baker's *The Development of Shakespeare as a Dramatist* (1907) and Brander Mathews's *Shakespere as a Playwright* (1913) treat the early comedies as exercises in plotting, but illustrate Shakespeare's ingenuity rather than his imaginative conceptions. J. R. Moore's paper in the University of Wisconsin's *Shakespeare Studies* (1916) and Richmond Noble's *Shakespeare's Use of Song* (1923) are more constructive, showing that the songs are not mere *divertissements* but of structural and thematic importance. These studies emphasize the subtleties of Shakespeare's art, but W. Robertson Davies's *Shakespeare's Boy Actors* (1939) suggests that Beatrice and Rosalind are such simple creations that they are seldom anything but 'witty'. If Davies had considered some non-Shakespearian roles he would not have presumed, following Granville-Barker, that the use of boy actors *forced* Shakespeare to avoid voluptuous scenes. The need for more precise knowledge about Elizabethan stage conditions is illustrated by the revaluation of Touchstone in Leslie Hotson's *Shakespeare's Motley* (1952); this book must out-date all vague references to the stock-in-trade of fools, for Hotson has reminded us to ask 'What kind of fool?', or even 'Which fool?'. The Elizabethan theatre had complex traditions, and it is becoming increasingly clear that all inferences based on *general* statements about stage conditions must be suspect.

In 1930 two books relating to the comedies added to the growing prestige of historical criticism, or the attempt to see Shakespeare's plays as Elizabethans saw them. G. W. Keeton's *Shakespeare and His Legal Problems* sought to allay modern doubts about Portia's conduct in the trial of Antonio, by arguing that she adopts the "attitude of the Court of Chancery at the period", and M. W. Latham's *Elizabethan Fairies* showed, with full documentation, that Shakespeare created his own fairies—they are not members of an "active and powerful commonwealth with their traditional ruler" but the "innocuous and almost negligible attendants upon two literary or mythological sovereigns". Such inquiries are typical of many; for example, H. P. Pettigrew and Hardin Craig have argued that, for an Elizabethan, the mercenary marriages of Bassanio and Claudio could also be love-matches (*Philological Quarterly*, XVI, 1937, and *An Interpretation of Shakespeare*, 1948), while Z. S. Fink, O. J. Campbell and E. E. Stoll have related Jacques's melancholy to the affectations and disorders of his contemporaries (*Philological Quarterly*, XIV, 1935, *Huntington Library Bulletin*, VIII, 1935, and *Modern Language Notes*, LIV, 1939). Shylock became a *cause célèbre*: in an article of 1911 Stoll put the case for a comic Shylock, arguing from the text of *The Merchant* and from contemporary opinion of Jews and usurers (expanded in *Shakespeare Studies*, 1927); in his *Contemporary Jew in Elizabethan Drama* (1925), J. L. Cardozo tried to prove that Shakespeare had never seen a Jew and would present Shylock as a fabulous bogey, but subsequently C. J. Sisson established beyond doubt that Jews did live in Shakespeare's London and maintained elements of their ancient worship and way of life (*Essays and Studies*, XXIII, 1938); in the meantime, in *The Review of English Studies*, V (1929), A. Tretiak had related Shylock to the 1595 anti-alien riots and suggested that *The Merchant*, like the 'Ill Mayday' scene in *Sir Thomas More*, was a plea for toleration, and in *Modern Philology*, XXXIII (1935), J. W. Draper had taken up Stoll's point about usury, arguing that Shylock should be hated as a villainous usurer; S. A. Tannenbaum countered Draper's arguments on the grounds that Shakespeare left money for Judith at interest and that usury is not a dominant theme in the play (*Shakespeare Association Bulletin*, X, 1935). Such divided counsel argues for the complexity of Shakespeare's plays and the diversity of Elizabethan opinion, and, together with Latham's proof that Shakespeare could reject time-honoured traditions, it suggests that historical criticism should be used as a guide, not as a commander.

For the early comedies, historical criticism has been chiefly concerned with elucidating difficult characters or themes, but J. W. Draper has led an attempt to provide a commentary from Elizabethan writings on many characters who have not hitherto perplexed the reader or audience. This produced a series of articles on subjects like Orlando as a younger brother suffering from the effects of primogeniture, or Orlando as a sanguine lover under Jupiter's influence (*Philological Quarterly*, XIII, 1934, and *Modern Language Quarterly*, II, 1941), and two books, both by Draper—*The Humors and Shakespeare's Characters* (1945) and *The Twelfth Night of Shakespeare's Audience* (1950), which describes Olivia's household as an Elizabethan one "in transition from easygoing feudal paternalism...to the modern era of a more stringent economy". Draper pieces out the imperfections of Shakespeare's sociology with details from real and fictional case-histories, and finds that the play centres on Sir Toby and Malvolio, and that its theme is "social security, generally attained through marriage".

The study of Shakespeare's life and times has brought to light a number of allusions to real persons and events. The scent has proved strongest in *Love's Labour's Lost*, which seems to allude to a quarrel between Gabriel Harvey and Thomas Nashe, and to a group of poets under Raleigh's patronage, which may have been known as the 'School of Night'. In her study of the play (1936), Frances Yates added to the possible allusions and attempted a synthesis of the earlier work of scholars such as Warburton, Fleay, A. Acheson, H. C. Hart, R. Taylor and Sir Edmund Chambers. In detail, the discoveries are debatable, but the general direction of the satire seems reasonably clear. For a succinct and judicious account of the work on this subject, it is best to refer to Richard David's new Arden edition of 1951. In *Shakespeare versus Shallow* (1931) Hotson has argued that *The Merry Wives of Windsor* was written for the Garter Feast of 23 April 1597, and that Shallow and Slender are satiric portraits of William Gardiner and his stepson, William Wayte, with whom Shakespeare had been involved in a lawsuit. Hotson presented Shakespeare as a "personal satirist", and in this he belongs to a considerable group of scholars. In *As You Like It*, Jacques has been seen as a satire of Jonson or of Sir John Harington (A. Gray, *How Shakespeare 'Purged' Jonson*, 1928, and *The Times Literary Supplement*, 3, 10 and 17 January 1929), and the de Boys family as the family of that name from Weston-in-Arden, the Rainsfords, or the Howards (*Notes and Queries*, 26 May, 30 June and 1 September 1928, and *Review of English Studies*, XII, 1936). T. W. Baldwin suggested that *The Comedy of Errors* has allusions to the execution of William Hartley at Holywell on 5 October 1588 (*William Shakespeare Adapts a Hanging*, 1931) and E. I. Fripp that further allusions to a Star Chamber case were added for performance at Gray's Inn in 1594 (*Shakespeare: Man and Artist*, 1938). Prototypes for Malvolio have been seen in Sir Ambrose Willoughby, Sir William Knollys,[3] and Sir William Ffarington (*Book of Homage*, 1916; E. K. Chambers, *Shakespeare, a Survey*, 1925; and *Shakespeare Association Bulletin*, VII, 1932). There has even been an attempt to see Shylock as Philip Henslowe. In general such identifications have been received with caution.

Characters, Themes and Language

By far the most common way of studying Shakespeare's comedies is to study the characters in them. This has been encouraged by the constantly repeated dictum—Dowden, Baker, Charlton, Palmer, and Parrott have given their authority to it—that the heart of Shakespeare's comedy lies in his characters. So Cumberland Clark's studies of *The Merchant* and *As You Like It* (1927 and 1931) are mainly character studies, and John Palmer's *Comic Characters of Shakespeare* (1946) deals broadly with Shakespeare's conception of comedy. From this character study, some generalizations have emerged. Particularly since Raleigh's *Shakespeare* (1907), critics have stressed Shakespeare's tolerance and sympathy, his ability, as Palmer put it, to identify himself "imaginatively with all sorts and conditions of men and women". More fruitful perhaps, has been the realization that the characters are significantly related to each other—Palmer stressed this with regard to *As You Like It*. S. C. Sen Gupta's *Shakespearian Comedy* (1950) is probably the most straightforward attempt to create a theory of the comedy of character: Gupta believed that Shakespeare's "principal purpose" was to "portray character in all its complexity and depth" and that instead of inviting the audience to enter into the characters' emotions, as in the tragedies, Shakespeare "places his characters in certain situations in which they learn the deeper secrets of their own hearts"—it is a drama of 'contrasts', not of 'conflicts' within individuals.

This stress on characters has had some important consequences: *The Comedy of Errors*, *The Shrew* and *The Merry Wives* are neglected as mere farces; *A Midsummer Night's Dream* is considered to be *sui generis*, a 'symbolical' or masque-like play; Shylock, who appears in only five scenes, is made the centre of *The Merchant*; Hero and Claudio are thought to be of little interest to Shakespeare or the audience; the masque of Hymen is passed over as an unauthoritative accretion; Malvolio is sometimes allowed to play for tragedy; and the endings of *The Two Gentlemen*, *Much Ado* and *Twelfth Night* are called precipitous and unsatisfying. Few critics would doubt Shakespeare's increasing mastery of characterization or the universality of his sympathy, but there does seem to be something wrong with a theory of Shakespeare's comedy which implies that all his successes are so considerably blemished.

Critics who have dealt primarily with plot and construction have been less apt to find fault with the early comedies. The studies of *The Merchant* and *Twelfth Night* in W. H. Fleming's *Shakespeare's Plots* (1902) are early examples of this; Fleming was at pains to show Shakespeare's ingenuity, but he also showed the unity of the plays, how Viola, for instance, is the structural and thematic centre of *Twelfth Night*. Later M. P. Tilley elaborated this particular point in *PMLA*, XXIX (1914). In keeping with such studies, F. E. Schelling found the "interest of the comedies" to lie in their "kaleidoscopic groupings" and called them "comedies of incident rather than comedies of character". W. P. Ker's 'Note on the Form of Shakespeare's Comedies' (*Edda*, VI, 1916) also stressed the importance of contrasts between characters, and suggested that by this means Shakespeare developed his own form for comedy and history plays alike. A. Y. Fisher's *Introduction to a Study of Shakespearean Comedy, Part One* (1931) and W. Jacobi's *Form und Struktur der Shakespeareschen Komödien* (1937) are somewhat mechanical analyses, but Jacobi has useful comparisons with non-Shakespeare plays, and Fisher shows how the complications are of situation and plot rather than of character or character development.

The imagery, verse and style of the early comedies has been little studied except in general works such as those of Rylands, Caroline Spurgeon, Wilson Knight, and Clemen. Wilson Knight's *Shakespearian Tempest* (1932) has the most to say about the comedies. He has read them listening above all else for "poetic colour and suggestion", and although his views tend to be uncorrected by reference to plot, character, or situation, and sometimes give undue importance to trivial details—see, for example, his passage on the symbolic importance of the ducking of Falstaff—he has taught others to look for implicit value-judgements in passages which have often been dismissed as merely poetic or descriptive, and has shown a way to a new view of the coherence and thematic unity of the comedies. Granville-Barker's treatment of III, ii, of *The Merchant*, in his *Preface* to that play (1939), is an example of what might be achieved by a close study of verse and style; a fine sense of theatre and a sensitive appreciation of Shakespeare's dialogue has reinstated a scene which has sometimes been dismissed as frigid and over-fanciful. Hardin Craig's paper on 'Shakespeare's Bad Poetry' in *Shakespeare Survey*, 1 (1948) is a tactful and constructive attempt to find dramatic reasons for some archaic and comparatively unfinished verse in the comedies.

It remains to consider those critics who have tried to discover a theme which can be more closely defined than the presentation of life or nature. Some such attempts have been discussed already, as Charlton's study of comic form, the medieval approaches of Gollancz, Coghill and Frye, the investigation of sources by Prouty, and various kinds of structural analysis, but other critics have worked more directly, asking 'What are these plays about?' From the first it has been asked with regard to *Love's Labour's Lost*, where the plot is slight and the contrast of characters is obviously significant; in 1902, for example, Charlotte Porter and Helen A. Clarke stressed the importance of Mercade's entrance for the simple moral theme which they saw in the play (*Poet Lore*, XIV). John Masefield, in his *William Shakespeare* (1911), was more adventurous, and with a poet's insight tried to discover what interested Shakespeare in his plots; so he saw *As You Like It* as a play about the "gifts of Nature and the ways of Fortune", and *Twelfth Night* as a presentation of images of self-deception. Masefield was sympathetic towards the earliest comedies; for noting that vow-breaking is a "pole-star of dramatic action" at all stages of Shakespeare's career, he saw *The Two Gentlemen* as an exploration of the "moral blindness" that leads to vow-breaking. Such intuitive discernment is always open to question: for instance, H. T. Price differed widely from Masefield, believing that *The Two Gentlemen* is critical in tone and that Shakespeare "set out to prove Valentine a fool" (*Philological Quarterly*, XX, 1941). The critic's personal disposition has influenced such criticism: J. Smith took Touchstone seriously, and so he stressed the 'unromantic' elements of *As You Like It* (*Scrutiny*, IX, 1940; for another analysis, see *Philological Quarterly*, XXI, 1942). Max Plowman thought Shylock was the "enemy because he would check the free flow of money", and for him the theme of *The Merchant* was the "interdependence of human beings in civilised society" (*Adelphi*, 1931). Such judgements need to be examined in the light of historical criticism, close scrutiny of the texts, and comparison with the sources and with other plays in the canon.

There have been a few attempts to trace certain ideas through all the early comedies. Although C. H. Herford's *Shakespeare's Treatment of Love and Marriage* (1921) is directed towards problems of chronology, it was a first analysis of this theme. It makes the important point that usually Shakespeare was concerned only with the love and wooing that lead to marriage, and so "touched only the fringes of the Comedy of love"; the comedies do not make love ridiculous except through some fact or situation external to it. Stoll, in *Shakespeare's Young Lovers* (1937), made much the same general points, but, discussing *Romeo and Juliet* along with the comedies, added that most of Shakespeare's lovers in tragedy could be in comedy, and *vice versa*; as the comedy is external, so are the obstacles to happiness, for the lovers are "too naive, too sound and open-hearted, to get into serious inner complication". A. Harbage, in *Shakespeare and the Rival Traditions* (1952), made a comparative study of this theme, and suggested that Shakespeare was unusual in avoiding scenes dealing with fornication and adultery. Recognizing these qualities in the comedies, Charles Williams, in *The English Poetic Mind* (1932) and *Reason and Beauty in the Poetic Mind* (1933), suggested that the constancy and purity of Shakespeare's heroines is a 'figure' of his ideal of beauty; so the progression of the comedies is a poet's quest for beauty, his attempt to find a local habitation for an "undetermined sense of unknown modes of being".

Some other themes have been considered. In his *Shakespearean Comedy* (1930), A. Jha argued that none of the comedies is simply light-hearted, but that all contain an awareness of winter and rough weather. D. L. Stevenson's *Love-Game Comedy* (1946) discusses the theme of courtship in *Love's Labour's Lost*, *As You Like It* and *Much Ado*. Two recent studies from America consider moral themes; Harbage's *As They Liked It* (1947) suggests that the outcome of each comedy is the enjoyment of life in the simplest and most available ways, and D. A. Stauffer's *Shakespeare's World of Images* (1949) that the "golden comedies" image an ideal harmony "achieved through unselfish love". E. T. Sehrt has discussed the development of Shakespeare's idea of Mercy and Justice in *Vergebung und Gnade bei Shakespeare* (1952), and in *The Development of English Humor* (1952) L. Cazamian has found Shakespeare's humour to be "part of the English heritage, being a policy of wise self-repression in the quiet enjoyment of inevitable contrasts".

Few of these writers would presume that the theme of one of Shakespeare's early comedies can be simply described. But the attempt to analyse it increases one's awareness of his comic vision, and has been an important corrective to an exclusive interest in character portrayal. Some critics have thought it irrelevant to ask for themes or meanings, but "A jest's prosperity lies in the ear of him that hears it", and it is no discredit to the gaiety and humanity of Shakespeare's creations to analyse and compare. So a comedy which is appreciated yearly by audiences of many kinds may yet reserve the full prosperity of its jest and beauty to be, in the words of Muriel Bradbrook, the "last reward of Elizabethan studies".

II. The 'Dark', or 'Problem' Comedies

Since Dowden's *Shakespere: a Critical Study of his Mind and Art* (1875), *All's Well, Troilus and Cressida*, and *Measure for Measure* have been known as 'dark' comedies; they were thought to be the products of a dark period of Shakespeare's life, a period which found its proper expression in the intensity of tragedy. Few questioned the term 'dark' until W. W. Lawrence summed up fifteen years' work in his *Shakespeare's Problem Comedies* (1931). He preferred 'problem' because the plays raise, but do not resolve, important intellectual issues, and because he did not accept Dowden's biographical inferences (*Shakesperian Studies*, 1916). The *coup de grâce* to the assumption that these plays must reflect Shakespeare's personal sorrows was given by C. J. Sisson in his lecture on 'The Mythical Sorrows of Shakespeare' (1934). The darkness, cynicism, and bad workmanship which had been found in these plays seemed to be occasioned by plots and themes which were familiar to Lawrence in medieval analogues, and therefore he concluded that Shakespeare had adopted them willy-nilly from his sources. According to Lawrence, Shakespeare's task was "not so much the logical and realistic working out of a given situation as the psychological rationalization of a pre-existing story"; Shakespeare was not responsible for ridiculing love and honour in *Troilus*, for he "could no more have whitewashed Cressida than he could have whitewashed Richard the Third" (*Shakesperian Studies*, 1916). In this judgement Lawrence was supported by J. S. P. Tatlock and H. E. Rollins (*Sewanee Review*, XXIV, 1916, and *PMLA*, XXXII, 1917). *All's Well* had been considered cynical because of the impropriety of Helena's action, but in *PMLA*, XXXVII (1922) Lawrence argued that she is the heroine of a 'Clever Wench' type of 'virtue-story' which exalted the devotion of a woman to a man who treats her badly, and that the 'bed-trick' by which she makes Bertram lie with her is a virtuous act because it is so in the analogues. Lawrence also defended the psychological inadequacy of the ending, for like Cinderella and her prince, they must live happily ever after. His defence of *Measure for Measure* was two-fold: first, the Duke's ruse for substituting Mariana for Isabella presented no difficulty because betrothal conferred marriage rights, and secondly, the Duke's policies and omniscience, the bed-trick, and Angelo's conversion "must be viewed as belonging in the realm of story-telling, not as serious discussion of moral issues, or as a transcript of life". Here Lawrence was supported by R. W. Chambers in 'The Jacobean Shakespeare and *Measure for Measure*' (1937).

By reminding critics that drama is not always directly realistic, Lawrence helped to stimulate a new interest in these comedies. His attempt to relieve Shakespeare of responsibility for a wanton Cressida and his assumption that his aims were similar to those of the authors of the non-dramatic sources were less fortunate, but provoked immediate and useful disagreement. In 1922 M. Hewlett pointed out that since there is no recognition of Helena's virtue in the final scene of *All's Well*, the play is not a true 'virtue-story' and requires a different response from that appropriate to Boccaccio's version (*The Nineteenth Century*). Murry's *Shakespeare* (1936) makes this point more generally, finding a 'harmony of values' in Boccaccio but not in Shakespeare. G. F. Taylor argued that Lawrence had not explained why Shakespeare's *Troilus* is stronger in revulsion than any other treatment of the theme (*PMLA*, XLV, 1930). Such disagreement forced the question of Shakespeare's dramatic intentions into prominence, and critics, freed from the need to interpret the plays solely in terms of realistic character and situation, offered new explanations.

All's Well has been seen as a play dealing with abstract issues. In 1938 Fripp equated Helena with 'Grace' and saw Parolles and Lavache as morality figures, and, in 1950, Muriel Bradbrook stressed the Elizabethan theme of 'true' nobility and its relation to nobility by birth (*Review of English Studies*, n.s., 1). But few critics believe that it is a successful play; E. M. W. Tillyard, in his influential book on *Shakespeare's Problem Plays* (1950), found that the dramatic outcome was that Bertram merely "yields to the pressure of numbers", while Miss Bradbrook concluded that the "social problem" conflicts with the "human problem" which Shakespeare drew forth from his plot. Tillyard defended certain passages of archaic verse on the grounds that Shakespeare, for the sake of his moral theme, was "deliberately evading drama and substituting ritual and cloudy incantation", but the last scene, where Shakespeare refuses the poetic possibilities of the situation and greatly complicates the action, remains virtually undefended by those who see a moral in the play. Stoll, however, was satisfied with it, for he thought that the play was designed so that the audience could relish "a fine and delicate character" in an indelicate situation (*From Shakespeare to Joyce*, 1944).

New critical inquiry has rescued *Troilus and Cressida* from being regarded as one of the least successful of Shakespeare's plays, with no unity and too much undramatic and cynical reflection. The new Variorum edition of 1953 brings together a great deal of work on the play; G. F. Reynolds has written on the staging, Alice Walker and P. Williams on the relation and authority of the texts, H. N. Hillebrand on the recurrent psychological terms, and W. Keller and R. K. Presson on the sources. But while many critics agree on the interest of the play, there is considerable disagreement on its interpretation. In *The Wheel of Fire* (1930), Wilson Knight saw its meaning in a contrast; the Trojans stand for "human beauty and worth", and the Greeks for the "bestial and stupid elements of man". For him, Troilus is the centre of interest, and his love, "hallowed" through its constancy, is glorified. Knight was one of the first to sense a passionate feeling in this play, but his analysis has not been generally accepted: for example, Pettet believed that *Troilus* was written to expose the "shallowness and sham" of romantic love and honour, and Presson that each of the Trojans is "blinded" by concepts "unsanctioned by Reason" (*Shakespeare and the Romance Tradition*, and *Philological Quarterly*, XXXI, 1952). Another, though related, view was stated by D. A. Traversi (*Scrutiny*, VII, 1938) and, with some modification, by Tillyard; for them both parties are criticized, the Trojans for following a "false idealism", founded only on instinct, and the Greeks for following "judgment", while being out of touch with the instinctive sources of action. Traversi supported his thesis with subtle analysis of language and verse, and argued that *Troilus* was a new kind of play, expressing unresolved contradictions.

It has often been said that *Troilus* is different in tone from any other Shakespeare drama. In 1928 Peter Alexander suggested that it was not written for the Globe, but for one of the Inns of Court (*The Library*, IX). O. J. Campbell went further, and, in his *Comicall Satyre and Shakespeare's Troilus and Cressida* (1938), argued that it was based on the satirical drama of Marston and Jonson. Some incidental satire of Jonson had long been seen in the person of Ajax (the view was defended by W. Elton, *PMLA*, LXIII, 1948, and denied by Hotson, *Shakespeare's Sonnets Dated*, 1949), but as F. P. Wilson's *Elizabethan and Jacobean* (1945) points out, Campbell did not account for the extent to which our feelings are engaged, nor can Ulysses be accepted as a 'sound' commentator on the action. The strangeness of the play was otherwise accounted for by

T. W. Baldwin in *Shakespeare Studien, Festschrift für Heinrich Mutschmann* (1951); he saw it as the first part of a two- or three-part chronicle play about the downfall of Troy, and hinted that the second part was needed to give proper perspective for the first.

Another interpretation has developed from noting the appearance-reality theme. Williams's *English Poetic Mind* (1932) sees the crux of the play in Troilus's speech in v, ii, "...this is, and is not, Cressid"—all that he had thought was fair has shown itself to be foul. Conflicting critical opinions about the characters show how treacherous appearances are in this play, and L. C. Knights in *Scrutiny*, xviii (1951) has considered the whole as an investigation of the world of appearance—an investigation that leaves the audience involved in the labyrinth. It used to be said that the indecisive ending was a sign of Shakespeare's lack of interest in his theme or of textual patchwork, but now it is generally praised: it is appropriate to the appearance-reality theme, to Miss Ellis-Fermor's idea that Shakespeare was giving dramatic form to an impression of chaos (*The Frontiers of Drama*, 1945), and to Tillyard's belief that he was presenting two complementary and flawed attitudes to life.

Measure for Measure has also been much studied since 1930; F. E. Budd and R. H. Ball have worked on the sources, and D. P. Harding has usefully examined Lawrence's defence of the bed-trick, showing that betrothal *de praesenti* was not as good as marriage in the eyes of the Church or of those laws which condemned Claudio (*Journal of English and Germanic Philology*, xlix, 1950). The play has continued to puzzle critics, and some, like Williams and Tillyard, have discerned an abrupt change of tone and technique half-way through. Others, however, have seen it as a clear Christian parable. Wilson Knight found a "studied explication" of the Gospel injunction "Judge not, that ye be not judged..."; when Mariana prays for Angelo's life, Isabella is softened and, like Angelo, is changed, and this is marked by marriage with the Duke, the marriage of understanding with purity. R. W. Chambers found no fault of rigour in Isabella, nor the inconsistency of characterization which Quiller-Couch had noticed (New Cambridge ed., 1922), and saw the play as a parable of forgiveness culminating in Isabella's prayer for Angelo. Muriel Bradbrook suggested that it might be named 'The Contention between Justice and Mercy', and she was supported by Elizabeth M. Pope, who glossed the action with extracts from Elizabethan writings on justice and mercy (*Review of English Studies*, xvii, 1941, and *Shakespeare Survey*, 2, 1949). R. W. Battenhouse saw it as an allegory of Christian atonement (*PMLA*, lxi, 1946). For some critics, this 'Christian' interpretation left nothing to be explained, but others believed that much was being left carefully unsaid. Clifford Leech voiced their uneasiness in *Shakespeare Survey*, 3 (1950); he believed that the Christian colouring is only intermittent, and complained that the characters who were supposed to be the spokesmen for orthodoxy are "too shifty, too complacent, too ignorant of their own selves, and...are nowhere explicitly reproved".

Other interpretations have been suggested. In 1912 S. J. Mary Suddard thought the play was a study in Puritanism (*Studies and Essays*); in the Duke, Shakespeare censures a slack morality, in Angelo shows the danger of giving supreme power to Puritans, and in Isabella presents Puritanism in its most favourable aspect—to plead for Claudio is against her creed, yet she gives in and so pleads for Christ's mercy and grace. L. C. Knights saw this theme of liberty and restraint in more general terms, and suggested that the 'moral' was the need for self-knowledge and sympathy (*Scrutiny*, x, 1942; this contains a rejoinder by Leavis). The critical tone of some passages led O. J. Campbell to see the play as an unsuccessful attempt to write a second comical satire (*Shake-*

speare's Satire, 1943), but W. Empson more subtly suggested that Shakespeare wrote an ostensibly romantic comedy while "keeping the audience's teeth slightly but increasingly on edge", and thereby expressed his feeling that "the whole business of public justice is fatuous and hideous, whether compared to the mercy of Christ or the humanity of private life" (*Southern Review*, IV, 1938; reprinted in *The Structure of Complex Words*, 1951). Clearly it is not an easy play, and, at the end of the most recent and sustained study, Mary Lascelles has suggested that Shakespeare's "unconfined thought" has transcended the bounds of the story he used (*Shakespeare's Measure for Measure*, 1953).

Critical interest in these three plays continues. Possibly an age of anxiety overestimates their success and relative importance among Shakespeare's works, but it is certainly true that no previous age has appreciated them so fully.

NOTES

1. Much of the work in this field has been summed up in Madeleine Doran's comprehensive *Endeavors of Art: A Study of form in Elizabethan Drama* (1954).

2. Kenneth Muir's 'Pyramus and Thisbe: A Study in Shakespeare's Method', *Shakespeare Quarterly*, V (1954), discusses Shakespeare's use of his sources. Muir promises a book giving a general account of Shakespeare's sources.

3. Hotson's *The First Night of Twelfth Night* (1954), published after this article went to press, supports this allusion.

B*

COMIC FORM IN *MEASURE FOR MEASURE*[1]

BY

NEVILL COGHILL

I

Long before there was any inkling that Shakespeare had ever written a 'dark' comedy, *Measure for Measure* had been judged morally shocking, a play horrible in its tragedy, disgusting in its comedy[2] and scandalous in its conclusion,[3] one that gave

> advantage
> To stubborn critics, apt without a theme
> For depravation.

Since the discovery of a working Shakespeare chronology this view has strengthened, for the play falls squarely in the 'Tragic Period' thereby revealed; it lies deep in what Dowden called 'The Depths'. The turbid sexual anguish, the manifold treacheries, the squalor and injustice of the play found in this fact their explanation.

Then came a tendency to account for Shakespeare's seven-year contemplation of Evil in terms of some disaster in his private life, some huge personal despair, of which the plays (it was thought) might be in some sense a record; and, after that, it seemed that the despairs of our own age chimed in so readily with those attributed to him that it was almost as if a full understanding of these plays was a privilege reserved for the sorrowful century in which we live.

The most eloquent expression of this view known to me is that of Dover Wilson; *Measure for Measure* he says[4]

is written in much the same key as *Point Counter Point* and others of Mr Aldous Huxley's novels. The hatred of sentimentalism and romance, the savage determination to tear aside all veils, to expose reality in its crudity and hideousness, the self-laceration, weariness, discord, cynicism and disgust of our modern 'literature of negation' all belonged to Shakespeare about 1603.

More recently Clifford Leech, in a passage hardly less stimulating, has written of *Measure for Measure*[5]

We are disturbed by it, not because its Christian doctrine is strict and uncompromising...but because the very spokesmen for orthodoxy in the play repel us by their actions and the manner of their speech.

And he particularly instances the antipathy which the Duke has aroused in many readers during the past hundred years; "We should note" he adds

that he claims to know Angelo's mind by virtue of being Angelo's confessor. One does not have to be deeply religious to be affronted by this piece of impertinence.

These are ideas of a kind important to producers, and when met with should be applied to a production, real or imaginary, to see their implications in detail.

Now the leading principle of *Point Counter Point* is the discovery of base, odious or imbecile motives in every living person, and a producer who applies this to *Measure for Measure* will find the text wonderfully patient of such a treatment. He will discover in the Duke an unctuous fraud who abdicates his already neglected duties in order to play the unsavoury part of eaves-dropper; a man who sneaks, under the guise of holiness, from one dark corner to another, smelling out other peoples' consciences. The producer will be careful to note what Lucio says of this Duke[6] and will contrive in some of these dark corners a glimpse of him at grips with a mouthing beggar of fifty, and the ring of a ducat in a clack-dish.

Angelo will rise before him in the image of puritanism, lubricity, blackmail, treachery, hypocrisy and injustice; Isabella will be distinguished by frigidity and sex-nausea, Mariana by a lush but spinsterly uxoriousness and Claudio by plain cowardice. Pompey Bum, Abhor-son and Mistress Overdone will seem figures out of a Hogarthian nightmare; Elbow and Mr Froth will take their place among the imbeciles, where, by a little forcing of his disposition—some ready producer's trick, a stammer, perhaps, or a repeated nervous tick—Escalus may join them. The spokesman for orthodoxy—the orthodoxy of disillusion—will of course be Lucio.

A producer will find some difficulty over the scene between the Friar-Duke and Juliet[7] for although it shows his hateful impertinence in searching Juliet's heart under the false pretences so well noted by Leech, that gain to a *Point Counter Point* production may well be lost in the beauty of Juliet's humility and penitence. One dare not risk the suggestion that she is holy; in *Point Counter Point* holiness belongs only to a late Beethoven quartet.[8] It will probably be better to cut the scene. As Bottom so truly says, "there are things in this comedy...that will never please".

If decor is used there will be opportunity for lurking horror and deformity in the brothel-streets and prison-cells of Vienna, sharply contrasted with the puffy opulence of ducal baroque. Much can be done by a sinister lighting-plot.

But it will be in the action and grouping that a sensitive producer will achieve his greatest effects. He needs scarcely to be prompted, in the sermon he is preaching, to show the prudish savagery of Isabella in her shameful scene with the quivering Claudio, for who (properly self-lacerated) could hope for a better chance to show the repellent selfishness of chastity? But it may be well to remind him that really imaginative handling and careful rehearsal will be needed if the full flavour of disgust is to be elicited from the final scene. It is not enough that it should seem the cynical get-out of a bored dramatist; that would do justice neither to Shakespeare nor to Huxley. It is the supreme moment; for the infamies of sex are at last to receive their crown in matrimony. Here he should show us the reunited Claudio and Juliet, speechless (as Shakespeare left them) and in recoil, standing at gaze in mutual loathing, after the sin, the terror and the disgrace that they have brought upon each other and that now irrevocably joins them; Angelo, freed from death only to be fettered for ever to Mariana's infatuation, eyeing her with freshly-poisoned memories of a certain "garden circummured with brick"; the Duke, hot to enjoy what Angelo had been cheated of, though it cannot be denied to *him*, and Isabella forgetting her ambition to be a prioress in the sudden certainty of becoming a duchess. Lastly there would be Lucio, the only likable fellow in the play, compelled to marry a punk, Kate Keep-Down. This would be lofty. But would it be Shakespearian?

There are certainly some who would think not, who would even think it

> worse than worst
> Of those, that lawless and incertain thought
> Imagine howling.

It is indeed the lawlessness and incertainty of the cynical and pessimistic view of this play that call for attention. There seems nothing to support it but a romantic assertion of private moral or sentimental attitudes, plus a heavy reliance on the fact that the play falls within the so-called 'Tragic Period'. The argument from chronology, however, can lead by a series of doubtful premises and false syllogisms into many dangerous superstitions; such as that Shakespeare's tragic vision, being concerned with self-torture and waste,[9] is a vision of disillusion and despair; that Art is Self-expression [10] and that therefore a man capable of such a vision must himself be in a condition of disillusion and despair; that such a man will eschew comedy altogether unless he can find in it a further means to vent his edifying blasphemy at the Abyss and die, or a chance to extend Timon's welcome to his theatre-patrons:

> Uncover, dogs, and lap.

II

But if a 'dark' interpretation of *Measure for Measure* is a lawless conjecture, what is the alternative? May we trust the Christian context to which it has been so movingly referred by other critics—Wilson Knight,[11] the late R. W. Chambers,[12] Roy Battenhouse [13] and Miss Pope? [14] Clifford Leech thinks not; in the article to which I have referred he writes:

> This Christian colouring is...not more than intermittent in the play: it wells up, as it were, from Shakespeare's unconscious inheritance, and it does not determine the play's characteristic effect.

Let us look at this Christian colouring. Wilson Knight has given us chapter and verse from the Gospels; he declares the plot to be an inversion of the parable of the unmerciful servant in Matthew xviii. The central theme, according to him, is taken from the Lord's Prayer: *Forgive us our debts as we forgive our debtors.* According to R. W. Chambers it is *Judge not; for with what measure ye mete it shall be measured to you again.* It does not appear that Chambers had read Knight's article, yet he seems to have reached an almost identical conclusion as to the main theme. He has also shown how Shakespeare removed the barbarities from his source in *Promus and Cassandra* in fashioning from it *Measure for Measure*, so as to fit the story as far as possible to Elizabethan notions of Christian decency. Battenhouse discerns a congruence between the Duke's actions and the Incarnation, Second Coming and Judgement of Our Lord. Miss Pope has shown that the ideas of rulership and justice ambient in the play exhibit Shakespeare as a man clarifying the ordinary Christian doctrine of the Renaissance in such matters. All the criteria offered by these critics can claim a high degree of objectivity, and can be verified on something more solid than a private moral pulse.

But if these claims are true, the Christian colouring of the play can hardly be "no more than intermittent"; on the contrary it must certainly "determine the play's most characteristic effect";

it must even be pervasive, for to be pervasive is the nature of the theme in any great work of art. Leech wisely bids us beware of "imposing a pattern on Shakespeare's thought"; and so we must. But what if the pattern is really there? May we not recognize it? He also seems to commend in the play "a complexity of meaning...that enables the theatrical producer to aim at a new 'interpretation'". But, as it seems to me, what is here involved is not complexity but contradiction. We have two sharply-defined and widely-held views diametrically opposed to each other; at least one of them must be wrong, and by 'wrong' I mean 'hostile or contrary to Shakespeare's understanding of it'—an understanding which it is often the excellent foppery of producers to ignore, or to dismiss as unascertainable.

The evidences advanced, and for which considerable objectivity can be claimed, are pointers towards an understanding of the play which is at least likely to have been his, and it is my hope that by bringing the test of comic form to bear upon it, that likelihood will seem a certainty.

III

In an essay called 'The Basis of Shakespearian Comedy'[15] I attempted, not long ago, to establish certain things concerning the nature of comic form, as it was understood at Shakespeare's time. Since I cannot presume that essay to be at all well known, I am obliged to recapitulate the gist of it as briefly as I may. I showed that there existed in the sixteenth century two opposed conventions as to the nature of comedy; the first, then losing ground among the critics, was the medieval, defined toward the middle of the thirteenth century by Vincent de Beauvais[16]

> *Est autem comædia poesis, exordium triste, laeto fine commutans.*

This is comedy as Dante, Chaucer and Lydgate knew and understood it. *The Divine Comedy* was its greatest exemplar, and it is to Dante also that we owe a very full exposition of its nature, in his famous letter to Can Grande.

Such a comedy, then, has this known, certain and necessary shape, that it starts in trouble and ends in joy, and this is the convention manifestly followed by Shakespeare in almost every instance, as, in that essay, I tried to show.

The other and opposed convention, though in fact of equal antiquity with the medieval form (for both, as I showed, go back to the Latin grammarians of the fourth century) first came to the fore at the Renaissance and may be defined in the words of Sir Philip Sidney:[17]

> Comedy is an imitation of the common errors of our life, which he representeth in the most ridiculous and scornefull sort that may be; so that it is impossible that any beholder can be content to be such a one.

This was the tradition of comedy embraced by Ben Jonson.

To return, however, to Dante. He explains that his work (the *Paradiso*) is a comedy and is to be interpreted allegorically, according to the usual medieval fourfold scheme; and he gives us an example of how to do this: (*a*) The Children of Israel (he reminds us) went from servitude in Egypt to the milk and honey of the Promised Land; their story is therefore a comedy as defined. (*b*) So we, in our redemption made through Christ, passed from the bondage of ignorance to the light of the Gospel. (*c*) So the soul, in its exchange of the state of sin for a state of grace, is also to be understood in the image of the Exodus. (*d*) So the righteous pass at death from this body of corruption into eternal glory. Comic form was, in other words, a picture of ultimate reality, as Dante knew it. Comic form was cosmic form. Its heart was love.[18]

Shakespeare's comedies also begin with trouble, end in joy and are centred in love, albeit human love. The joyful *solemnitas* of marriage is an image of happiness that ends his comedies almost as invariably as death ends a tragedy. Unless *Measure for Measure* be an exception in his use of this image, there are no exceptions. Wherever else it comes in his comedy, it betokens joy.

To draw argument from allegory, we must follow, as Dante did, the narrative movement. It is here that we will find the pattern, if there is a pattern, that we are not to impose. Yet—and I apologize for so long and perhaps so *triste* an *exordium* of my own—I must first make a little clearer what I believe Dante would have meant by allegory in the context of this play, and I gladly begin with a quotation from F. P. Wilson on the subject:[19]

The non-naturalistic temper of Shakespeare's plays admits always an element of the morality play, though this is more disguised with him than with his contemporaries because of his unparalleled gift of creating character.

Wilson continues by instancing the Duke as a "presiding if enigmatical Providence", who, had he remained on that level, would have been of "little interest"—Providence worsted by Levity or marrying itself to Chastity, and so forth.

This criticism is eminently just, so far as it goes; but it does not wholly fit the case, for it interprets the allegory on the moral plane only and not in the fuller medieval senses. Morality Plays are the one-stringed fiddles of allegory, deficient in all other tones. *Measure for Measure* is in an older and better tradition than any mere morality play; it is, as Wilson Knight has pointed out, in the tradition of the parables of Christ, that is, something fully human, like the narrative of the Prodigal Son (*sensus litteralis*), which has moral overtones easily perceived (*sensus moralis*) and pictures a typical human situation in which we find the likeness of our own personal situations (*sensus allegoricus*). In short it shows a human world in an eternal situation, not a series of abstractions in a contrived predicament, like a Morality Play or like the comedies of Ben Jonson.

In our own literature Chaucer showed the way to this kind of allegory; he too excelled in the gift of creating character and could intermix allegory with comedy upon occasion; the *locus classicus* is the Clerk's Tale of Patient Griselda, one of the most tenderly and barbarously human in all Chaucer, yet with overtones on every plane:

> This storie is seyd, nat for that wyves sholde
> Folwen Grisilde as in humilitee,
> For it were importable, though they wolde;
> But for that every wight, in his degree,
> Sholde be constant in adversitee
> As was Grisilde; therfor Petrark wryteth
> This storie, which with heigh style he endyteth.

> For, sith a womman was so pacient
> Un-to a mortal man, wel more us oghte
> Receyven al in gree that god us sent;

> For greet skile is, he preve that he wroghte.
> But he ne tempteth no man that he boghte,
> As seith seint Iame, if ye his pistel rede;
> He preveth folk al day, it is no drede,
>
> And suffreth us, as for our excercyse,
> With sharpe scourges of adversitee
> Ful ofte to be bete in sondry wyse;
> Nat for to knowe our wil, for certes he,
> Er we were born, knew al our freletee....

Now this is like, and it is not like, *Measure for Measure*. It is like it in that both are stories of human testing, trial or assay, seen in relation to both God and man. It is unlike in that the reason given by Chaucer for God's testing us is that we must exercise our virtues as an athlete exercises his muscles, not to know if they are there, but to keep them fit. In *Measure for Measure* the reason is the one given in the Sermon on the Mount:

Let your light so shine before men that they may see your good works and glorify your Father which is in heaven.

Or, to use the Duke's words:

> Heaven doth with us as we with torches do,
> Not light them for themselves; for if our virtues
> Did not go forth of us, 'twere all alike
> As if we had them not.

Now these words govern the entire action of the play, which pictures the world as a place where all are continually liable to tests, and some to tests increasingly severe, that they may show their virtues. Isabella and Angelo are tested to the core.

Of course the Duke knows, before the play begins, that there is some reason to suspect Angelo's integrity; indeed he gives him the strongest possible hint that he knows of his not wholly creditable past when he tells him that one who has observed his history could unfold his character. The hint wears a polite veil of ambiguity, but it is a warning to him none the less: [20]

> There is a kind of character in thy life,
> That to the observer doth thy history
> Fully unfold.

Angelo's mettle is to be tested. Of course he falls at the first fence, though I believe the point has not been noted. He falls at the test of his faithfulness in elementary matters of justice, when he is to adjudicate in the case of Mr Froth and Pompey Bum; instead of doing his duty he exhibits the insolence of office, refuses the tedium of sifting evidence and departs with a pun and a flick of cruelty, leaving the patient Escalus to do his work for him:

> This will last out a night in Russia,
> When nights are longest there: I'll take my leave,
> And leave you to the hearing of the cause;
> Hoping you'll find good cause to whip them all.

Then comes the greater testing when he is confronted by the pleading beauty of Isabella, and the anguish of his spirit expresses itself in two soliloquies of a quality not inferior to those of Hamlet. From then on he continues to fail and fall under successive test, more and more hideously up to the instant of discovery.

It was the action of the devious Lucio in persuading Isabella to intercede for her brother with Angelo that had brought him to this pass; it also brought Isabella to the test of her chastity. The fact that she resisted in that brought her to the further test of her courage: she had to tell her condemned brother that he must die. She could easily have lied to him, need never have told him of the one condition upon which life had been promised to him. But she preferred to tell the truth. In these two tests she is seen to triumph; but, as Langland has said,[21]

> chastite with-outen charite . worth cheyned in helle.

She has still, as Chambers has so well noted,[22] to be searched for charity of heart. When the time comes, she is found to have that also; perhaps she learnt it during the play.

Isabella is in turn a means of testing Claudio. Does he value her soul above his own life? At first he does, nobly responding   Thou shalt not do't.

He had been prepared for this test by the Friar Duke, who had sought to give him what he needed most—the cardinal virtue of fortitude—but he could not hold on to it. Down he went at the third step, like St Peter when he left the boat and tried to walk on the waters. He does not drown, for the Duke steps in to save him with a white lie, so offensive even to those not deeply religious:

> Son, I have overheard what hath past between you and your sister. Angelo had never the purpose to corrupt her; only he hath made an assay of her virtue.... I am confessor to Angelo, and I know this to be true; therefore prepare yourself to death.

The Duke has been criticized by some for preaching a stoical rather than a Christian sermon; yet John Donne was a Christian preacher, and one has only to finger through his sermons to find passages of no less stoical admonition on the contempt of life:

> Wee are all conceived in close Prison; in our Mothers wombes, we are close Prisoners all; when we are borne, we are borne but to the liberty of the house; Prisoners still, though within larger walls; and then all our life is but a going out to the place of Execution, to death. Now was there ever any man seen to sleep in the Cart, between New-gate, and Tyborne? between the Prison, and the place of Execution, does any man sleep? And we sleep all the way....[23]

The white lie remains an offence to critics, but apparently without evil effect in the play. Indeed it sets the stricken Claudio upon his feet again, for he replies to it:

> Let me ask my sister pardon. I am so out of love with life, that I will sue to be rid of it.

He is safely back in the boat.

Meanwhile Juliet has also been put to test in the exquisite scene I have already mentioned as unsuited to a *Point Counter Point* production. She responds with what by Christian standards, or by whatever standards may be invoked, is the answer of a soul in a state of grace:

> I do repent me, as it is an evil,
> And take the shame with joy.

These are the principal strands in the pattern of testing that runs through the play, though lesser soundings are made among other characters; Pompey Bum is brought to the admission that his trade of pimp "does stink in some sort", Barnardine demands more time to prepare himself for death, and gets it, and even Mistress Overdone reveals in herself a natural charity; she had looked after Lucio's bastard, begotten on Kate Keep-Down, for a year and a quarter at her own expense. These are not figures from the pit. Not one of them would necessarily qualify for the *Inferno*. Pompey Bum indeed gives every sign of running straight when given a fresh chance as an under-hangman; economics, not *malitia* had made a sinner of him. He may be murky, but Hell is murkier.

To return to the narrative design; we have seen who the tested are. Who is the tester? In all cases, sometimes directly and sometimes at one or two removes, it is the Duke. He is the *primum mobile* of the play.

What else do we know of him? We know that he had long since ordained laws the breach of which he has never himself punished, because his personal intervention would seem 'too dreadful' (I, iii, 34); he has withdrawn himself into invisibility from the world of which he is the Lord, but remains as it were omnipresent and omniscient, in the guise of a priest, seeking to draw good out of evil; he reappears "like power divine" (v, i, 372) in righteousness, majesty and judgement in the last scene. It is not very difficult to see what is here suggested on the anagogical plane, without taking away a particle of the Duke's humanity on the literal plane. One has to think both thoughts at once, to be 'multi-conscious' as S. L. Bethell has so well explained.[24]

Nevertheless that does not mean one is allowed to think any thoughts one pleases; there must be a discipline in these things and it is especially needed when the actions of God are anthropomorphically represented. For instance, if we say 'underneath are the everlasting arms', the human metaphor carries no risk of misinterpretation; but if we say with the psalmist "God is about my path and about my bed and spieth out all my ways", misinterpretation is easy. We mean it as an image for an omnipresent, an omniscient and a divine care, but it is open to any *fâcheux*, willing to misunderstand us, to seize on the irrelevant and unintended aspect of the anthropomorphic image, and say "So He's a spy, is He? Hiding behind the curtains to catch you out, a Fantastical Duke of Dark Corners!" And that is precisely what Lucio does call him.

The twisting of interpretation is a very ancient form of tiresomeness; even Langland has a word for those learned clerks and lewd fellows who like to show their wit at dinner by impious theological ingenuity:[25]

> Atte mete in heor murthe . whon munstrals beoth stille,
> Thenne telleth thei of the trinite . hou two slowen the thridde ...
> Thus thei drauelen on heore deys . the deite to knowe,
> And gnawen god with the gorge . whan her gutte is fulle.

It is of course intellectually possible to twist the story of the Incarnation so as to make it seem as if God the Father and God the Holy Ghost had conspired to slay God the Son. That is what Langland calls "drivelling on the dais" and "gnawing God with the gorge". In like manner we are drivelling on the dais if we accent what is irrelevant or distort what is apparent in the behaviour of the Duke—if we complain that he pretends to be what he is not, that he lies to Claudio, that he pimps for Mariana, and so on. What is important to notice in the 'bed-trick' (as it has been called) is not what happens to Mariana, but what happens to Angelo. The bed-trick puts him in exactly the same position (with regard to the law which he is charged to administer) as Claudio, whom he had condemned, is in. Both have lain with their contracted wives before marriage; both are equally guilty. That is the whole point, and to glance wryly at the morality of substituting Mariana for Isabella is to refuse proper attention to what Shakespeare is trying to do with the story he found. It is to underline what is accidental and irrelevant instead of what is pertinent and essential, the very core of the situation, long since announced with un-conscious but self-condemning irony by Angelo himself:

> When I, that censure him, do so offend,
> Let mine own judgement pattern out my death,
> And nothing come in partial. Sir, he must die.

Handy-dandy, which is the justice, which is the thief? With the marvellous adroitness noted by F. R. Leavis[26] of the last Act, the irony is brought home, full circle, in the denouement:

> 'An Angelo for Claudio, death for death!'
> Haste still pays haste, and leisure answers leisure;
> Like doth quit like, and MEASURE still for MEASURE...
> We do condemn thee to the very block
> Where Claudio stoop'd to death, and with like haste.

Would it be sensible at such a moment to remark that the Duke is lying again, since, as well he knows, Claudio is alive and just about to be pardoned? It would not. More sensible would be to note that Angelo, like Claudio, is repentant, and, like him, is forgiven. That is the only block on which they have to stoop. The parallel between them is maintained to the end; yet I am defrauded of saying so in one detail, for we do not know from the text that Claudio will marry Juliet as certainly as we know that Angelo has married Mariana; but, as Dover Wilson has pointed out,[27] the text seems almost certainly to have suffered from intruding hands. Marriage seems at least to be the Duke's idea of a right solution for problems of incontinence. Lucio, no less guilty in this kind, as Mistress Overdone tells us,

Mistress Kate Keep-Down was with child by him in the Duke's time, he promised her marriage...

is obliged to keep his promise.

The mention of Lucio at last raises the question where he is to be fitted into the grand allegorical design. Before this can be answered there are some strange things to be noted about him that, I think, have not received proper attention.

To begin with what is simple and obvious, Lucio is the only major character who is not tested; no assay is made on whatever virtue he may be thought to have. In this respect he seems to be in a class by himself. Next it should be noted that he performs two useful dramatic functions in the play: first, he lures Isabella from her convent into the plot: secondly, he is there to bait the Duke. About each of these functions there is something further to be said.

He is, as I have said, the instrument by which Isabella is led into temptation, in a scene which shows him gallant and agreeable; he treats her brother's sin as a thing for which, in his opinion, Claudio should be rewarded rather than punished, and when he is rebuked by Isabella for this levity, he tells her that he holds her "as a thing ensky'd and sainted", which, from the general tone of his conversation, seems hardly probable. It is rather a piece of alluring humbug, for, as he says himself, it is his familiar sin to play the lapwing with maids; and here he is at his lapwing tricks. The next time we see him he has brought her to Angelo and is warming her to her work with him, with worldly-wise asides.

Thereafter his function in the play is virtually confined to being rude to the Duke; if anyone in the audience has felt an impulse to "drivel on the dais", for instance by criticizing the Duke for duplicity, the crudity of Lucio's slanders ought to throw him back onto the Duke's side of the fence.[28] Amusing as he is, Lucio is a foul-mouthed liar, and that fact should restore us to our senses; but it may not succeed with everybody. Some of the mud will cling perhaps. "I am a kind of burr; I shall stick", as he says himself. Whether or not this be so, his function is that of comic adversary to the Duke.

All this is fairly straightforward, but now there must be mentioned a point in the presentation of Lucio that is both startling and difficult to argue, more especially as the authenticity of his character has been impugned by Dover Wilson, who thinks him largely the product of a revising botcher, and is especially suspicious of the passages of prose dialogue in which he occurs.[29] It may therefore be that Lucio's part in the allegorical design has been obscured; nevertheless I hope to recover it. I would first draw attention to the fact that both in the verse and in the prose he speaks, Lucio gives us reason to think that he knows all the time who the Friar-Duke is. This fact was first brought to my notice, in a production of the play I did about ten years ago, by the actor who was playing the part of Lucio.[30] Was he, or was he not, to suggest in his performance that he had penetrated the Duke's disguise?

The question was at once referred to the text, when the following passages seemed to emerge with new meaning. The first, from I, iv, is part of Lucio's conversation with Isabella at the convent:

> The duke is very strangely gone from hence;
> Bore many gentlemen, myself being one,
> In hand and hope of action: but we do learn
> By those that know the very nerves of state,
> His givings-out were of an infinite distance
> From his true-meant design.

From whom could Lucio have had this information, since neither Angelo, nor Escalus knew it? Who were the very nerves of the State, if not they? What had the Duke himself said to Friar Thomas?

> And he supposes me travell'd to Poland;
> For so I have strew'd it in the common ear,
> And so it is received.

And if it be conceded that Lucio had learnt it somehow,[31] for what reason does he impart it to Isabella? There is no natural reason why she should be told this State-secret at that moment, and it looks as if the lines were there to inform the audience that Lucio is in some sense 'in the know', just as of course the audience itself is. This passage, taken alone, would not be conclusive; but it should be compared with another in III, ii.

Lucio. Go to kennel, Pompey; go.
      What news, friar, of the duke?

Duke. I know none. Can you tell me of any?

Lucio. Some say he is with the Emperor of Russia; other some, he is in Rome: but where is he, think you?

Duke. I know not where; but wheresoever, I wish him well.

Lucio. It was a mad fantastical trick of him to steal from the state, and usurp the beggary he was never born to.

The beggary he was never born to. How did Lucio know the Duke had become a mendicant?[32] No one else thought so. The only answer we have is his own, that he knew what he knew; and that is a line that can hardly be said without searching innuendo:

> Come, sir, I know what I know.

If Lucio did not know, but was pretending to, it was an amazing guess, just as it was a rare coincidence that he should broach such a subject to the Duke himself, and to him only. Is it a wholly satisfactory explanation to say the coincidence is no more than a stage-situation contrived to raise a laugh? It seems to carry a hint beyond that.

Let me gather together these observations about Lucio. He is never tempted himself: he is the instrument by which Isabella and Angelo are led into temptation: he is the Duke's adversary and mocker: it is hinted that he has recognized the Duke in the Friar, and he is not afraid of him.[33] It seems almost too obvious what part Lucio plays in the parable of the play. Like the Duke, he suggests an anagogical plane of meaning, on which he stands for what Hardy would have called the Spirit Ironic or the Spirit Sinister; or Satan, as he is called in that other play of testing, *The Book of Job.* He is very far, of course, from Milton's Satan, being still on mocking-terms with God and able to stroll into the presence with a gibe, in the best Old Testament manner:

> Doth Job fear God for naught?

But we must not let Milton bedazzle us about Satan; Lucio is not of his calibre, nor even of that of Lucifer, though the name is suggestive;[34] he is hardly more than a minor fiend, like that fiend in *The Friar's Tale*, who claims to be sometimes an instrument of God:

> For som-tyme, we ben goddes instruments
> And menes to don his comandements,

and, when a man is, by divine permission, tempted,

> Whan he withstandeth our temptacioun
> It is a cause of his savacioun;
> Al-be-it that it was nat our entente
> He sholde be sauf, but that we wolde him hente.

This suggestion, grounded in the text such as we have it, completes the shadowy shape of the human world as a testing-ground, and of an even shadowier world above it which together make the meaning of the play. The allegorical should neither supplant nor overbear the literal, human meaning; it should on the contrary enrich it by such touches in production as will make audiences imaginatively conscious of an extra depth. They need not be able clearly to define it, but it should remain an overtone which hearing they may hear and not understand. There is no need to be heavy-handed in the matter.

What then happens at the end, when Lucio unmasks the Duke? If Lucio knew all along who the 'Friar' was, how can that be reconciled with his tearing off his cowl? Job's Satan and Chaucer's fiend, being comedy characters as well as Immortals, should be able to pass the situation off; and so can Lucio. He makes a joke of it. After calling him a "bald-pated, lying rascal" and bidding him show his "sheep-biting face", he reveals his Duke to the assembly. There is a general movement of stupefaction. For an instant Lucio strikes the pose of a conjuror who has produced a white rabbit out of a black hat, and then he slinks tiptoe away, leaving stage-centre to more important characters, with a line that carries a grimace and raises a laugh:

> This may prove worse than hanging.

And indeed Shakespeare concludes the play in a comic and a forgiving mood; Lucio must of course be kept down, but only by Kate Keep-Down. What matters more is that we are in a swift mood of general amnesty and the uniting of lovers; and the Duke will govern them and lift them up for ever. The play bursts into a sudden *Paradiso* not untouched by hilarity, and I do not see why all the bells in Vienna should not ring, organs peal, *Te Deums* soar, trumpets blow and all the populace dance round the united couples in a general and harmonious happiness. If there is more joy in Heaven over one sinner that repenteth, there should be more joy in Vienna too.

It seems worth adding, for the sake of objectivity, that in *Promus and Cassandra* there is no character that corresponds to Mariana, no character that corresponds to Lucio, and no character that corresponds to the Friar-Duke; for the King of Hungary who comes so tardily in towards the end of Whetstone's double-decker ten-act play is a mere *Deus ex machina*. The omnipresent Friar-Duke is Shakespeare's invention; so are Lucio, Mariana and Barnardine. There is no scene in the source corresponding to that which shows the penitence of Juliet, and, most significant of all, Shakespeare has turned Cassandra, who is described merely as "a very vertuous and bewtiful Gentlewoman",[35] into Isabella, about to enter the cloister and become a votarist of St Clare, and the bride of Christ.

Can changes such as these 'well up from the unconscious'? Do they not necessarily indicate some meditated purpose? I have attempted to present a coherent meaning that accounts for them and for other changes in the play; of course there may be some other and better explanation; but it cannot be objected that I have imposed an unwarrantably religious pattern upon it, for it is Isabella and the Friar-Duke who import religion into the play, not I.

I would, however, rather refer the matter once more to that deceptively simple medieval formula for comedy. It will then at once become apparent why a religious basis for the design of this particular play is inevitable; the reason is that the subject-matter is sin.

Exordium triste laeto fine commutans. That is the difference between the *exordium triste* in *Measure for Measure* and in those other, earlier comedies; in them the causes of sadness that haunt their beginnings are separations, misunderstandings, crossings in love, exiles, shipwrecks, paternal wrath, mistaken identity, false report, fickleness, shrewishness and other light afflictions; such things are easily supplied with happy endings, they belong to the "golden World".[36] But can there be happiness for a world bursting with sin and misery? Must Evil always end in Tragedy?

c

It may call for a mind at the top of its energies and a man in good heart to hold up a mirror to nature so that it reflects what is truly dark and diseased, yet still can show how it may turn to health and joy. To do so was possible to Shakespeare in the midst of his so-called 'Tragic Period', and that it is possible has always been the mainstay of Christian imagination; we live in a fallen world and yet have hope of salvation. It is the comedy of Adam.

If a 'dark' comedy is one in which pessimism or cynicism is uppermost, it has yet to be shown that there is any such thing in Shakespeare. *Measure for Measure* is as easily embraced by the medieval definition of comedy as any other that he wrote, for that definition includes sin as a root-cause of sorrow, as it is also a cause of all Christian joy:

O felix culpa! O necessarium peccatum Adae![37]

NOTES

1. Part of the substance of a lecture delivered at the Stratford-upon-Avon Shakespeare Conference of 1953.
2. T. M. Raysor (ed.), *Coleridge's Shakespeare Criticism* (1930), I, 113.
3. A. C. Bradley, *Shakespearean Tragedy* (1904), Lecture II.
4. J. Dover Wilson, *The Essential Shakespeare* (1932), p. 117.
5. Clifford Leech, 'The Meaning of *Measure for Measure*', *Shakespeare Survey*, 3 (1950), 67.
6. III, ii, 129–30, 187–8.
7. II, iii.
8. *Opus* 132 in A minor.
9. Bradley, *op. cit.* Lecture I.
10. An opinion widely held in the 1920's.
11. G. Wilson Knight, *The Wheel of Fire* (1930), Chapter IV. Reference should also here be made to the full and sensitive study by Mary Lascelles, *Shakespeare's Measure for Measure* (1953), not published at the time this lecture was written, a fact which must excuse its neglect of her views on the play.
12. R. W. Chambers, *Man's Unconquerable Mind* (1939), pp. 277–310.
13. R. W. Battenhouse, '*Measure for Measure* and the Christian Doctrine of Atonement', *PMLA*, LXI (1946), 1029–59.
14. E. M. Pope, 'The Renaissance Background of *Measure for Measure*', *Shakespeare Survey*, 2 (1949), 66–82.
15. *Essays and Studies collected for the English Association*, 1950.
16. *Speculum Maius Vincentii Burgundi, Praesulis Beluacensis*, Venice 1591. Vol. II, Book 3, p. 53.
17. 'An Apologie for Poetrie' in Gregory Smith (ed.), *Elizabethan Critical Essays*, I, 176–7.
18. It should be remembered that both in his letter to Can Grande and in the *Convivio* (which also treats of allegory) Dante is offering First Aid to Critics, a technique of critical analysis appropriate to the understanding of a certain tradition of vision. He is not offering advice to creative writers, and it is not here suggested that Shakespeare had read him. It is suggested that this technique of interpretation turns out to be appropriate to *Measure for Measure* and perhaps to some other Shakespeare plays.
19. F. P. Wilson, *Elizabethan and Jacobean* (1945), pp. 117–18.
20. I, i, 28–30. "History" and not "character" is the subject of "unfold".
21. *Piers Plowman*, Passus B I, l. 192.
22. *Op. cit.* p. 302.
23. Sermon XXVII.
24. S. L. Bethell, *Shakespeare and the Popular Dramatic Tradition* (1944), *passim*.
25. *Piers Plowman*, A Text, Passus XI, ll. 39–43 and B Text, Passus X, l. 57.
26. F. R. Leavis, 'The Greatness of *Measure for Measure*', *Scrutiny*, X (1942), 243.
27. *Measure for Measure*, New Cambridge Edition, 1922, pp. 97–113.

28. Lucio has a function not unlike that of Thersites in *Troilus and Cressida*. He is there to say the worst that can be said against people or things we should admire. Chivalry and love to Thersites are nothing but war and lechery. But this, as the play shows us, is the opinion of "a very filthy rogue", and we agree with him at our peril. Thersites is partly intended to turn sympathy towards Hector as Lucio is mainly intended to turn sympathy towards the Duke.

29. *Measure for Measure*, New Cambridge Edition, pp. 99 *et seq.*

30. A. W. Ashby, of Exeter College, Oxford.

31. See note on I, i, 1 of the New Cambridge Edition, where it is offered as a guess that the abrupt beginning of the play as we have it might be an abridged form of a scene in which perhaps the Duke may have given this information, in spite of what he says (in the lines quoted above) to Friar Thomas in I, iii.

32. Usurping the beggary he was never born to has an overtone reference to the Incarnation.

33. *Lucio.* I fear you not. (III, ii, 173.)

34. Battenhouse thinks the name suggests lightness (levity) not light (Lucifer). *Op. cit.* p. 1036 n.

35. From the *Argument* of *Promus and Cassandra*, 1578.

36. I take this phrase not from *As You Like It* but from *Promus and Cassandra*.

37. *Piers Plowman*, C Text, Passus VIII, l. 126. Langland seems to be freely quoting (according to Skeat's note) from the Holy Saturday canticle *Exultet* in the Sarum Missal.

TROILUS AND CRESSIDA[1]

BY

KENNETH MUIR

Troilus and Cressida has always been something of a puzzle. The title-page of the Quarto described it as a History, the Epistle to the Reader spoke of it as a Comedy, and the Folio as an afterthought put it between the Histories and the Tragedies. Oscar J. Campbell calls it a comical satire. John Palmer spoke of it as a tragedy in 1912, and as a comedy in 1914. To Hazlitt it was loose and desultory; Coleridge found it hard to characterize; Swinburne said it was a hybrid which "at once defies and derides all definitive comment". Heine said much the same thing more decoratively:

> It is as though we should see Melpomene dancing the Cancan at a ball of grisettes, with shameless laughter on her pallid lips, and with death in her heart.[2]

The stage-history has been equally baffling. We do not know whether it was ever performed in Shakespeare's lifetime and the first recorded performance—apart from those of Dryden's adaptation—was at Munich in 1898. We do not know whether the play was Shakespeare's contribution to the War of the Theatres; we do not know whether Achilles was intended as a portrait of Essex; we do not even know when the play was written. After the first modern performance in England, *The Times* said that the play was better left unacted; and after the first performance in New York, as recently as 1932, most of the critics said the same thing. If the play has now become relatively popular on the stage, and if modern critics have come to appreciate it more in the study, we may suspect that audiences and critics have been taught by two world wars and by changes in society to see what Shakespeare was trying to do.

Mutability is a common subject in Elizabethan poetry, and the power of Time is one of the main themes in Shakespeare's *Sonnets*, besides being the subject of a not wholly relevant digression in *The Rape of Lucrece*. Whatever the literary genetics of the theme, Shakespeare seems to have been poignantly conscious of the irreparable outrages of Time. Time is mentioned in about a third of the *Sonnets*, and in many of them it is the implacable enemy of youth and beauty, of fame, and even of love. Shakespeare's beloved "among the wastes of Time must go". In the early sonnets the poet declares that marriage is the one sure way of making war "upon this bloody tyrant, Time" and in the later ones that beauty may live for ever in his "eternal lines":

> you shall shine more bright in these contents
> Than unswept stone besmear'd with sluttish time.

Time becomes a symbol, almost a synonym, for mortality:

> Since brass, nor stone, nor earth, nor boundless sea,
> But sad mortality o'er-sways their power,
> How with this rage shall beauty hold a plea,
> Whose action is no stronger than a flower?

28

> O, how shall summer's honey breath hold out
> Against the wrackful siege of battering days,
> When rocks impregnable are not so stout,
> Nor gates of steel so strong, but Time decays?

The poet protests that he will remain constant despite Time with his scythe, and proclaims that:

> Love's not Time's fool, though rosy lips and cheeks
> Within his bending sickle's compass come.

But he is agonizingly aware, as Troilus is, that he cannot expect constancy in others. He knows that although his own love would not alter when it alteration found, love is often "converted from the thing it was".[3]

Here in the *Sonnets*, then, whether they are fact or fiction, or a blend of both, we have a fore-runner of the Troilus situation—an obsessive concern with the power of Time and a realization of the vulnerability of constancy. In *Lucrece*, it may be observed, the heroine's tirade against Opportunity and Time (ll. 876–1024) precedes the long and vivid description of the painting of Troy Town (ll. 1366–1568). Time is described as "mis-shapen", "carrier of grisly care", "eater of youth", "virtue's snare", "the ceaseless lackey to Eternity". Some of the imagery used in the poem links up with four famous speeches in *Troilus and Cressida*:

> Thou grant'st no time for charitable deeds...   (l. 908)

> Time's glory is to calm contending kings...   (l. 939)

> To ruinate proud buildings with thy hours,
> And smear with dust their glitt'ring golden towers...   (ll. 944–5)

> To feed oblivion with decay of things...   (l. 947)

> Let him have time a beggar's orts to crave,
> And time to see one that by alms doth live
> Disdain to him disdained scraps to give.   (ll. 985–7)

Ulysses's speech on Time[4] is spoken in answer to Achilles's question: "What, are my deeds forgot?" And in the course of his reply Ulysses mentions "good deeds past", the scraps which are "alms for oblivion", the charity which is subject to "envious and calumniating time", and the "gilt o'er-dusted" which is no longer praised. In the next act, when Troilus parts from Cressida, he makes use of Lucrece's epithet:

> Injurious time now with a robber's haste
> Crams his rich thievery up, he knows not how:
> As many farewells as be stars in heaven,
> With distinct breath and consign'd kisses to them,
> He fumbles up into a loose adieu,
> And scants us with a single famish'd kiss,
> Distasted with the salt of broken tears.   (IV, iv, 44–50)

29

C*

Here we have the same image of Time with a wallet, and also the cooking imagery first pointed out by Walter Whiter,[5] to the significance of which we shall have occasion to return. When Ulysses prophesies the destruction of Troy, Hector replies:[6]

> the end crowns all,
> And that old common arbitrator, Time,
> Will one day end it.

The fourth speech having links with the lines quoted from *Lucrece* is spoken by Troilus after he has witnessed Cressida's unfaithfulness:

> The fractions of her faith, orts of her love,
> The fragments, scraps, the bits and greasy relics
> Of her o'er-eaten faith, are bound to Diomed. (v, ii, 158–60)

Some of the food images in *Lucrece* and the *Sonnets* are connected with the Ovidian idea of devouring Time; the remainder associate sexual desire with feeding, and its satisfaction with surfeiting. The association is a natural extension of the various meanings of the word *appetite*. Tarquin considers that

> the profit of excess
> Is but to surfeit;

his lust is compared to the "sharp hunger" of a lion; and he is described after his crime as "surfeit-taking":

> His taste delicious, in digestion souring,
> Devours his will, that liv'd by foul devouring.

A few lines later, we have another image of surfeiting:[7]

> Drunken Desire must vomit his receipt,
> Ere he can see his own abomination.

There are some twenty-five food images in *Lucrece* and more than three times that number in *Troilus and Cressida*. In the poem there is a link between the Time imagery and the Food imagery: Time is not merely a devourer, but also a bloody tyrant; and the ravisher is not merely a devourer of innocence, but a tyrant as well.

The painting of Troy enables us to compare Shakespeare's early attitude to the story with that he held at the turn of the century, when he may be supposed to have written *Troilus and Cressida*. In both, of course, he adopted the traditional medieval and Elizabethan view of the matter. He sympathized with the Trojans, and he was critical of the Greek heroes. Achilles is not described in the painting. In Ajax is to be seen "blunt rage and rigour". Ulysses is "sly". Pyrrhus is a brutal killer, as he is in *Hamlet*. Sinon is a hypocrite. On the other side Helen is "the strumpet that began this stir", and the lust of Paris is said to be the firebrand that destroyed Troy. Priam is blamed for not checking his son in time and for being deluded by Sinon:[8]

> Priam, why art thou old and yet not wise?

But the Trojans as a whole ought not to have been punished for the sins of Paris:

> Why should the private pleasure of some one
> Become the public plague of many moe?
> Let sin, alone committed, light alone
> Upon his head that hath transgressed so;
> Let guiltless souls be freed from guilty woe:
> > For one's offence why should so many fall,
> > To plague a private sin in general? (ll. 1478–84)

The main difference in *Troilus and Cressida* is that both sides are presented more critically. The debate in Troy enables the poet to show that the blame must be shared by all the Trojan leaders; and the Greek heroes are all presented in as unflattering light as possible. Even in the *Iliad* Hector is a more attractive figure than his killer; but in the play, even if we discount the railings of Thersites, Achilles is singularly unpleasant, and his murder of Hector is more brutal than the account given in Shakespeare's sources. Caxton's Achilles catches Hector partially unarmed and kills him single-handed. For this incident Shakespeare substituted the murder by Achilles and the Myrmidons, which he took from the Caxton-Lydgate story of Troilus's death.

The difference between Shakespeare's attitude to his lovers and that of Chaucer may largely be explained by the hardening of opinion towards Cressida in the intervening two hundred years. She had become a type of inconstancy, as Pandarus was the archetypal pimp. There is another reason: Chaucer, in writing a narrative poem, was able to slide over uncomfortable facts. We do not see Cressida's actual surrender to Diomed. It takes place after a lapse of time; it is 'distanced' by the poet and given excuses and motives—all except the obvious one. But once the story was dramatized—and it had been put on the stage before Shakespeare tried his hand— the evasions of narrative were no longer possible. The tempo was necessarily quickened, and Cressida's rapid capitulation stamps her as a daughter of the game so clearly that we hardly need the official portrait by Ulysses. To make her fall plausible Shakespeare has to suggest in the early scenes that she is something of a coquette. But she is as genuinely in love with Troilus as her shallow nature will allow, and Dame Edith Evans was wrong to play her as a Restoration heroine.[9] We are told that in the scene in which she parts from Troilus she was shown

pinning on her hat, visibly intent on her looks and on her change of fortune, while Troilus is boring her with his repeated "But yet be true". "Oh, heavens! be true again!" retorts the lady in her impatience to get his entreaties done with.

But Cressida means her protestations of eternal faithfulness, as Troilus means his.

Nor is Troilus the "sexual gourmet" with the "educated sensuality of an Italianate English roué" described for us by Oscar J. Campbell.[10] He fears, it is true, that the joy of intercourse will be too subtle for him to appreciate, "tuned too sharp in sweetness for the capacity" of his "ruder powers", and he is afraid of losing distinction in his joys.[11] But in this speech he is expressing precisely the same feelings as those of the chaste Portia when Bassanio chooses the right casket.[12] Campbell thinks that the bawdy benchers would have laughed at Troilus's later speech in which he answers Cressida's wise saw about the incompatibility of love and wisdom:

> O that I thought it could be in a woman—
> As, if it can, I will presume in you—

> To feed for aye her lamp and flames of love;
> To keep her constancy in plight and youth,
> Outliving beauty's outward, with a mind
> That doth renew swifter than blood decays!
> Or that persuasion could but thus convince me,
> That my integrity and truth to you
> Might be affronted with the match and weight
> Of such a winnow'd purity in love;
> How were I then uplifted! but, alas!
> I am as true as truth's simplicity
> And simpler than the infancy of truth.   (III, ii, 165–77)

These lines, underlined in Keats's copy of the play and partly quoted by him in a letter to Fanny Brawne,[13] can hardly be taken to mean that Troilus fears that Cressida "will never be able to satisfy the demands of his discriminating, if voracious, sensuality".[14] Nor is Troilus a Mr Pinchwife who married only because he could never keep a mistress to himself. The whole point of the story is that Troilus is a faithful lover and that Cressida proves unworthy of him. He is not exactly a Romeo; Donne, it may be said, had intervened. The audience at one of the Inns of Court—if the play was performed there, as several critics have thought— would recognize Troilus as one of themselves. If he is satirized, it is not as a lecher but as an idealist. Indeed, some of his most characteristic speeches are concerned with the contrast between the idea and the reality, and with the inadequacy of the flesh to express the desires of the heart:

> This is the monstruosity in love, lady, that the will is infinite and the execution confined, that the desire is boundless and the act a slave to limit.   (III, ii, 87–90)

Troilus the idealist is displayed in the debate in Troy. He speaks, as Hector points out,

> not much
> Unlike young men, whom Aristotle thought
> Unfit to hear moral philosophy: (II, ii, 165–7)

for he brushes on one side all considerations of wisdom and justice, arguing merely from Helen's beauty:

> a Grecian queen, whose youth and freshness
> Wrinkles Apollo's, and makes stale the morning...
> Is she worth keeping? why, she is a pearl,
> Whose price hath launch'd above a thousand ships,
> And turn'd crown'd kings to merchants.   (II, ii, 78–83)

Earlier in the play Troilus had spoken scornfully of Helen as a war-aim; but the full extent of his unwisdom in this scene is revealed later in the play. We may discount Diomed's bitter attack, as that hard-boiled cynic is likely to be prejudiced:

> For every false drop in her bawdy veins
> A Grecian's life hath sunk; for every scruple
> Of her contaminated carrion weight,
> A Trojan hath been slain.   (IV, i, 69–72)

But the devastating scene at the beginning of the third act makes it clear that the face that launched a thousand ships[15] belongs to a woman of extreme silliness and affectation. Troilus is as unlucky in his idealizing of Helen as he had been in his idealizing of Cressida—though, to be sure, it might be said that Troilus, like many who fix their affections on an unworthy object, is not quite so blind as he tries to be. He has suspicions that Cressida is not quite as innocent as she pretends, and if he were certain of her constancy he would not exhort her quite so much.

The function of Pandarus throughout the play and of the Helen scene is to show that Troilus's love is thwarted not merely by Cressida's unworthiness but also by his environment. "Sweet love is food for fortune's tooth"[16] partly because of human frailty:

> something may be done that we will not:
> And sometimes we are devils to ourselves,
> When we will tempt the frailty of our powers,
> Presuming on their changeful potency.   (IV, iv, 95–8)

but partly because Troy is an amoral world, and because the house of Pandarus is a place where bedding is more important than wedding.

We have seen how Shakespeare would have found the matter of Troy associated with the imagery derived from time and food in his own *Lucrece*. Ulysses's great speech on Time does not merely serve as part of his device to arouse the sulky Achilles: it also illuminates the coming together and the parting of the lovers, the scenes which precede and follow it. Love, we are warned, is subject to envious and calumniating Time. But we have just heard the lovers swear they will be true for ever; and we are about to hear Troilus's description of injurious Time. Cressida's frailty and the accident of war speeds up what Ulysses regards as an inevitable process. This Time-theme has, of course, been analysed by G. Wilson Knight, D. A. Traversi, Theodore Spencer and L. C. Knights;[17] but it should, perhaps, be said, that there are more references to Time in twenty-eight of the plays than in *Troilus and Cressida*, and only seven with fewer references. *Macbeth* has twice as many, though it is a much shorter play. The critics are nevertheless right to stress the Time-theme in *Troilus and Cressida* since Time makes a memorable and significant appearance at the key-points of the play in the passages to which I have referred.

As we have seen, the food imagery is linked with the Time-theme. It is because sexual desire is an appetite that it is bound to fade with its satisfaction, and because love is linked with desire that it is likely to be involved in its decay. The "fragments, scraps, the bits and greasy relics" of Cressida's faith are given to Diomed; and Menelaus, in seeking to recover Helen, "would drink up The lees and dregs of a flat tamed piece".[18] Troilus is right to claim that his fancy is

> More bright in zeal than the devotion which
> Cold lips blow to their deities,   (IV, iv, 28–9)

but therein lies his tragic error. His mad idolatry is criticized by Hector in his speech on Value:

> value dwells not in particular will;
> It holds his estimate and dignity
> As well wherein 'tis precious of itself
> As in the prizer: 'tis mad idolatry
> To make the service greater than the god;
> And the will dotes that is attributive
> To what infectiously itself affects,
> Without some image of th'affected merit. (ii, ii, 53–60)

The food imagery is not confined to the love-scenes; there are about twice as many food images in the other scenes, those relating to the war; and it is reasonable to assume from this, either that Shakespeare was showing that the appetite for glory was as liable as the sexual appetite to lead to revulsion, or else that the atmosphere of the love scenes is carried over, whether deliberately or accidentally, into the remainder of the play. There is, for example, a sexual undertone in the dialogue between Ulysses and Nestor in i, iii: "conception", "shape", "seeded", "blown up", "rank", "nursery", "grossness", "barren", "palate", "pricks", "baby figure", "mutual act", "a man distill'd Out of our virtues", "miscarrying". The appetite for power is a wolf that at last eats up itself, as lechery eats itself. It is still common to apply the sexual term of rape to wars of conquest; and Sartre in *Le Sursis* juxtaposes in the same sentence the rape of his heroine and the signing of the Munich agreement which led to the rape of Czechoslovakia.

Certainly the play is meant to expose the false glamour of sex and war.[19] Both Helen and Cressida are worthless. The war is fought about "a cuckold and a whore; a good quarrel to draw emulous factions and bleed to death upon".[20] The Homeric heroes are vain, self-seeking, beef-witted, brutal individualists; and the great deed at the climax of the *Iliad* is converted into a cowardly murder. On the Trojan side, Priam is an ineffective chairman of committee; and Hector, who is wise enough to make an eloquent plea for the restoration of Helen, suddenly decides against his own arguments:

> For 'tis a cause that hath no mean dependance
> Upon our joint and several dignities. (ii, ii, 192–3)

He deliberately jettisons justice in favour of prestige. His sudden *volte-face* provides a theatrical surprise more effective than A. P. Rossiter's ingenious rearrangment of the speeches.[21] In the last act, Troilus chides Hector for the "vice of mercy" he displays in battle.[22] The "fair play" proper to a medieval tournament is unsuitable in war. Hector, for all his charm and heroism, is doomed: he does not realize that the age of chivalry is dead. Indeed, as the Elizabethans would be acutely aware, all the Trojans are doomed; and it is partly because of the doom which hangs over them that we are willing to judge them leniently.

Wilson Knight, Theodore Spencer and S. L. Bethell[23] are right in suggesting that the debates in Troy and in the Greek camp are designed to present the values which are violated in the action. Just as Hector is the spokesman for sanity in Troy, so Ulysses speaks for sanity in the camp. But in both cases what they say has little effect. Ulysses makes a superb diagnosis of the chaos caused by the lack of order, but his Machiavellian stratagem to put an end to Achilles's sulking has no effect on the action, since the latter is roused only by the death of Patroclus. Shakespeare characteristically suppresses all mention of the genuine grievance that Homer gives Achilles; instead, there is a belated and casual revelation that he is in love with Polyxena.[24]

That the play is concerned with the nature of Value is borne out by the imagery relating to distribution and exchange—there is similar imagery in *Cymbeline*[25]—though in fact the presentation of values is done directly as well as by means of imagery, and there are three other groups of images of greater importance. The numerous images related to sickness are concerned partly with sex, and partly with the sickness of anarchy in the Greek camp, so that these images serve to link the two plots together. The group of images connected with movement suggests the continual revolutions of Time and the agitated striving of Emulation's thousand sons. Even larger is the group of animal images, the great majority of which are confined to the Greek scenes. As Audrey Yoder has pointed out in *Animal Analogy in Shakespeare's Character Portrayal*,[26] the satiric portraiture is mostly put into the mouth of Thersites, and

there is little doubt that satire implemented by animal characterization does play a great part in the depreciation of such characters as Achilles, Ajax, Patroclus, Menelaus, and Thersites, who receive the greatest amount of such characterization.

However much we discount Thersites's railings, some of the mud he throws is bound to stick; and after we have heard Ajax compared to a bear, an elephant, a mongrel, an ass, a horse, and a peacock; after we have heard Achilles compared frequently to a cur; after Menelaus has been described as worse than a herring without a roe or than the louse of a lazar—they cannot climb again on to their Homeric pedestals. The greater sympathy we feel for the Trojans is partly due to the fact that they are largely spared Thersites's satire. Yet Wilson Knight exaggerates when he suggests that[27]

The Trojan party stands for human beauty and worth, the Greek party for the bestial and stupid elements of man, the barren stagnancy of intellect divorced from action, and the criticism which exposes these things with jeers.

For the only real intellectual in the Greek camp is Ulysses, and even *his* speeches are no more intellectual than those of Hector. Hector's actions, moreover, have little relation to his considered opinions, while Ulysses does carry out the one plan he proposes, futile as it is. Nor can it be said that the Greeks stand for intellect and the Trojans for emotion; for pride and the pursuit of self-interest are no less emotional than sexual desire and the pursuit of honour. The motives of Achilles are love, both of Polyxena and Patroclus, and excessive pride. Ajax is moved merely by brutish vanity. Diomed is moved by a sexual desire that is uncontaminated by respect or affection for the object of the desire. Wilson Knight in the course of his essay makes or implies some of these qualifications. But his assumption that Shakespeare's two primary values were Love and War, and that in *Troilus and Cressida* they "exist in a world which questions their ultimate purpose and beauty"[28] seems to make the mistake of replacing the idols Shakespeare was anxious to overturn. Whatever views one may deduce from a study of the whole canon, Hector and Priam, as well as Diomed and Thersites, agree that Helen is an unsatisfactory war-aim; and the one glimpse we have of her only confirms their opinion. Whatever else Shakespeare was doing he was not setting her up as an absolute value.

T. W. Baldwin, for reasons which are both learned and unconvincing, believes that Ulysses's speech on Order is unShakespearian.[29] At least it has a very Shakespearian purpose. It is dramatically necessary to build up a conception of Order, so that its destruction by Cressida's unfaithfulness may be the more devastating. In several of the books suggested as possible sources of the speech, it is Love, rather than Order or Law, which preserves the universe from chaos. It is so in Chaucer's *Troilus and Criseyde*. Order is more appropriate than Love to the war-plot, but the background of the speech facilitated its application to the love-plot. Ulysses argues that the stars in their courses obey the same ultimate laws as the people and classes in a well-ordered State, and he goes on to state that with the removal of degree civil war and anarchy on earth will be reflected in great natural upheavals. The life of man becomes "nasty, brutish and short". If the order is disturbed at one point, chaos everywhere results. Cornwall blinds Gloucester, and nothing but divine intervention can prevent the return of chaos:

> Humanity must perforce prey on itself,
> Like monsters of the deep. (IV, ii, 49–50)

"When I love thee not", cries Othello[30] while he still loves Desdemona, "Chaos is come again." So chaos comes again to Troilus:

> If beauty have a soul, this is not she;
> If souls guide vows, if vows be sanctimonies,
> If sanctimony be the gods' delight,
> If there be rule in unity itself,
> This is not she. O madness of discourse,
> That cause sets up with and against itself!
> Bi-fold authority! where reason can revolt
> Without perdition, and loss assume all reason
> Without revolt: (V, ii, 138–46)

Cressida's unfaithfulness upsets order both in the microcosm and in the macrocosm—or so Troilus thinks. But before the end of the play he has apparently forgotten his feud with Diomed; he is concerned only with wreaking vengeance on the great-sized coward, Achilles, for the murder of Hector.

Shakespeare, I believe, was more detached than some critics have allowed, though less detached, I hope, than Oscar J. Campbell believes. Charles Williams seemed to imply that the crisis expressed in Troilus's speech was in some sense Shakespeare's own.[31] Even Una Ellis-Fermor argues[32] that the content of the poet's thought is "an implacable assertion of chaos as the ultimate fact of being", though the "idea of chaos, of disjunction, of ultimate formlessness and negation, has by a supreme act of artistic mastery been given form." We may agree about the artistic mastery, but not that Shakespeare was asserting that life was meaningless. He was asserting something much more limited, and much less pessimistic. He was saying that men are foolish enough to engage in war in support of unworthy causes; that they are deluded by passion to fix their affections on unworthy objects; that they sometimes act in defiance of their consciences; and that in the pursuit of self-interest they jeopardize the welfare of the State. He was not saying, as far as one can judge, that absolute values are illusions. He was certainly not saying that all women are Cressids; for Troilus himself, at the very moment of disillusionment, dissociates himself from any such position:

> Let it not be believed for womanhood!
> Think, we had mothers; do not give advantage
> To stubborn critics, apt, without a theme,
> For depravation, to square the general sex
> By Cressid's rule.
>
> (v, ii, 129–33)

T. S. Eliot's early critics, confronted with the unflattering picture of modern civilization given in *The Waste Land*, generally assumed that the poet was expressing his own disgust and disillusionment, though we can see now that it should not have been difficult to recognize the religious implications of the poem. In a similar way, the violation of order and the betrayal of values in *Troilus and Cressida* do not mean that the Order does not exist, or that all values are illusions. There is clearly a strong element of satire in the play, though it is tragical rather than comical satire. We sympathize with Troilus and Hector: we do not laugh at them. Even Campbell has to admit that the half-grim, half-derisive mood expected in comical satire was not suited to Shakespeare's genius: [33]

His mind was unable to assume the required flippancy in the face of human aberrations capable of producing as serious results as those issuing from the abysmal follies of the Greeks and Trojans. The sustained intensity of his mind...lent to the play a depth of tone which makes his satire ring with universal meanings.

One of the reasons why *Troilus and Cressida* has been interpreted in so many different ways is that we are continually made to change our point of view. In nearly all the other plays we look at the action through the eyes of one or two closely related characters. We see *Hamlet* through Hamlet's eyes, never through those of Claudius; *King Lear* through Lear's eyes—or Cordelia's, or Kent's—but never through the eyes of Goneril; *The Tempest* through Prospero's eyes. It is true that another point of view is often given, and a character such as Horatio or Enobarbus may sometimes act as a chorus. But in *Troilus and Cressida* the point of view is continually changing. At one moment we watch events through the eyes of Troilus, and the war seems futile. In a later scene we see the events through the eyes of Hector, and Troilus in advocating the retention of Helen seems to be a romantic young fool. In the Greek camp we see everything from Ulysses's point of view; and then, a little later, however much we despise and dislike Thersites, we become infected with his views on the situation:

Lechery, lechery; still, wars and lechery; nothing else holds fashion: a burning devil take them!
(v, ii, 196–7)

It is this shifting of emphasis which makes the play so difficult to grasp as a unity; but although Tillyard complains [34] that Shakespeare failed to fuse his heterogeneous materials into a unity, I believe the unity is there. Yet we distort the play if we make any one character to be Shakespeare's mouthpiece. The worldly standards of Ulysses are not Shakespeare's, though Shakespeare apparently shared, until the end of the sixteenth century, some of his views on Order. In general Ulysses appears more of a Baconian than a Shakespearian in his attitude. Others have argued that Shakespeare speaks mainly through the mouth of Thersites, though Thersites was renowned for his knavish railing in all Shakespeare's sources, including the *Iliad*, and also in Heywood's play about the Trojan war, written afterwards. Shakespeare could enjoy writing his curses, as we can enjoy hearing them, without sharing the bitterness of his creature. Others, again, suppose that Hector is Shakespeare's real spokesman, though perhaps his attitude to the character was not unlike his attitude to Hotspur.

Tillyard thinks that Shakespeare was "exploiting a range of feelings more critical and sophisticated than elemental and unfeignedly passionate", that he plays "with the fire of tragedy without getting burnt", and that "he meant to leave us guessing". We may agree with him that the play provides "a powerful if astringent delight", but doubt whether it is necessary to make all these qualifications.[35] It is quite possible to be critical and sophisticated at the same time as one is elemental and unfeignedly passionate. This, surely, is what the metaphysical poets accomplish when they are at their best; and if we are to place *Troilus and Cressida* it is not with the banned satirists, or even with the satirical plays of Marston and Jonson, it is rather as Shakespeare's excursion into the metaphysical mode. The most remarkable thing about the play is perhaps the way in which the poet managed to fuse thought and feeling, to unify an extraordinary mass of materials, and to counter the sense of chaos and disruption, not so much by the sense of order implicit in the artistic form, as by his establishment of the values denied or corrupted in the action. Cressida does not stain our mothers. In reading most of Anouilh's plays we feel that the sordid compromises of adult life make suicide the only proper solution for an idealist. As we quaff our dose of hemlock we murmur: "But for the grace of God (if there were a God) we might have gone on living." But although *Troilus and Cressida* is a kind of *pièce noire*, we should never be in danger, after seeing it performed, of thinking that it gives Shakespeare's verdict on life, at any rate his permanent verdict. Cressida did not cancel out Rosalind and Viola or make it impossible for him to create Desdemona or Cordelia. He did not "square the general sex by Cressid's rule".

The play, from one point of view, in its exposure of 'idealism', might be regarded as the quintessence of Ibsenism as interpreted by Shaw. From another point of view, as we have seen, it is a dramatic statement of the power of Time. From a third point of view it shows how "we are devils to ourselves": the world and the flesh make the best the victims of the worst. We may admit that the fusing of these themes required extraordinary imaginative power—a power which Shakespeare on the threshold of the tragic period amply demonstrated. The real problem about the play is the failure of most critics to appreciate it.

NOTES

1. A lecture delivered to the Shakespeare Conference at Stratford-upon-Avon, 18 August 1953.
2. Cf. the New Variorum *Troilus and Cressida*, edited H. N. Hillebrand and T. W. Baldwin (Philadelphia, 1953), pp. 382, 554, 520, 522, 523.
3. *Sonnets* XII, XVI, XVIII, LV, LXV, CXVI, XLIX.
4. *Troilus and Cressida*, II, ii, 145 ff.
5. *A Specimen of a Commentary* (1794), p. 136.
6. *Troilus and Cressida*, IV, v, 224–6. Lucrece had said that her words in railing on Time were "weak arbitrators".
7. *The Rape of Lucrece*, ll. 138–9, 421–2, 699–700, 703–4.
8. *Lucrece*, ll. 1398–9, 1467, 1471, 1550.

9. Cf. New Variorum, p. 218.

10. *Comicall Satyre* (San Marino, 1938), p. 212.

11. *Troilus and Cressida*, III, ii, 22 ff.

12. *The Merchant of Venice*, III, ii, 111 ff.

13. C. F. E. Spurgeon, *Keats' Shakespeare* (1928), p. 165; Keats, *Letters*, ed. M. B. Forman (1935), p. 501.

14. Campbell, *op. cit.* p. 213.

15. *Troilus and Cressida*, II, ii, 82.

16. *Troilus and Cressida*, IV, v, 293.

17. G. Wilson Knight, *The Wheel of Fire*, ed. 1949, pp. 65 ff.; D. A. Traversi, *Scrutiny*, VIII (1938), 301–19; T. Spencer, *Studies in English Literature*, XVI (Tokyo, January 1936), 1 ff.; L. C. Knights, *Scrutiny*, XVII (1951), 144–57.

18. *Troilus and Cressida*, IV, i, 61–2.

19. Cf. Bonamy Dobrée (ed.), *Troilus and Cressida* (1938), p. xii.

20. *Troilus and Cressida*, II, iii, 78–80.

21. *T.L.S.* 8 May 1948, p. 261.

22. *Troilus and Cressida*, V, iii, 37.

23. S. L. Bethell, *Shakespeare and the Popular Dramatic Tradition* (1944), pp. 98–105.

24. *Troilus and Cressida*, III, iii, 208.

25. Cf. A. A. Stephenson, *Scrutiny* (1942).

26. *Op. cit.* (New York, 1947), pp. 41–3.

27. *Op. cit.* p. 47.

28. *Op. cit.* p. 47.

29. New Variorum, p. 410.

30. *Othello*, III, iii, 92.

31. *The English Poetic Mind* (Oxford, 1932), pp. 60 ff.

32. *The Frontiers of Drama* (1945), pp. 71–3.

33. Campbell, *op. cit.* p. 234.

34. E. M. W. Tillyard, *Shakespeare's Problem Plays* (1950), p. 86.

35. *Op. cit.* p. 86. I have produced the play for an audience which was both unsophisticated and unbewildered.

AS YOU LIKE IT[1]

BY

HAROLD JENKINS

A masterpiece is not to be explained, and to attempt to explain it is apt to seem ridiculous. I must say at once that I propose nothing so ambitious. I merely hope, by looking at one play, even in what must necessarily be a very fragmentary way and with my own imperfect sight, to illustrate something of what Shakespeare's method in comedy may be. And I have chosen *As You Like It* because it seems to me to exhibit, most clearly of all the comedies, Shakespeare's characteristic excellences in this kind. This is not to say that *As You Like It* is exactly a representative specimen. Indeed I am going to suggest that it is not. In this play, what I take to be Shakespeare's distinctive virtues as a writer of comedy have their fullest scope; but in order that they may have it, certain of the usual ingredients of Shakespeare's comedy, or indeed of any comedy, have to be—not of course eliminated, but very much circumscribed. In *As You Like It*, I suggest, Shakespeare took his comedy in one direction nearly as far as it could go. And then, as occasionally happens in Shakespeare's career, when he has developed his art far in one direction, in the comedy which succeeds he seems to readjust his course.

If our chronology is right, after *As You Like It* comes, among the comedies, *Twelfth Night*. And while we may accept that *Twelfth Night* is, as Sir Edmund Chambers says, very much akin to *As You Like It* "in style and temper", in some important respects it returns to the method and structure of the previous comedy of *Much Ado About Nothing*. Sandwiched between these two, *As You Like It* is conspicuously lacking in comedy's more robust and boisterous elements—the pomps of Dogberry and the romps of Sir Toby. More significantly, it has nothing which corresponds to the splendid theatricalism of the church scene in *Much Ado*, nothing which answers to those crucial bits of trickery by which Benedick and Beatrice in turn are hoodwinked into love. Even if, as may be objected, they are not hoodwinked but merely tricked into removing their hoods, still those stratagems in Leonato's orchard are necessary if the happy ending proper to the comedy is to be brought about. These ambushes, if I may call them so—they are really inverted ambushes—are paralleled, or should one say parodied, in *Twelfth Night* in the scene where Malvolio is persuaded that he too is beloved. And this ambush too is necessary if, as the comedy demands, Malvolio is to have his sanity called in question and his authority undermined. The slandering of Hero in *Much Ado* also is to have its counterpart in *Twelfth Night*. For the slandering of Hero, with its culmination in the church scene, forces one pair of lovers violently apart while bringing another pair together. And in *Twelfth Night* the confusion of identities holds one pair of lovers—Orsino and Viola—temporarily apart, yet forces another pair—Olivia and Sebastian—with some violence together. A satisfactory outcome in *Much Ado* and *Twelfth Night* depends on such embroilments; and the same is even more true in an earlier comedy like *A Midsummer Night's Dream*. In *As You Like It* I can hardly say that such embroilments do not occur, but they are not structural to anything like the same degree. Without the heroine's masculine disguise Phebe would not have married Silvius any more than in *Twelfth Night* Olivia would have married Sebastian; but the confusions of identity in *As You Like It* have no influence whatever upon the ultimate destiny of Rosalind and Orlando, or of the kingdom of Duke Senior, or of the estate of Sir Rowland de Boys. Yet these are the destinies with which the action of the play is concerned. It is in the defectiveness of its action that *As You Like It* differs from the rest of the major comedies—in its dearth not only of big theatrical scenes but of events linked together by the logical intricacies of cause and effect. Of comedy, as of tragedy, action is the first essential; but *As You Like It* suggests that action is not, if I may adapt a phrase of Marston's, "the life of these things". It may be merely the foundation on which they are built. And *As You Like It* further shows that on a very flimsy foundation, if only you are skilful enough, a very elaborate structure may be poised. But the method has its dangers, and though Shakespeare's skill conceals these dangers from us, *Twelfth Night*, as I said, returns to a more orthodox scheme.

The story which provides the action for *As You Like It* belongs to the world of fairy-tale or folk-lore. This is a world which supplied the plots of a number of Shakespeare's plays, including the greatest, notably *King Lear*. And fairy-tales have many advantages for the dramatist, among which is their total disregard of practical probabilities. In fairy-tales, for example, evil is always absolute, clearly recognized, and finally overthrown; all of which may have something to do with the Aristotelian theory that while history records what has happened, poetry shows what should happen. Relaxing the more prosaic demands of verisimilitude, the fairy-tale invites the imagination. It can certainly provide a convenient road into the Forest of Arden. And this is not less true for Shakespeare because the road had already been built for him by Lodge.

A man has died and left three sons. Three is the inevitable number, and though Shakespeare, like Lodge, forgets to do much with the middle one, he is not therefore unimportant. The eldest brother is wicked, the youngest virtuous—and does fabulous feats of strength, notably destroying a giant in the shape of Charles the wrestler, who has torn other hopeful youths to pieces. Orlando therefore wins the princess, herself the victim of a wicked uncle, who has usurped her father's throne. This is the *story* of *As You Like It*. And Shakespeare, making the journey of the imagination far more quickly than Lodge, gets most of it over in the first act. That is what is remarkable. By the time we reach the second act Rosalind has already come safe to the Forest of Arden, by the aid of her man's disguise. From this disguise, as everybody knows, springs the principal comic situation of the play. But such is the inconsequential nature of the action that this comic situation develops only when the practical need for the disguise is past. The course of true love has not run smooth. But most of its obstacles have really disappeared before the main comedy begins. It only remains for the wicked to be converted, as they duly are at the end, all in comedy's good but arbitrary time, when the wicked eldest brother makes a suitable husband for the second princess. Or a most *un*suitable husband, as all the critics have complained. But this, I think, is to misunderstand. Instead of lamenting that Celia should be thrown away on Oliver, he having been much too wicked to deserve her, we should rather see that Oliver's getting this reward is a seal set on his conversion, and a sign of how good he has now become.

The first act of *As You Like It* has to supply the necessary minimum of event. But, Quiller-Couch notwithstanding, this first act is something more than mechanical.[2] It is for one thing a feat of compression, rapid, lucid and, incidentally, theatrical. In fifty lines we know all about the three brothers and the youngest is at the eldest's throat. In three hundred more we know all about the banished Duke and where and how he lives, and the giant has been destroyed before our eyes. But there is more to the first act than this. Before we enter Arden, to "fleet the time

D

carelessly, as they did in the golden world", we must be able to contrast its simple life with the brittle refinement of the court. This surely is the point of some of what 'Q' called the "rather pointless chop-logic"; and also of the courtier figure of Le Beau, a little sketch for Osric, with his foppery of diction and his expert knowledge of sport. Le Beau's notion of sport provokes Touchstone's pointed comment on the courtier's values: "Thus men may grow wiser every day: it is the first time that ever I heard breaking of ribs was sport for ladies." This *is* the callousness one learns at a court ruled by a tyrannous Duke, whose malevolent rage against Rosalind and Orlando not only drives them both to Arden but completes the picture of the world they leave behind.

This first act, then, shows some instinct for dramatic preparation, though we may grant that Shakespeare's haste to get ahead makes him curiously perfunctory. He is in two minds about when Duke Senior was banished; and about which Duke is to be called Frederick; and whether Rosalind or Celia is the taller. He has not quite decided about the character of Touchstone. I do not think these are signs of revision. They simply show Shakespeare plunging into his play with some of its details still but half-shaped in his mind. The strangest of these details is the mysterious middle brother, called Fernandyne by Lodge but merely "Second Brother" in *As You Like It*, when at length he makes his appearance at the end. Yet in the fifth line of the play he was already christened Jaques. And Shakespeare of course afterwards gave this name to someone else. It seems clear enough that these two men with the same name were originally meant to be one. As things turned out Jaques could claim to have acquired his famous melancholy from travel and experience; but I suspect that it really began in the schoolbooks which were studied with such profit by Jaques de Boys. Though he grew into something very different, Jaques surely had his beginnings in the family of De Boys and in such an academy as that in Navarre where four young men turned their backs on love and life in the belief that they could supply the want of experience by study and contemplation.

Interesting as it might be to develop this idea, the important point of comparison between *As You Like It* and *Love's Labour's Lost* is of another kind. And to this I should like briefly to refer before I come to discuss the main part of *As You Like It*. *Love's Labour's Lost* is the one play before *As You Like It* in which Shakespeare sought to write a comedy with the minimum of action. Four young men make a vow to have nothing to do with a woman; each breaks his oath and ends vowing to serve a woman. That is the story; far slighter than in *As You Like It*. Yet, in contrast with *As You Like It*, the careful and conspicuous organization of *Love's Labour's Lost* distributes its thin action evenly through the play. And the characters always act in concert. In the first act the men, all together, make their vow; in the second the ladies, all together, arrive and the temptation begins. The climax duly comes, where you would expect it, in a big scene in Act IV, when each in turn breaks his vow and all together are found out. *Love's Labour's Lost* is the most formally constructed of all the comedies. When the ladies and gentlemen temporarily exchange partners, this is done symmetrically and to order. Indeed the movement of the whole play is like a well-ordered dance in which each of the participants repeats the steps of the others. But this is exactly what does *not* happen in *As You Like It*, where the characters do *not* keep in step. When they *seem* to be doing the same thing they are really doing something different, and if they ever echo one another they mean quite different things by what they say—as could easily be illustrated from the little quartet of lovers in the fifth act ("And so am I for Phebe.—And

42

I for Ganymede.—And I for Rosalind.—And I for no woman"), where the similarity of the tune they sing conceals their different situations. The pattern of *As You Like It* comes not from a mere repetition of steps, but from constant little shifts and changes. The formal parallelisms of *Love's Labour's Lost* are replaced by a more complex design, one loose enough to hold all sorts of asymmetries within it.

But of course the effect of variations upon a theme instead of simple repetitions is not new in *As You Like It*. It is the tendency of Shakespeare's comedy from the start. In *Love's Labour's Lost* itself the courtly gestures of the four young men are burlesqued by those of a fantastic knight, and while the four young men are vowing not to see a woman, Costard the clown is "taken with a wench". Moreover, one of the four, though he goes through the movements with the others, has some trouble to keep in step, and is always threatening to break out of the ring. Even when he makes his vow with the others, he knows that necessity will make him break it. As he joins in their purposes he knows them to be foolish and he mocks at ideals which he at the same time pursues. Human activity offers itself to the dramatist in a large variety of forms and the same individual can play contradictory parts. The drunken tinker in *The Taming of the Shrew* does not know whether he may not really be a noble lord. Although Shakespeare did not invent this situation, it was just the thing to appeal to him. For he knew that a man is very easily "translated". In the middle of his fairy play he put a man with an ass's head. In perhaps the most remarkable encounter in Shakespeare the daintiest fairy queen caresses a man turned brute, who, with a fairy kingdom around him, can think only of scratching his itch. When the animal appears in a man it may terrify his fellows; it may also attract to it his finest dreams and fancies, corrupting them, or being uplifted by them to a vision of new wonder. Shakespeare of course does nothing as crude as *say* this. He knows as well as the Duke in Arden that sermons may be found in stones, but much better than the Duke that it is tedious to preach them, a thing, incidentally, he does not permit the Duke to do. What Shakespeare characteristically does in his comedy is to set together the contrasting elements in human nature and leave them by their juxtaposition or interaction to comment on one another.

In *As You Like It* the art of comic juxtaposition is at its subtlest. It is to give it fullest scope that the action can be pushed up into a corner, and the usual entanglements of plotting, though not dispensed with altogether, can be loosened. Freedom, of course, is in the hospitable air of Arden, where convenient caves stand ready to receive outlaws, alfresco meals are abundantly provided, with a concert of birds and running brooks, and there is no worse hardship than a salubrious winter wind. This is "the golden world" to which, with the beginning of his second act, Shakespeare at once transports us, such a world as has been the dream of poets since at least the time of Virgil when, wearied with the toilings and wranglings of society, they yearn for the simplicity and innocence of what they choose to think man's natural state.[3] It is of course a very literary tradition that Shakespeare is here using, but the long vogue of the pastoral suggests that it is connected with a universal impulse of the human mind, to which Shakespeare in *As You Like It* gives permanent expression. But this aspect of the play is merely the one which confronts us most conspicuously. There are many others. *As You Like It* has been too often praised for its idyllic quality alone, as though it were some mere May-morning frolic prolonged into a lotos-eating afternoon. A contrast with the ideal state was necessitated by the literary tradition itself, since the poet seeking an escape into the simple life was expected to hint at the ills of the society he was escaping from. That meant especially the courts of princes, where life—it was axiomatic —was at its most artificial. And the vivid sketching in of the courtly half of the antithesis is, as I have shown, an important function of *As You Like It*'s maligned first act. With the first speech of the banished Duke at the opening of the second act, the complete contrast is before us; for, while introducing us to Arden, this speech brings into sharp focus that first act which has just culminated in the usurper's murderous malice. "Are not these woods more free from peril than the envious court?" Though the contrast is traditional, it comes upon us here, like so many things in Shakespeare, with the vitality of fresh experience. The Forest of Arden comes to life in numerous little touches of the country-side, and the heartless self-seeking of the outer world is concentrated into phrases which have the force of permanent truth. The line that 'Q' admired— "And unregarded age in corners thrown"—might have come from one of the sonnets, and when Orlando observes how "none will sweat but for promotion" we recognize the fashion of our times as well as his. As the play proceeds, it is easy enough for Shakespeare to keep us ever aware of the forest, what with Amiens to sing for us, the procession home after the killing of the deer, an empty cottage standing ready for Rosalind and Celia, surrounded by olive-trees beyond a willow stream, and a good supply of oaks for Orlando or Oliver to lie under. It cannot have been quite so easy to keep us in touch with the court life we have now abandoned; but nothing is neater in the construction of the play than those well-placed little scenes which, by despatching first Orlando and then Oliver to the forest, do what is still required by the story and give the illusion that an action is still going briskly forward, while at the same time they renew our acquaintance with the wicked world. After the first scene in the ideal world of Arden and a sentimental discourse on the deer, there is Frederick again in one of his rages, sending for Oliver, who, an act later, when we are well acclimatized to the forest, duly turns up at court. Then occurs a scene of eighteen lines, in which Shakespeare gives as vivid a sketch of the unjust tyrant as one could hope to find. The tyrant prides himself upon his mercy, punishes one man for his brother's sins, and finds in his victim's excuses further cause of offence. Oliver's plaint that he had never loved his brother brings the instant retort, "More villain thou. Well, push him out of doors." As this eruption dies down, there appears in the Forest of Arden the cause of all the trouble quietly hanging his verses on a tree.

The contrast between court and country is thus presented and our preference is very plain. Yet as a counterpoise to all this, there is one man in the country-side who actually prefers the court. Finding himself in Arden, Touchstone decides: "When I was at home, I was in a better place." It is no doubt important that he is a fool, whose values may well be topsy-turvy. But in one word he reminds us that there are such things as domestic comforts. And presently we find that the old man whom society throws into the corner is likely in the "uncouth forest" to die of hunger and exposure to the "bleak air". There is clearly something to be said on the other side; the fool may anatomize the wise man's folly. And there is also Jaques to point out that the natural life in Arden, where men usurp the forest from the deer and kill them in their "native dwelling-place", while deer, like men, are in distress abandoned by their friends, is as cruel and unnatural as the other. When Amiens sings under the greenwood tree and turns "his merry note unto the sweet bird's throat", inviting us to shun ambition and be pleased with what we get, Jaques adds a further stanza to the song which suggests that to leave your "wealth and ease" is the act of an ass or a fool. Most of us, I suppose, have moods in which we would certainly agree with him, and it is a mark of Shakespeare's mature comedy that he permits this criticism of his ideal world in the very centre of it. The triumphal procession after the killing of the deer, a symbolic ritual of the forester's prowess, is accompanied by a mocking song, while the slayer of the deer is given its horns to wear as a somewhat ambiguous trophy.

It is Jaques, mostly, with the touch of the medieval buffoon in him, who contributes this grotesque element to the songs and rituals of Arden. Like Touchstone he is not impressed by Arden, but unlike Touchstone he does not prefer the court. Indeed, as we have seen, he is able to show that they are very much alike, infected by the same diseases. No doubt his is a jaundiced view of life, and it is strange that some earlier critics should have thought it might be Shakespeare's. Shakespeare's contemporaries would hardly have had difficulty in recognizing in Jaques a variant of the Elizabethan melancholy man—the epithet is applied to him often enough—though I remain a little sceptical when I am told by O. J. Campbell that from the first moment they heard Jaques described, the Elizabethans would have perceived "the unnatural melancholy produced by the adustion of phlegm".[4] Whatever its physiological kind, the important thing about his melancholy is that it is not the fatigue of spirits of the man who has found the world too much for him, but an active principle manifesting itself in tireless and exuberant antics. Far from being a morose man, whether he is weeping with the stag or jeering at the huntsman, he throws himself into these things with something akin to passion. His misanthropy is a form of self-indulgence, as is plain enough in his very first words:

> *Jaques.* More, more, I prithee, more.
> *Amiens.* It will make you melancholy, Monsieur Jaques.
> *Jaques.* I thank it. More, I prithee, more. I can suck melancholy out of a song.

His own comparison with a weasel sucking eggs suggests what a ferocious and life-destroying thing this passion is. Shakespeare's final dismissal of Jaques is profound. Far from making Celia a better husband than Oliver, as George Sand apparently thought, he is the one person in the play who could not be allowed to marry anyone, since he can have nothing to do with either love or generation. His attempt to forward the nuptials of Touchstone and Audrey serves only to postpone them. He is of course the one consistent character in the play in that he declines to go back with the others to the court that they have scorned. Yet how *can* he go back when the court has been converted? Jaques's occupation's gone. And he will not easily thrive away from the social life on which he feeds. It is notable that the place he really covets, or affects to, is that of the motley fool, licensed to mock at society, indulged by society but not of it. Yet, seeking for a fool, he has only to look in the brook to find one; and it is the romantic hero who will tell him so.

Shakespeare, then, builds up his ideal world and lets his idealists scorn the real one. But into their midst he introduces people who mock their ideals and others who mock *them*. One must not say that Shakespeare never judges, but one judgement is always being modified by another. Opposite views may contradict one another, but of course they do not cancel out. Instead they add up to an all-embracing view far larger and more satisfying than any one of them in itself.

Now when Orlando tells Jaques that he may see a fool by looking in the brook, this is not the first time that Jaques and Orlando meet; and the relations between the two of them are worth a moment's glance. Their first encounter occurs in public when the Duke and his retinue are met for one of their forest repasts. Jaques has just been eloquent about the vices of mankind and is justifying the satirist who scourges them, when he is confronted with the romantic hero in his most heroic attitude, rushing into the middle of the scene with drawn sword,[5] crying, "Forbear, and eat no more." But Jaques is not the man to be discomposed, even when a sudden interruption throws him off his hobby-horse. When he has inquired, "Of what kind should this cock come of?", the heroic attitude begins to look extravagant. The hero stands his ground: "Forbear, I say: He dies that touches any of this fruit"; at which Jaques nonchalantly helps himself to a grape, saying, "An you will not be answered with reason (raisin), I must die." Heroism now appears thoroughly deflated, or would do if Jaques were attended to by the company at large. The hero is in fact saved by the Duke's "civility"; and their talk of "gentleness" and "nurture" even throws back into perspective Jaques's recent attack upon society. The situation as a whole retains its equilibrium. And yet as a result of this little incident we are bound to feel that the romantic hero is very vulnerable to the ridicule of the satirist, until their duel of wit in the following act readjusts our view by allowing Orlando his retort.

There is a formal point to notice here, easy to miss but full of meaning. The wit-combat between Jaques and the hero is matched an act or so later—there is no strict regularity about these things—by a similar wit-combat between Jaques and the heroine. On each occasion Jaques is worsted and departs, leaving Rosalind and Orlando to come together. In fact the discomfiture of Monsieur Melancholy by one or other of the lovers is the prelude to each of the two big love-scenes of the play. And this arrangement makes a point more prettily than any action-plot involving Jaques could do. The mocking words of Jaques's farewell are in each case illuminating: "Farewell, good Signior Love"; and "Nay, then, God be wi' you, an you talk in blank verse." The gibe at blank verse is not an incidental or decorative jest. It makes it clear that, however we judge of them, the melancholy spirit of Jaques and the romantic emotion of Rosalind and Orlando cannot mingle. Shakespeare dismisses the melancholy man before he gives the lovers their scope. And in this I follow his example.

So far I have dealt only with the immigrants to Arden. There is of course a native population. The natural world of the poet's dreams has always been inhabited by shepherds, who from the time of Theocritus have piped their songs of love. And Rosalind and Celia have been in the forest for only twenty lines when two shepherds appear pat before them. In an earlier comedy perhaps these might have been a similar pair singing comparable love-ditties. But in *As You Like It*—Shakespeare making the most of what is offered him by Lodge—they are a contrasting pair. One is young and one is old, one is in love and one is not. The lover is the standard type. But the notion of love has undergone a change since classical times and the shepherds of Renaissance pastorals have all been bred in the schools of courtly love. So young Silvius is the faithful abject lover who finds disdain in his fair shepherdess's eye and sighs "upon a midnight pillow"— Shakespeare always fixes on a detail in which a whole situation is epitomized. There are of course many other lovers in the play, but the story of Silvius and Phebe is of the pure pastoral world, the familiar literary norm against which all the others may be measured. First against Silvius and Phebe are set Rosalind and Orlando, and the immediate result of this is that Rosalind and Orlando, though they clearly belong to the pastoral world, seem much closer to the ordinary one. Indeed, since Silvius and Phebe relieve them of the necessity of displaying the lovers' more extravagant postures, Rosalind and Orlando are freer to act like human beings. Rosalind need only play at taunting her adorer while allowing her real woman's heart to be in love with him in earnest. In an earlier comedy like *The Two Gentlemen of Verona* the heroes themselves had to undergo those "bitter fasts, with penitential groans, With nightly tears and daily heart-sore sighs", and these are what, as H. B. Charlton says, may make Valentine look a fool. But with Silvius to take this burden from him, Orlando can really be a hero, performing the traditional hero's fabulous feats, and upon occasion may even be a common man like ourselves. He has, for example, the very human trait of unpunctuality; he is twice late for an appointment. And although on one occasion he has the perfect excuse of a bloody accident, on the other he has nothing to say, beyond "My fair Rosalind, I come within an hour of my promise." Such engaging casualness is of course outside Silvius's range. And although Orlando has his due share of lovers' sighs and is indeed the "unfortunate he" who hangs the verses on the trees, in so human a creature these love-gestures appear not as his *raison d'être* but as an aberration. A delightful aberration, no doubt—"I would not be cured, youth", he says—but still an aberration that can be the legitimate subject of our mockery. Lying contemplating his love under an oak, he seems to Celia "like a dropped acorn", and both the ladies smile at his youthful lack of beard. But Orlando is robust enough to stand their mockery and ours, and Shakespeare's superb dramatic tact arranges that Orlando shall draw our laughter towards him so that he may protect the fragile Silvius from the ridicule which would destroy *him*. Rosalind alone is privileged to make fun of Silvius; and that because searching his wounds, she finds her own. The encounters which do not occur have their significance as well as those which do: Touchstone is only once, and Jaques never, allowed a sight of Silvius before the final scene of the play. Silvius has not to be destroyed or the play will lack something near its centre.

If in a pastoral play the ideal shepherd is satirized it must be indirectly. But that he is, through his complete unreality, a likely target for satire has been commonly recognized by the poets, who have therefore had a habit of providing him with a burlesque counterpart to redress the balance and show that they did know what rustics were like in real life. As Gay was to put it in his proem to *The Shepherd's Week*, the shepherd "sleepeth not under myrtle shades, but under a hedge"; and so when Gay's shepherd makes love it is in a sly kiss behind a haycock to the accompaniment of the lady's yells of laughter. This may have been the method of Shakespeare's William, for, far from inditing verses to his mistress, William is singularly tongue-tied; though he is "five and twenty" and thinks he has "a pretty wit", the biggest of his eleven speeches is only seven words long. And his partner is just as much a contrast to the shepherdess of pastoral legend. She thanks the gods she is not beautiful, does not even know the meaning of "poetical", and her sheep, alas, are goats.

Shakespeare, then, presents the conventional pastoral, and duly burlesques it. But with a surer knowledge of life than many poets have had, he seems to suspect that the burlesque as well as the convention may also miss the truth. Do shepherds really sleep under hedges? In order to be unsophisticated, must they be stupid too? So among his varied array of shepherds, Silvius and Ganymede and William, Shakespeare introduces yet another shepherd, the only one who knows anything of sheep, whose hands even get greasy with handling them. It does not matter that Shakespeare got the hint for Corin from Corydon in Lodge. For Lodge found Corydon in literature and for Corin Shakespeare went to life. Lodge's Corydon, though he may make the king smile with his clownish salutation, has evidently been bred at court himself. Would he ever else accost a lady in distress in strains like these

If I should not, fair damosel, occasion offence, or renew your griefs by rubbing the scar, I would fain crave so much favour as to know the cause of your misfortunes.

Shakespeare's Corin speaks at once of grazing and shearing and an unkind master; and when he talks about the shepherd's life he shows that he knows the value of money and that fat sheep need good pasture. His greatest pride is to see his ewes graze and his lambs suck. This is the note of his philosophy, and if it has its limitations, it is far from despicable and is splendidly anchored to fact. His attitude to love is that of the fully sane man undisturbed by illusions. Being a man, he has been in love and can still guess what it is like; but it is so long ago he has forgotten all the details. How little he belongs to Arcadia may be discovered from Sidney, whose shepherd-boy went on piping "as though he should never be old". In *As You Like It* perpetual youth is the happiness of Silvius, and his fate. *That* much of the difference between Silvius and Corin is apparent from the short dialogue of twenty lines which first introduces them together to us.

In Corin Shakespeare provides us with a touchstone with which to test the pastoral. Corin's dialogue with the Touchstone of the court, dropped into the middle of the play, adds to the conventional antithesis between courtier and countryman a glimpse of the real thing. Our picture of the court as a place of tyranny, ambition and corruption is no doubt true enough. But its colours are modified somewhat when Touchstone gives us the court's plain routine. For him, as he lets us know on another occasion, the court is the place where he has trod a measure, flattered a lady, been smooth with his enemy and undone three tailors. Though Touchstone seeks to entangle Corin in the fantastications of his wit, his arguments to show that the court is better than the sheepfarm have a way of recoiling on himself. What emerges from the encounter of these two realists is that ewe and ram, like man and woman, are put together and that though the courtier perfumes his body it sweats like any other creature's. In city or country, *all* ways of life are at bottom the same, and we recognize a conclusion that Jaques, by a different route, has helped us to reach before.

The melancholy moralizings of Jaques and the Robin Hood raptures of the Duke, though in contrast, are equally the product of man's spirit. There has to be someone in Arden to remind us of the indispensable flesh. It was a shrewd irony of Shakespeare's to give this office to the jester. Whether he is wiser or more foolish than other men it is never possible to decide, but Touchstone is, as well as the most artificial wit, the most natural man of them all; and the most conscious of his corporal needs. After the journey to the forest Rosalind complains of a weariness of spirits, to which Touchstone retorts "I care not for my spirits, if my legs were not weary." And when he displays his wit at the expense of Orlando's bad verses, saying "I'll rhyme you so eight years together", he remembers to add "dinners and suppers and sleeping-hours excepted." A "material fool", as Jaques notes. This preoccupation with the physical makes Touchstone the obvious choice for the sensual lover who will burlesque the romantic dream. So Touchstone not only deprives the yokel William of his mistress, but steals his part in the play, making it in the process of infinitely greater significance. However, Shakespeare from the beginning cast Touchstone for this burlesque role, though he may not have seen at first what form the burlesque would take. When Silvius first exhibits his love to us, and reminds Rosalind of hers, Touchstone completes the trio on his discordant note:

I remember, when I was in love I broke my sword upon a stone and bid him take that for coming a-night to Jane Smile; and I remember the kissing of...the cow's dugs that her pretty chopt hands had milked.

This sort of extravagance—in the burlesque-chivalrous vein—is not, I think, developed; but an indecent jest about a peascod does point forward to the animal lust which propels him towards Audrey, and his amour with her forms the perfect contrast to the three idealized courtships of the play. If we need a formal juxtaposition of the two kinds of love to point the matter further, I note that it is just when Rosalind has met Orlando in the forest and Orlando has promised to woo her "by the faith of [his] love" and "with all [his] heart" that we see Touchstone courting the goat-girl, regretting that fair women should be honest and talking of sexual desire.

The fool is not only a material touchstone; he is also the time-keeper of the play. At least, in the forest, where "there's no clock", he carries a time-piece with him; and it provokes the reflection: "It is ten o'clock...'Tis but an hour ago since it was nine, And after one hour more 'twill be eleven." The people of Arcadia will do well to take note of this, but if all you can do with your hours is to count them, this undeniable truth may seem a trifle futile. Touchstone, to do him justice, goes on: "And so, from hour to hour, we ripe and ripe, And then, from hour to hour, we rot and rot." He dares to speak in Arcadia, where one can never grow old, of Time's inevitable processes of maturity and decay. By this the ideal life of the banished Duke is mocked, and since Touchstone's words are repeated by Jaques with delighted and uproarious laughter, the mockery is double. Yet, in accordance with the play's principle of countering one view with another, there are two things that may be noted: first, that in a later scene Touchstone, who sums up life as riping and rotting, is compared by Rosalind to a medlar, which is rotten before it is ripe; and second, that it is at this very point, when the ideal life is doubly mocked, that the Duke administers to the mocker Jaques a direct and fierce rebuke, charging the mocker of the world's vices with having lived a vicious life himself.

The satirist, of course, is far from silenced; it is now that he ridicules the romantic hero, and presently he delivers his famous speech on the seven ages of man, brilliantly summing up the course of human life, but omitting to notice anything in it that is noble or even pleasant. However, as has often been observed, though the seven ages speech ends with a description of man's final decrepitude—"sans teeth, sans eyes, sans taste, sans everything"—it has not yet left the speaker's tongue when an aged man appears who is at once addressed as "venerable". There is always this readjustment of the point of view. Senility and venerableness—are they different things or different ways of looking at the same? Certainly the entry of the venerable Adam does not disprove what Jaques says; Shakespeare seeks no cheap antithesis. "Sans teeth"—Adam himself has admitted to being toothless, Orlando has called him "a rotten tree", and his helplessness is only too visible when he is *carried* on to the stage. Yet he *is* carried, tenderly, by the master whom he has followed "to the last gasp, with truth and loyalty". Here is the glimpse of human virtue that the seven ages speech omitted. And then it is upon this moving spectacle of mutual affection and devotion that Amiens sings his song, "Blow, blow, thou winter wind, Thou art not so unkind As man's ingratitude." Placed here, this lovely lyric, blend of joy and pathos, has a special poignancy.

The arrangement of the play depends upon many such piquant but seemingly casual juxta-positions. *As You Like It* contemplates life within and without Arden, with numerous shifts of angle, alternating valuations, and variations of mood. As for action, incident—life in the Forest of Arden does not easily lend itself to those. I have suggested that Shakespeare does something to supply this want by a glance or two back at what is happening at court. And departures from the court are matched by arrivals in the forest. For events, of course, even in Arden do sometimes occur. Orlando arrives dramatically, even melodramatically. Presently Rosalind learns that he is about. A little later on they meet. Later still Oliver arrives and is rescued from a lioness. Shakespeare still keeps up a sense of things going on. But the manner of the play, when once it settles down in the forest, is to let two people drift together, talk a little, and part, to be followed by two more. Sometimes a pair will be watched by others, who will sometimes comment on what they see. Sometimes of course there is a larger group, once or twice even a crowded stage; but most often two at a time. When they part they may arrange to meet again, or they may not. Through the three middle acts of the play, though there are two instances of love at first sight (one of them only reported), it is rare that anything happens in any particular encounter between these people of the sort that changes the course of their lives, anything, that is to say, that goes to make what is usually called a plot. Yet the meetings may properly be called 'encounters', because of the impact the contrasting characters make on one another and the sparkle of wit they kindle in one another. What is important in each meeting is our impression of those who meet and of their different attitudes to one another or to one another's views of life, an impression which is deepened or modified each time they reappear with the same or different partners. As I describe it, this may all sound rather static, but such is the ease and rapidity with which pairs and groups break up, re-form, and succeed one another on the stage that there is a sense of fluid movement. All is done with the utmost lightness and gaiety, but as the lovers move through the forest, part and meet again, or mingle with the other characters in their constantly changing pairs and groups, every view of life that is presented seems, sooner or later, to find its opposite. Life is "but a flower in spring time, the only pretty ring time", but for the unromantic Touchstone there is "no great matter in the ditty" and he counts it but time lost—his eye no doubt still on his timepiece—"to hear such a foolish song". A quartet of lovers avowing their love is broken up when one of them says

Pray you, no more of this; 'tis like the howling of Irish wolves against the moon.

And the one who says this is she who cannot tell "how many fathom deep" she is in love. Dominating the centre of the play, playing both the man's and woman's parts, counsellor in love and yet its victim, Rosalind gathers up into herself many of its roles and many of its meanings. Around her in the forest, where the banished Duke presides, is the perfect happiness of the simple life, an illusion, much mocked at, but still cherished. She herself, beloved of the hero, has all the sanity to recognize that "love is merely a madness" and that lovers should be whipped as mad-men are, but admits that "the whippers are in love too". Heroine of numerous masquerades, she is none the less always constant and never more true than when insisting that she is counter-feiting. For she is an expert in those dark riddles which mean exactly what they say. Though things are rarely what they seem, they may sometimes be so in a deeper sense. What is wisdom and what is folly is of course never decided—you may have it "as you like it". Or, as Touchstone rejoined to Rosalind, after her gibe about the medlar, "You have said; but whether wisely or no, let the forest judge."

It may be possible to suggest that the forest gives its verdict. For if *As You Like It* proclaims no final truth, its ultimate effect is not negative. Longing to escape to our enchanted world, we are constantly brought up against reality; sanity, practical wisdom sees through our illusions. Yet in *As You Like It* ideals, though always on the point of dissolving, are for ever recreating themselves. They do not delude the eye of reason, yet faith in them is not extinguished in spite of all that reason can do. "I would not be cured, youth."

NOTES

1. A lecture delivered to the Shakespeare Conference at Stratford-upon-Avon, 18 August 1953.

2. Quiller-Couch, *Shakespeare's Workmanship* (1918), p. 130. In spite of some radical disagreement, I have got a number of hints from 'Q''s essay.

3. This is not to imply that Shakespeare's 'golden world' is at all the same as the primitive life of the mythical golden age, in which, by contrast with the Forest of Arden, there was no winter wind, sheep went unshorn, and man, at peace with all creatures, neither killed the deer nor was theatened by the snake and lion. Virgil associated the simplicity of pastoral life with the golden age, and the two ideals were frequently combined, not to say confused, by later pastoralists (cf. Roy Walker, *The Golden Feast* (1952), p. 133).

4. *Huntington Library Bulletin*, VIII (1935), 85.

5. "*Enter Orlando*" says the Folio simply, but the dialogue justifies Theobald's "*with Sword drawn.*"

THE INTEGRITY OF SHAKESPEARE: ILLUSTRATED FROM *CYMBELINE*

BY

J. M. NOSWORTHY

Of all the plays in the Shakespeare canon there is, perhaps, not one which, at first sight, presents quite such a glorious conglomeration of styles as *Cymbeline*. It is not surprising, therefore, that a vigorous tradition of doubt exists, that Furness and Granville-Barker in the twentieth century found themselves rejecting as non-Shakespearian all those things which Pope and Hanmer had already disposed of in the eighteenth. Hence, conjecture has played merrily around a lost play which Shakespeare half-heartedly refashioned; a collaborator; a Shakespeare bored to death; a Shakespeare drunk with the new wine which Beaumont and Fletcher were pouring into old bottles. It is unlikely that any of these possibilities will long survive in the convictions of any reader who cares to work through the complex body of source material which lies behind *Cymbeline*, for, *pace* Dr Johnson and his followers, the construction of the play, when viewed in relation to the basic raw material, is altogether too uniform to admit of more than a single creative activity—and one that is neither drunk nor bored.

The maligned Vision in Act v may serve to illustrate this contention. Wilson Knight, who regards it as authentic, has brought forward a useful set of Shakespearian parallels, but it must be reluctantly admitted that the sum total is not really enough to dispose effectively of two centuries of doubt. The whole section is archaic in tone and style and sounds remarkably unlike anything else of Shakespeare's. But it does sound quite like one of the songs from Underdowne's translation of the *Æthiopica* of Heliodorus, and this, as Posthumus's rejection of the disguised Imogen and the name 'Philarmonus' testify, was one of the minor sources of *Cymbeline*. And it is, if anything, even nearer to the theophany at the beginning of the old play of *Love and Fortune* which must be reckoned a major source. It is difficult, then, to resist the conclusion that the Vision, though uncharacteristic, is perfectly genuine.

There are, however, more closely integrated sections of the play which have from time to time promoted editorial consternation and their stylistic promiscuity is such that all doubts would be fully justified were it not for a kind of lurking evidence. One fairly common notion is that Shakespeare allowed scene after scene to ramble on and that some stage-hack, singular in his art, pruned away acres of such verbiage and rounded things off with a heroic couplet or two. Hence the 'whipping-boy' has been held responsible for:

> Cowards father cowards and base things sire base:
> Nature hath meal and bran, contempt and grace.   (IV, ii, 26–7)

> Lead, lead. The time seems long; their blood thinks scorn,
> Till it fly out and show them princes born.   (IV, iv, 53–4)

>   Let me make men know
> More valour in me than my habits show.

> Gods, put the strength o' the Leonati in me!
> To shame the guise o' the world, I will begin
> The fashion, less without and more within. (v, i, 29–33)

But it is, presumably, Shakespeare himself who offers parallels sufficiently close. To the first:

> Seeds spring from seeds and beauty breedeth beauty;
> Thou wast begot; to get it is thy duty. (*Venus and Adonis*, ll. 167–8)

to the second:

> But swords I smile at, weapons laugh to scorn,
> Brandish'd by man that's of a woman born. (*Macbeth*, v, vii, 12–13)

and to the third:

> I gin to be aweary of the sun,
> And wish the estate o' the world were now undone.
> Ring the alarum-bell! Blow, wind! come, wrack!
> At least we'll die with harness on our back. (*Macbeth*, v, v, 49–52)

Evidence of the same kind, though more subtle, testifies to the genuineness of the Soothsayer's interpretation of the label in v, v, 443–58:

> Thou, Leonatus, art the lion's whelp;
> The fit and apt construction of thy name,
> Being Leo-natus, doth import so much.
> The piece of tender air, thy virtuous daughter,
> Which we call 'mollis aer;' and 'mollis aer'
> We term it 'mulier': which 'mulier' I divine
> Is this most constant wife; who, even now,
> Answering the letter of the oracle,
> Unknown to you, unsought, were clipp'd about
> With this most tender air.
>
> .   .   .   .   .
>
> The lofty cedar, royal Cymbeline,
> Personates thee: and thy lopp'd branches point
> Thy two sons forth; who, by Belarius stol'n,
> For many years thought dead, are now revived,
> To the majestic cedar join'd, whose issue
> Promises Britain peace and plenty.

This, by Shakespearian standards, is stuff both strange and poor, and it is quite probable that a round three dozen of the plays would fail to provide any kind of precedent. Yet there is just one other place in which Shakespeare uses this word 'mulier', and that in a tedious elucidation comparable to that of the Soothsayer:

> There is no bar
> To make against your highness' claim to France
> But this, which they produce from Pharamond,
> 'In terram Salicam mulieres ne succedant:'

'No woman shall succeed in Salique land:'
Which Salique land the French unjustly gloze
To be the realm of France.... *(Henry V, I, ii, 35–41)*

Identity of authorship does not rest, of course, on mulieres or tedium, but on unquestionable similarities in what must be regarded as an 'occasional' style. The use and positioning of relative pronouns is one peculiarity. In *Cymbeline* we have: "Which we call 'mollis aer'", "which 'mulier' I divine", "who, even now, Answering the letter", "who, by Belarius stol'n", to set against a similar group in *Henry V*: "Which Salique land the French unjustly gloze", "Who, holding in disdain the German women", "Which Salique, as I said", and so on. The second common feature, the overweight of participles, is too obvious to require comment.

It is *Henry V* again which provides the starting-point for an extraordinarily interesting illustration of Shakespeare's stylistic continuity and integrity. The Prologue to Act III offers a pleasant naval scene:

Suppose that you have seen
The well-appointed king at Hampton pier
Embark his royalty; and his brave fleet
With silken streamers the young Phoebus fanning:
Play with your fancies, and in them behold
Upon the hempen tackle ship-boys climbing;
Hear the shrill whistle which doth order give
To sounds confused; behold the threaden sails,
Borne with the invisible and creeping wind,
Draw the huge bottoms through the furrow'd sea,
Breasting the lofty surge. (ll. 3–13)

It is probable that Shakespeare was already familiar with Plutarch's description of Cleopatra's barge which he so closely followed in Enobarbus's magnificent lines in *Antony and Cleopatra*, II, ii, 195–245, and there may be a measure of unconscious recollection. At any rate, "fanning", "tackle", "sails" and "wind" are common to *Henry V*, *Antony and Cleopatra* and to North's *Plutarch*. It is only the two plays, however, which claim "silken", "whistle/whistling", and "invisible". In the tragedy, then, two sets of impulses are merged and it is not easily possible to distinguish that which derives from North from that which is unprompted Shakespeare.

It is clearly evident that the Shakespeare of *Cymbeline* was still haunted by his own description of Cleopatra, for Imogen's bedchamber

was hang'd
With tapestry of silk and silver; the story
Proud Cleopatra, when she met her Roman,
And Cydnus swell'd above the banks, or for
The press of boats or pride. (II, iv, 68–72)

That there should be a certain stylistic overflow is, therefore, not surprising—though there are surprises in other respects. Belarius's commendation of the two princes in IV, ii is held by some to typify Shakespeare's reversion to Elizabethan poetic conventions, by others to establish his surrender to Fletcher—while Furness, if I understand him aright, completely repudiates Shakespeare's authorship. Such views cannot be condemned out of hand, for the passage has an unfamiliar look:

> O thou goddess,
> Thou divine Nature, how thyself thou blazon'st
> In these two princely boys! They are as gentle
> As zephyrs blowing below the violet,
> Not wagging his sweet head; and yet as rough,
> Their royal blood enchafed, as the rudest wind,
> That by the top doth take the mountain pine,
> And make him stoop to the vale. 'Tis wonder
> That an invisible instinct should frame them
> To royalty unlearn'd, honour untaught,
> Civility not seen from other, valour
> That wildly grows in them, but yields a crop
> As if it had been sow'd.   (ll. 169–81)

Yet, when we probe below the surface, we find that this passage is not really so far removed from Enobarbus's description of Cleopatra, that common elements of thought and imagery are quite abundant. "Nature" and "wind" appear in both, and the gentle violet of the one may be set against the "flower-soft hands" of the other. The idea of stooping is common ("And made their bends adornings" in *Antony and Cleopatra*): the verb "frame" occurs in both; and the "strange invisible perfume" has become a wonderful, that is strange, "invisible instinct". And so, different though the two passages are, there are, as it were, certain of Shakespeare's hall-marks to persuade us that we have not been duped. It may be added that the reader who grasps the significance of the princes, "their royal blood enchafed", is not likely to assign the great *Troilus and Cressida* prologue to Chapman or any other candidate put forward by the disintegrators.

Yet, to adapt Shakespeare's own paradox, the self is not the same. Belarius's speech, like so much of *Cymbeline*, is Elizabethan, and pastoral, and decorative, and even conventional. This does not mean that Shakespeare, in 1608 or thereabouts, went to school with Guarini or with Beaumont and Fletcher, but simply that he returned to his own earlier practices. *Venus and Adonis* and *The Rape of Lucrece* come back into the picture at this time, and it is surely significant that the name which Imogen invents, "Richard du Champ", should be none other than that of Richard Field, the stationer from Stratford who published these first heirs of the poet's invention. The famous bedchamber scene in *Cymbeline* may serve to illustrate Shakespearian continuity over what is practically the longest possible period.

The situation, that of furtive nocturnal assault upon an innocent person, would obviously provide the dramatist with several ready-made associations. Macbeth's trespass upon Duncan is one, and its impact upon the bedchamber scene has been duly demonstrated, notably by Ingleby. But it is clear that Shakespeare's mind travelled further back, to *Titus Andronicus* and the Philomel myth:

> She hath been reading late
> The tale of Tereus; here the leaf's turn'd down
> Where Philomel gave up.   (II, ii, 44–6)

and to *The Rape of Lucrece* itself:

> Our Tarquin thus
> Did softly press the rushes, ere he waken'd
> The chastity he wounded.   (II, ii, 12–14)

It is not surprising, then, that these early pieces, with *Venus and Adonis* thrown in, should exert stylistic influence, and herein lies the paradox of Iachimo's superb apostrophe—that it is as much the work of the prentice as of the master. By way of illustration I offer the following cento:

> Cytherea,
> How bravely thou becom'st thy bed! Fresh lily,
> Imprisoned in a gaol of snow, and teaching
> The sheets a whiter hue than white. To touch;
> But kiss, one kiss! Rubies unparagon'd,
> Dearly they kiss each other. Filling the chamber
> Comes breath perfumed. Now the flame o' the taper
> Bows toward her, and would underpeep her lids
> To see th'enclosed lights, now canopied
> Under the two blue windows, violet-veined,
> As if from thence he borrow'd all his shine.

Translation in terms of *Venus and Adonis* is not a very difficult matter. Adonis's retort:

> Mine ears, that to your wanton talk attended,
> Do burn themselves for having so offended.   (ll. 809–10)

might easily be that of Imogen to Iachimo, and Posthumus's meditations on death in v, iii, 68–73 are not far removed from:

> Hard-favour'd tyrant, ugly, meagre, lean,   (l. 931)

Again:

> A purple flower sprung up, chequer'd with white,
> Resembling well his pale cheeks and the blood
> Which in round drops upon their whiteness stood.   (ll. 1168–70)

could well be Arviragus lamenting the lost Fidele.

When we speak of Shakespeare's style, it is often, perhaps, with too narrow a conception of what that style really embraces. These passages from *Cymbeline*, several of which have sorely troubled highly responsible critics, amply illustrate that when he is least himself, or least what we might expect him to be, he is most himself—or, to take his own phrase, "When I most wink, then do mine eyes best see." *Cymbeline* is a stylistic gallimaufry, but, in the last analysis, all the styles are Shakespeare's, and what applies to this play must surely hold for others more closely integrated. There may yet be more profit in seeking for Shakespeare in that which purports to be his than in following Greene, Peele, Chapman, Wilkins, Middleton or Fletcher into the shadows.

SHAKESPEARE'S COMIC PROSE[1]

BY

LUDWIG BORINSKI

GENERAL CHARACTERISTICS OF SHAKESPEARE'S PROSE

Historically, Shakespeare's prose is more or less in that 'pre-classical' style which had its roots in the medieval period and survived until the middle of the seventeenth century.[2] Among its characteristics are redundancy, a love of epithets, emphasis and inversion, lengthy periods, a certain preference for nouns and abstracts before verbs, and finally a liking for 'architectural' patterns of expression.

About the middle of the sixteenth century the first signs of new tendencies appeared. This was the age which saw the birth of modern science. The new spirit of analysis tended to create a new prose style; the old clumsy periods became articulated into short, clear sentences; antithesis, the main instrument of intellectual clarification, became omnipresent; and the architectural patterns assumed a new form of almost mechanical rigidity. Metaphor, nearly non-existent before, symbolized the increasing intellectuality in its task of bringing together remote ideas. 'Wit' rapidly became the watchword of the new age; euphuism is only the culmination of a tendency apparent since 1550 or even earlier.

In Shakespeare's writings, it is true, we can readily trace the influence of the new intellectuality, but side by side with this remain the persisting qualities of the older style. Redundancy, the main feature of the old style, is already absent in Shakespeare, except where it is used for intentional comic effects. Thus we miss the characteristic tautologies, such as "intention and meaning", or "support and maintain", which figure in every paragraph of Spenser and Hooker. But his prose is still full of semipoetic *emphasis*, emphatic particles and short clauses, "faith", "pray", "by my troth", "I assure you", epithets in the superlative, exclamations of all sorts. Exaggeration or hyperbole is a feature common to all levels of Shakespeare's comic prose. The predominance of nouns and adjectives over verbs is universal—

So shall my anticipation prevent your discovery, (*Hamlet*, II, ii, 304)

I think the policy of that purpose made more in the marriage than the love of the parties.
(*Antony and Cleopatra*, II, vi, 126)

I was then frugal of my mirth. (*Merry Wives of Windsor*, II, i, 27)

This nominal style is semipoetic; it agrees with Shakespeare's predilection for the visual and concrete. Nouns denote things and adjectives qualities of things, whereas verbs express processes which cannot be seen, and can be conceived only intellectually. Hence the verbal character of the more intellectual classical prose of Dryden and Locke, or of Milton's poetry compared with Shakespeare's.

His metaphors are, as it were, transitional between the unintellectual, visual art of the earlier Renaissance (as it persists, for example, in Spenser) and the new intellectuality of the seventeenth century. Basically the metaphor, as a connexion of remote ideas, is the result of an intellectual

E

effort, and in mature classical prose, where it is frequent, its function is didactic, not picturesque. Locke says of children: "They are travelling newly arrived in a strange country"; this helps to explain the situation to us. It is the same with jests. A jest also presents a connexion between remote ideas; thus it has many qualities in common with the metaphor, and in mature classical prose the jest, like the metaphor, clarifies a complicated situation; we learn something from it. Jane Austen writes in *Mansfield Park*: "Selfishness must always be forgiven, you know, for there is no hope of a cure." This teaches us more than twenty pages of philosophy; the jest is a form of intellectual shorthand, again like a metaphor.

Shakespeare's prose, like his verse, is full of metaphors, and for the most part these metaphors are of a visual, highly concrete sort. Frequently indeed they assume a half-allegorical form—

And then comes repentance and, with his bad legs, falls into the cinque pace faster and faster, till he sink into his grave. (*Much Ado About Nothing*, II, i, 81)

...if justice cannot tame you, she shall ne'er weigh more reasons in her balance. (*Ibid.* v, i, 210)

They are mainly picturesque and quaint; they are not merely intellectually clarifying;[3] essentially they are poetic images. The same is true of his jests. They are quaint rather than 'witty' in the modern sense of the word, and a *bon mot* of the sort quoted from Jane Austen is hardly found in his prose. Closely connected with all this is another quality of Shakespeare's jests and images— often they are more far-fetched than happy. Although to associate remote ideas is in the nature of both, the greatest intellectual achievement does not necessarily consist in finding the remotest associations; that achievement consists in discovering the happiest comparison, a comparison which may well be fairly obvious. Locke's comparison of children with strangers might be considered almost commonplace, but it is marvellously appropriate. Forced metaphors, similes and jests, the peculiarity of Shakespeare's age, are intellectually less mature, although they have the compensating advantage of greater picturesqueness and poetic charm.

It is as easy to count atomies as to resolve the propositions of a lover (*As You Like It*, III, ii, 245)

—intellectually this is not particularly happy, but it is 'quaint' and charming; the same may be said of such a forced jest as:

I think he will carry this island home in his pocket and give it his son for an apple. And sowing the kernels of it in the sea, bring forth more islands. (*The Tempest*, II, i, 90)

Images and jests are the two main elements in a further quality of Shakespeare's style, its richness in association. Of all intellects ever born, Shakespeare comes nearest the divine quality of seeing all things and all relations between things in one single intuition. With every concept an infinite number of associations come crowding on his mind. Everything gives rise to an image, a jest, an allusion of some sort; hardly a sentence is free of them. His habit of generaliza- tion and reflexion is of the same pattern, though perhaps it is more pronounced in his verse than in his prose. Both association and generalization are common features of the age. Euphuistic or semi-euphuistic prose from Lyly to Sir Thomas Browne is the prose of metaphor, allusion, quotation, proverb, and 'sentence'. The ensuing classical age either did away with these things altogether, or reduced them to more modest proportions. It is highly significant that Le Bossu[4] in 1674 blames Seneca's style for its abundance of metaphor and 'sentence', while this is precisely why Seneca was so popular with the Elizabethans. Classical style is functional, whereas Elizabethan style is decorative. This is particularly true of Shakespeare's comic prose, and explains central features of its character. Not only are Shakespeare's prose metaphors and jests in themselves picturesque and quaint rather than intellectually revealing, their role in the whole is ornamental rather than functional. In Restoration comedy all dialogue has at least some remote connexion with the action of the play; it is, therefore, functional; but in Shakespeare's plays action is almost entirely confined to verse, and the prose scenes are more or less static, devoid of real dramatic action. This means that such prose scenes exist largely for the sake of ornamentation or of reflexion. Jests, images, allusions, thus become ends in themselves.

All this has further important consequences. The tempo of Shakespeare's prose is mostly slow, much slower than the tempo of his verse, precisely because this mass of ornamental detail swells the sentences. Along with this quality we note a most significant tendency: there is no steady progress of an argument, such as is always found in classical comedy, even in scenes where the dialogue contains little action. Shakespeare in his prose dialogues never sticks long to a train of ideas; clowns, fools, and courtiers have this in common—they shift from one subject to another; [5] and all subjects are more or less irrelevant, ornamental as their language, just as the plots of the purely comic portions of the comedies are irrelevant pranks and practical jokes.

Nevertheless, this love of the decorative has its very definite limits in Shakespeare's art. From the start, in his prose he does without the fantastic 'natural science' imagery of euphuism. In addition to the free use of images, the decorative spirit of Renaissance art was accustomed to express itself in purely verbal artistry, in word-play and the invention of grotesque words, as in the works of Rabelais. This tendency is reduced to very modest proportions by Shakespeare, though it is never entirely discarded. *Love's Labour's Lost* had been a youthful experiment in this line, yet the play itself contains his great renunciation of that kind of art (v, ii). When, later, long strings of grotesque terms of abuse are employed, such as Kent's apostrophe of Oswald in *King Lear*, ii, ii, 15, or when abstracts are made to serve as abusive epithets (an example is Falstaff's "thou unconfinable baseness", *Merry Wives of Windsor*, ii, ii, 21), we realize that the stylistic methods are being employed with conscious choice and artistic purpose. The rare examples of grotesque learning, of the kind found in Rabelais, are associated with the Host in *Merry Wives of Windsor*, the fools, and the pedants of *Love's Labour's Lost*. Word-play and purely verbal grotesque are thus no longer ends in themselves.

Finally, we note the prevailing architectural patterns of Shakespeare's prose—parallelisms, mostly antithetical and with the characteristic rigidity of euphuism, triadic figures of all kind, chiasmus, and especially long enumerations of words or short 'sentences'. Here may be discerned stereotyped larger architectural patterns. One such is a series of parallelisms, often three or four, followed by a concluding antithesis: [6]

One woman is fair, yet I am well; another is wise, yet I am well; another virtuous, yet I am well; but till all graces be in one woman, one woman shall not come in my grace.

(*Much Ado About Nothing*, ii, iii, 28–31)

Note here how other figures—chiasmus and the puns—are combined with the parallelism and antithesis; the profusion of architectural figures is hardly inferior to that of associative ornament.

At the end of a long speech or a scene we often get a figure, an exact counterpart to the rhymed couplets at the end of verse speeches or verse scenes—

the clown bore it, the fool sent it, and the lady hath it; sweet clown, sweeter fool, sweetest lady!

(*Love's Labour's Lost*, IV, iii, 16–18)

This love of architectural patterns is only another symptom of the non-functional character of Shakespeare's prose. In the absence of a functional whole such mechanical patterns are the only means to give structure to the mass of decorative detail of which this art consists, just as in Spenser's *Faerie Queene* an allegorical pattern connects a mass of incoherent episodes in the absence of an inner, functional unity of action. This is also the reason why sometimes Shakespeare appears so much more accomplished an artist in verse than he does in prose. In verse we take such patterns for granted; in prose the patterns, at least to this degree of rigidity, are felt as unnatural; they seem semi-poetic, they contradict what we regard as the nature of prose. Prose, we feel, demands a structure derived from the meaning expressed, that is to say, an organic, functional structure. Similarly, Shakespeare's long periods sound clumsy only in prose, not in verse, although in verse the periods are even longer, sometimes interminable: since in verse we hear only the rhythm of the metre, which articulates the sentence, the length and rhythm of the sentence itself become irrelevant. In true prose, however, form is derived from meaning; meaning itself must be well articulated and must not be burdened with decorative irrelevancies and associations if prose is to sound harmonious and well balanced. Shakespeare represents a stage in the development of prose where prose has not yet found itself, where it follows the laws of verse rather than its own intrinsic laws.

A curious consequence of all this is that Shakespeare largely inverts the use of verse and prose. One of his most eminent qualities is his realistic vividness of speech. He is perhaps the only dramatist of his age who makes his characters speak like living human beings in real situations; this is his distinctive quality from the very outset of his career, and it is the surest means of distinguishing the genuine and non-genuine portions of, for example, *1 Henry VI*. The Renaissance liked to tie expressions in patterns, whereas Shakespeare's expression is from the start free and natural; everything is alive and real, compared, for instance with Spenser's studied dream-like unreality. But all this applies only to his verse. Shakespeare is natural in his verse, but artificial in his prose. All his prose consists of highly conscious artistry. Evidently he still needed the mechanical prop of blank verse in order to feel entirely at his ease, while his sense of awkwardness in the total freedom of prose made him escape into artificiality. Shakespeare's prose is thus the great manifestation of the exquisite in his art, with a charm of its own beside and opposite to the full-blooded realism of his verse. In the following we shall demonstrate this on the various levels of his comic prose.

NATURALISTIC PROSE

If nearly all Shakespeare's speech is stylized, it is because his artistic tendencies, his 'style', demanded it. His was eminently a type of intellect in which the constructive faculties preponderated over the receptive. He was not primarily an observer, least of all an observer of detail. His creative power was stronger than his habit of observation; he built a character as a living whole out of his unique intuition, after which it assumed an independent life, and all details of behaviour derived spontaneously from this initial act of creation. His technique was the reverse of that of nineteenth-century authors, who were first of all observers, note-book authors who collected details and assembled a comic character from them. Falstaff is first created as a living whole and all he does or says follows from that whole; Mrs Gamp is assembled from a mass of comic detail collected beforehand, and Dickens's greatness lies in the way in which he transforms such an assemblage into a living person in which we still can believe. All this applies also to details of speech. Shakespeare creates speech, he does not reproduce what he observes. Even his naturalistic prose is therefore rather poorer in amusing phrases taken from life than that of nineteenth- and twentieth-century authors.

Low Comedy Prose

This is a clearly defined type in Shakespeare's works. It appears in the speech of Falstaff and his gang, of the comic parts of *Henry IV* and of *The Merry Wives of Windsor*, and exactly the same style occurs also elsewhere in similar characters. Jack Cade and Christopher Sly are preliminary studies in Falstaff, and the low comedy parts of *Twelfth Night*, *Troilus and Cressida* (especially Thersites) and *The Tempest* carry on this style. Here are found the first of the stylized types of speech. One preliminary word of caution is necessary. If we call such manner of speech 'stylized', we do not want to imply that it was quite without analogies in real life. In real life certain classes of persons may use artificial forms of speech—but this is due to the influence of artistic convention on real life and therefore is to be distinguished from naturalistic prose. The 'humour' was a fashion both in literature and in life. In a way, this tendency has always remained an English peculiarity. Every class in England has always more or less consciously stylized its behaviour and talk. The stylized humour of Dickens's Sam Weller, Mark Tapley, Dick Swiveller, who like Pistol speaks only in quotations, Bailey junior, etc., would be impossible in any other country. That Shakespeare, Ben Jonson, the eighteenth-century novelists and Dickens took their 'oddities' also from life, is confirmed even today. I have known cockney workmen who constantly indulged in the same artificial brag as Falstaff, if not quite with Falstaff's genius.

In this, Falstaff, Sly and Jack Cade are all self-stylized; they act a role on the stage of life and are conscious of it. Everything is turned by them into a jest or an allusion; they owe this to their reputation. As a result the level of comedy is uneven, much that is marvellous is intermingled with much that is cheap or forced, especially facile comic exaggeration.[7] In keeping with the less intellectual character of low comedy, the comic effects here are nearly always of the visual, not of the intellectual kind. Metaphors are rare, but comic similes abound, all highly concrete. The prince calls Falstaff "thou globe of sinful continents" (*2 Henry IV*, II, iv, 309), Falstaff says of himself "my skin hangs about me like an old lady's loose gown" (*1 Henry IV*, III, iii, 4). All is full of striking pictures, and Falstaff sees himself as a grotesque, vivified by strange comparisons: he talks to his diminutive page:

I am not only witty in myself, but the cause that wit is in other men. I do here walk before thee like a sow that hath overwhelmed all her litter but one. (*2 Henry IV*, I, ii, 11)

E*

This more than anything confirms our opinion of Falstaff's style as conscious self-stylization and of Falstaff as the actor of his own role. He continues:

If the prince put thee into my service for any other reason than to set me off, why then I have no judgement.

There is a great deal of highly conscious aestheticism in all of this.

It is specially significant that even in the few cases where the jests are of a more intellectual kind, consisting of a surprising association of ideas, they take their start from a visual picture. The Lord Chief Justice rebukes Falstaff:

You have misled the youthful prince.
Fal. The young prince hath misled me: I am the fellow with the great belly, and he my dog.

(*2 Henry IV*, I, ii, 163–5)

This is marvellous repartee, truly witty, but again based on a grotesque picture—a visual comic style which is a counterpart in comedy to the prevailing Renaissance cult of the picturesque.[8] Even more obviously in the style of contemporary Renaissance grotesque is Falstaff's description of Shallow as an undergraduate:

When a' was naked, he was, for all the world, like a forked radish, with a head fantastically carved upon it with a knife. (*2 Henry IV*, III, ii, 333–5)

Falstaff's self-conscious, self-stylized irony expresses itself above all in a very interesting form of parody: he uses all the means of 'elevated' style, but his metaphors are nearly always ironic:

Your lordship, though not clean past your youth, hath yet some smack of age in you, some relish of the saltness of time. (*2 Henry IV*, I, ii, 110–12)

The weakness of contemporary style for abstracts, nouns and hard words in general is also given an ironic turn:

Thou art essentially mad. (*1 Henry IV*, II, iv, 541)

Discharge yourself of our company! (*2 Henry IV*, II, iv, 147)

Euphuistic style in general is parodied:

for, Harry, now I do not speak to thee in drink, but in tears, not in pleasure but in passion, not in words only, but in woes also. (*1 Henry IV*, II, iv, 457–9)

It is highly interesting that this sort of sophistication was already known to the Elizabethans.

One of the finest qualities of Shakespeare's art of prose is his subtle differentiation of speech and its use for atmospheric effects. The different frequency of nouns and abstracts on various levels of speech and the restriction of naturalistic prose to women of the lowest class have already been mentioned. Even the speech of one and the same person is differentiated in diverse scenes. Falstaff's parodistic style is most pronounced when he is talking to the Lord Chief Justice; Mrs Page's and Mrs Ford's style is different from Mrs Quickly's because they are better educated. Their husbands' style is again different; their intellectual level is higher than their wives', so their speech is even fuller of nouns and abstracts and complicated periods; they too use metaphors, but of a more refined kind. While the two women and their husbands are thus differentiated, the level of stylization in their speech is not highly advanced. The Host, on the other hand, is clearly stylized, though less self-stylized than Falstaff; his manner of speech has rather the qualities of a traditional 'humour'. Here is a mixture of superiority and affected broad geniality, with an unpleasant whiff of business advertising and the use of stereotyped phrases. Shallow, too, is stylized. His talk has the commonplace peculiarities of a silly old man, extreme slowness produced by constant repetitions and digressions. But all this is purposely forced and overdone, and thus it assumes the additional artistic and decorative quality of the grotesque, like Falstaff's exaggerations, though here in a much more discreet form. But this is not the only 'overtone' in the Shallow scenes; they also serve to create an atmosphere. As soon as we get into the country, Shakespeare, who throughout his work is a conscious representative of the provincial Englishman, deliberately creates an air of homely comfort, the air of provincial old England. This poetic flavour can be felt in all the various styles of speech as a common additional overtone. Shallow's sentimental harking back to the days of his youth; his grotesque deviations:

Certain, 'tis certain; very sure, very sure: death, as the Psalmist saith, is certain to all; all shall die. How a good yoke of bullocks at Stamford fair? (*2 Henry IV*, III, ii, 40–3)

—all this is not pure silliness, it is also poetic. And so are Falstaff's ironic answers, here all in his best vein of parodistic metaphor. Shallow asks Falstaff about Jane Nightwork:

Doth she hold her own well?
Fal. Old, old, Master Shallow...
Shal. Ha, cousin Silence, that thou hadst seen that that this knight and I have seen! Ha, Sir John, said I well?
Fal. We have heard the chimes at midnight, Master Shallow. (*2 Henry IV*, III, ii, 217–29)

The Clown

In all plays the clown-scenes are dominated by certain stereotyped forms of speech. First, there is the long comic soliloquy, a feature common to all types of Shakespeare's prose, but in the clown-scenes mostly with an impersonation of a dramatic scene in short sentences of direct speech (*Two Gentlemen of Verona*, II, iii, *Merchant of Venice*, II, ii, etc.).[9] Secondly, there are the comic catechisms, exemplified in *Comedy of Errors*, II, ii, *Two Gentlemen of Verona*, III, i, Falstaff's catechism of honour, etc. Thirdly, closely related with the foregoing is a form which we may call the vexing dialogue, a complicated system of never getting to the point by means of diverting answers, puns, quibbles, etc. (*Two Gentlemen of Verona*, II, v, *The Merchant of Venice*, II, ii, 38, the gravedigger-scene in *Hamlet*, etc.). Something similar appears also in the comic soliloquies, where the Clown sometimes confuses himself in an impersonated dialogue, for example *The Two Gentlemen of Verona*, III, i, 264–9:

He lives not now that knows me to be in love; yet I am in love; but a team of horse shall not pluck that from me; nor who 'tis I love; and yet 'tis a woman; but what woman, I will not tell myself; and yet 'tis a milkmaid; and yet 'tis not a maid....

All this is only a special form of burlesque dialectics, itself nothing but a further type of Renaissance grotesque. Shakespeare's immediate forerunner is in this case Lyly (e.g. *Campaspe*, III, ii), whom he clearly imitates.

It has been stressed that Shakespeare in all his prose pursues a deliberate artistic purpose, even in his seeming shortcomings. He is sometimes silly and artificial, and often his jests are not really laughable, but normally this is not for any lack of ability, but rather for highly sophisticated artistic reasons. This becomes specially clear from the development of the Clown. Shakespeare starts from the natural, and his characteristic style is only the result of a gradual and deliberate evolution. In *The Comedy of Errors* the Clowns still talk in a more or less natural style, and their jests are laughable if rather commonplace. *The Two Gentlemen of Verona* is already full of eccentric quibbling; the process of stylization begins; Shakespeare starts working out his peculiar technique. For the first time we find stylized silliness, that is to say, silliness which is so extreme that it looks quaint and grotesque rather than ridiculous:

my sister crying, our maid howling, our cat wringing her hands...my grandam, having no eyes, look you, wept herself blind at my parting.   (*The Two Gentlemen of Verona*, II, iii, 7–15; see also IV, iv)

In *The Merchant of Venice* the same type of clown-talk is fully developed, revealing a fundamental principle of Shakespeare's mature comic art: the style of his comic passages is brought into close harmony with the total atmosphere and subject of the play. Launcelot Gobbo is an almost exact replica of Launce and Speed, because *The Merchant of Venice* is the same type of semi-realistic, semi-romantic play as *The Two Gentlemen of Verona*. And in *A Midsummer Night's Dream* the clown-scenes are entirely dominated by 'poetic' silliness, because the atmosphere of the whole play is now purely lyrical and poetic. There is no really laughable and witty jest, which is clearly intentional. We hear of the "lamentable comedy", "roaring gently", "in a monstrous little voice". Even the trades of the Clowns have something of the quaintly absurd: "Francis Flute, the bellows-mender." Even here, however, the characters are carefully differentiated. Quince is the pedant whose talk abounds in redundancies; Bottom is no fool and has real wit, and accordingly he alone has sufficient imagination for witty associations, as, for instance, when he talks to the fairies; these associations are once more half funny, half picturesque and quaint, in keeping with the atmosphere of the play:

Good Master Mustardseed, I know your patience well: that same cowardly, giantlike oxbeef hath devoured many a gentleman of your house...I desire your more acquaintance, good Master Mustardseed.

(III, i, 196–201)

In *The Winter's Tale* the poetic element is even more pronounced than in *A Midsummer Night's Dream*, and again it is in keeping with the atmosphere of the play. Nevertheless its prose is basically much more naturalistic than that in any other Clown Scenes, because these clowns are real peasants, their intellectual level is inferior even to that of Launce, Speed and Launcelot. Their images are of the homeliest kind: "as you'd thrust a cork into a hogshead" (III, iii, 95). Yet their speech is nevertheless stylized. In such a passage as

the men are not yet cold under water, nor the bear half dined on the gentleman: he's at it now.

(III, iii, 107–9)

the effect is produced by means which might be deemed overdone in a purely realistic comedy; here is stylization with poetic overtones. Autolycus is differentiated from the peasants; he is a clever rogue, and accordingly his speech is more intellectual, with a high proportion of nouns and abstracts, even learned allusions and especially metaphors, always the surest sign of intellectuality. He is full of irony, but his irony is different from Falstaff's; it is finer, gentler, in keeping with the atmosphere of the play. There is poetry in his roguery. While he is picking the Clown's pocket he says: "Softly, dear sir; good sir, softly. You ha' done me a charitable office", and he declines his victim's offer of money, because "that kills my heart". The peculiar poetic atmosphere is thus again all-pervading; not even the rogue's speeches are at variance.

PROSE OF THE COURT

In the prose used by courtly characters, Shakespeare's art undergoes a clear evolution, produced by his partial emancipation from euphuism. All Shakespeare's prose has some resemblance to euphuism, but euphuism proper is confined to his immature comic style. It appears, though only in occasional patches, in *Love's Labour's Lost*, and it dominates courtly conversation in *The Merchant of Venice*, I, ii. Portia uses a euphuistic device in her parallel variations of generalized antithetic sentences, indulging even in euphuism's favourite alliterations. But Nerissa's speeches are not euphuistic; they are in ordinary 'elevated' prose with an abundance of nouns and abstracts in fairly long periods. Differentiation again. In his later comedies Shakespeare has passed beyond this euphuistic stage, or rather he has developed it further into his own style of courtly conversation. This conversation is more natural and less sententious than the euphuistic, and is characterized by a great deal of repartee expressed in very short, scrappy sentences. Shakespeare thus takes a step further in the evolution of courtly dialogue, a tradition which in England was founded by his immediate predecessor Lyly.

For the rest, this style has, surprisingly, much in common with that of the Clown and the Fool, especially in its dialectics and syllogism, its comic catechisms, its long comic monologues and its forced comic exaggerations. But in spite of all the forced wit the level of comedy here has this in common with the Falstaff scenes, that it is uneven rather than low; we get frequent flashes of really brilliant repartee, but this wit too, like the Clown's, is half poetic and has a quaint flavour:

Oh God, that I were a man! I would eat his heart in the market-place.
(Beatrice in Much Ado About Nothing, IV, i, 308)

In addition, we observe once more how it is modified to express delicate differentiation and atmosphere. Thus in *Much Ado about Nothing* dialectics are confined to Beatrice, as in *The Merchant of Venice* euphuism was the privilege of Portia, in both cases to indicate the superior talents of the heroine compared with those of Benedick or Nerissa. In purely male conversation, too, we find a quality of irony absent in repartee between the sexes (for example, *The Merchant of Venice*, V, i, and *The Tempest*, II, i).

By creating this style of courtly conversation Shakespeare made his contribution to the development of classical prose. Classical prose is in its very essence conversational; the fluent and witty conversation of high comedy is its masterpiece. But, apart from its forced wit and poetic flavour,

Shakespeare's conversational prose is distinguished from that of Restoration comedy by the staccato quality of its repartee. This has its exact parallel in the work of other contemporary forerunners of classical prose, for example, in Bacon's *Essays*. Even Dryden's sentences are shorter than Addison's and Swift's. Extreme terseness was the only way to overcome the unwieldy periods of pre-classical prose. It was also in keeping with the strong nervous tension of the age and formed another variant of the quaint and picturesque.

THE PROSE OF THE 'TOWN'

We cannot, however, regard this as the most important forerunner of classical prose in Shakespeare's age. The stage was also the place where a much maturer form of classical prose was being developed, but to find this we must go not to Shakespeare's still half-euphuistic courtly dialogue, but to the dramatic prose of his fellow-playwrights. In his comic prose Shakespeare is almost isolated among his contemporaries; his prose is nearly all stylized and romantically artistic, whereas they write in a more or less natural, lifelike manner. Theirs is the realistic comedy of the Town, whereas Shakespeare in his generation is the almost solitary representative of the older Renaissance comedy of the Court. The Town and the Court are two worlds which must be clearly distinguished. Classical civilization is the creation of the Town, not of the Court, which lost its leading role with the last traces of the Renaissance under Charles I. Between 1580 and 1660 the 'Town' was growing up, and English comedy outside Shakespeare is from its very start closely bound up with this growth. Therefore classical prose, the central achievement of classical civilization, arose first on the stage. The prose of Ben Jonson, Beaumont and Fletcher, Middleton, Shirley, etc. must not be confused with the naturalistic speech of Mrs Quickly. The so-called naturalness of classical prose is an artificial product of rationalization, of art looking like nature. Its sole example in Shakespeare is to be found in his only experiment in the comedy of the 'Town', namely in the brothel and prison scenes of *Measure for Measure*. This prose stands completely by itself among all Shakespeare's works. It is almost without any traces of romantic stylization, 'quaintness' and poetic atmosphere. Even his predilection for nouns and abstracts is almost gone. It is significant that an attempt at the riddling dialogue is pointedly cut short: "Come sir, leave me your snatches, and yield me a direct answer" (IV, ii, 6–7). The jests are jokes of a cruelly modern variety: "Pray, Master Barnadine, awake till you are executed, and sleep afterwards" (IV, iii, 34–5). The whole is another confirmation of Shakespeare's principle of conformity to atmosphere, and, besides, it forms an additional proof that he could be both natural and 'modern', in prose, if he wanted to, and that his other styles spring from a conscious artistic purpose.

CONCLUDING REMARKS

One last peculiarity of the poet, his habit of expressly calling our attention to the characteristics of his art, must be held firmly in mind. The word-play in *Love's Labour's Lost* is repeatedly advertised, so are the puns in the clown-scenes (*The Two Gentlemen of Verona*, III, i, 283; Launcelot is called a witsnapper, *Merchant of Venice*, III, v, 55), Launcelot introduces his riddling speeches with "I will try confusions with him" (II, ii, 38), Touchstone's character as a wise fool is several times pointed out by the Duke, and he is called "fantastical" by Martext (III, iii, 107); the strongly poetic quality of repartee in *As You Like It* is underlined by Jaques; "You are full of pretty answers" (III, ii, 287) he says.[10]

These self-characterizations offer, again, still more proof that Shakespeare was a thoroughly conscious artist in his prose, with his subtle differentiation of character and even situation, and his principle, consistently observed, of conformity with the total atmosphere of the play. A word-by-word analysis of a passage or a scene would show how the smallest detail, and the choice of practically every word, is the result of a conscious or semiconscious intention. I may add one further example. When in *The Merry Wives of Windsor* Falstaff's little page gives a message from his master, he suddenly falls into ironic metaphor, because he quotes Falstaff:

> My master knows not of your being here and hath threatened to put me into everlasting liberty if I tell you of it.
> (III, iii, 29–31)

The result is a wealth of comic and artistic resource which is unique. And the unique quality is to be seen in more ways than one. Shakespeare is not fond of clichés and so he deliberately avoids certain items in the stock-in-trade of comedy. He completely dispenses with anecdotes, one of the favourite forms of the Renaissance;[11] we miss the paradoxes dear to his contemporaries, and only very sparingly does he use the (mostly alliterative) formulas of the type 'wit—will—wisdom', 'profit—pleasure', 'nature—nurture', 'nature—fortune', etc., which are among the most conspicuous features of seventeenth-century prose and are ubiquitous in his predecessor Lyly. (One of the rare examples in Shakespeare is in *As You Like It*, I, ii, 43.) This unique character of Shakespeare's prose (his verse has much more in common with his fellow-playwrights) should furnish a very useful method of deciding questions of authenticity, at least if analysis is accurate and detailed.

To sum up: euphuism proper and the purely verbal artistry of the late Renaissance are only a transitory phenomenon in Shakespeare's early development. *Love's Labour's Lost* would therefore deserve a separate study. Even this one-sided cerebralism has its peculiar charm of high-wrought elegance and brittle lightness. It survives in his mature style, but there it takes second place to a new and specifically Shakespearian art of poetic atmosphere, subtle shades of character, and extreme delicacy of touch, qualities which have so far passed unobserved in his prose, and which become apparent only to the minutest analysis. Alongside this the peculiar nervous tension of the age makes itself felt. Shakespeare evolves a complete technique of excentric association, of scraps of sentences, and of quaint dialectics; even his puns and quibbles and riddling dialogues are not merely traditional or concessions to the vulgar, but are evolved only gradually as a further means of creating this atmosphere, which is continually on the increase in Shakespeare's work. The disintegration of logic in Feste's talk is a further step on this road, at the end of which is the feigned madness of Hamlet and Edgar and the real madness of Lear and Ophelia, whose speeches and songs are an exact parallel of Feste's. Chaos is a dominating motif in Shakespeare's mature tragic art, and we see how intimately the most modest elements of his early comedies, the puns and quips of his Clowns, are connected with these profoundest aspects of his work. This holds good also for other techniques of his comic prose: parody, which we found in Falstaff, becomes a dominating influence in European literature round about 1600 with Cervantes's *Don Quixote* and Tassoni's *La Secchia Rapita*, and Shakespeare makes his contribution to the new style with the parodistic elements in *Troilus and Cressida*. The conscious conformity to atmosphere discernible in his prose has its parallel in the great tragedies: the black-and-white technique of character in *King Lear*, the rigid parallelisms of the two plots, the symbolism of the play (otherwise rare in Shakespeare), are all in keeping with its total atmosphere of primeval myth in archaic surroundings, just as the subtle psychology, the rationalism, and the sophistication of *Othello* conform to its 'modern' milieu. In *Troilus and Cressida*, too, the parodistic tone is underlined by a curiously artificial language. Shakespeare's expositions and initial scenes chiefly serve to create atmosphere. Above all, in his comedies Shakespeare is the master of romantic atmosphere and of fine shades, integrated out of a wealth of artistic detail, to which his comic prose thus makes an important contribution. But it is not only his art of creating atmosphere, it is also his subtle differentiation of style according to character and situation and his art of irony and parody that are manifestations of this all-pervading technique of fine shades. His own whimsical and cryptic personality, hidden and elusive behind his characters, has something of this quality. And he was perfectly conscious of this overall character of his comic art. Falstaff gives us a complete philosophy of wit in *2 Henry IV*, IV, iii, where we hear about the brain, which must become "apprehensive, quick, forgetive, full of nimble, fiery and delectable shapes...". Ariel is its symbol and the words 'fancy' and 'fantastical' occur again and again in his comedies. This helps also to explain certain undeniable shortcomings in his art of prose. In its profusion of inventive detail it is original rather than perfectly shaped. We miss the steady level of refinement prevalent in the dialogue of Congreve. It is full of the quaint irregularity of the late Renaissance, and it lacks the evenness—but also the reduced originality—of late maturity.

NOTES

1. The present article is based on a paper read at the Shakespeare Conference, Stratford-upon-Avon, in August 1953. Deliberately no attention has been paid to the language of Shakespeare's Fools—which is a subject demanding a special essay.

2. For the historical background of Shakespeare's prose see R. W. Chambers, *On the Continuity of English Prose from Alfred to More and his School* (Oxford, 1932), and my *Englischer Geist in der Geschichte seiner Prosa* (Freiburg, 1951) and *Der Stil König Alfreds* (Leipzig, 1934). Milton Crane's *Shakespeare's Prose* (Chicago, 1951) deals with other problems, and so does most of the older work on Shakespeare's prose. There are some good remarks in J. Churton Collins, *Studies in Shakespeare* (Westminster, 1904).

3. For these two functions of the image cf. Wolfgang Clemen's fine remarks in *Shakespeares Bilder* (Bonn, 1936), p. 44.

4. *Traité du Poème Épique* (Paris, 1674), ch. 6. Ben Jonson in his *Discoveries* has already the same standpoint; he is also a forerunner of classical prose, cf. p. 66.

5. Orlando and Jaques, *As You Like It*, III, ii, 268 ff., is a good example, but the Falstaff Scenes are not fundamentally different.

6. All this has its exact parallel in verse.

7. Falstaff's very figure is such a grotesque exaggeration.

8. Cf. Clemen, *loc. cit.* p. 116.

9. Elsewhere Shakespeare uses such scraps of direct speech, cf. the Prince's impersonation of Hotspur (*1 Henry IV*, II, iv, 110), Touchstone in *As You Like It*, V, iv, etc.

10. Similarly *Twelfth Night*, I, v, 35 about Feste. Even double entendre is advertised, *Romeo and Juliet*, II, iv, 120, *2 Henry IV*, II, iv, 58. This should be a warning against seeing too much of it in Shakespeare.

11. A problematic exception is in *Measure for Measure*, I, ii, but this is only a further confirmation of the peculiar character of this play.

A NOTE ON A PRODUCTION OF
TWELFTH NIGHT

BY

NGAIO MARSH

Each decade creates its own fashions in Shakespeare and only actors of distinction can survive them. The Shakespearian costumes of Macready's stage now 'date' almost as markedly as the crinoline itself. Is it not probable, moreover, that if we could look through the wrong end of our opera glasses at the Lyceum of the 1880's, the mannerisms of the lesser players would make us titter while Ellen Terry or Irving would still command our applause? In the portrait of Garrick as Lear the authentic look of madness in his eyes effaces the oddness of his wig and costume. One is able to believe that his performance, if we could see and hear it, would transcend the mannerisms of his period.

Fashions in acting and presentation are as extreme as those that control the garments worn by the actors. The points of view held by producers, critics, actors and designers are forever changing: there is a feverish anxiety in our theatres to keep up with, or better still, anticipate the mode. It is in the presentation of Shakespeare's comedies that this kind of stylistic snobbism is seen at its extremity and it is about an attempt to escape from fashion that I propose to write, with specific reference to the comedy of *Twelfth Night*.

The modern producer of Shakespeare's comedies believes himself to be up against a number of difficulties. Much of the word-bandying is, he says, disastrously unfunny while many of the allusions are obscure and some so coarse that it is just as well that they are also incomprehensible. He must cut great swathes out of his script and for the rest depend on comic 'business' funny enough in its own right to amuse the audience while the words may look after themselves. If he is honest he dreads the obligatory laughter of the Bardolators as much as he fears the silence of unamused Philistia. These are reasonable fears, and, in my opinion, he does well to entertain them.

There are, however, contemporary producers who in their search for a new treatment of an old comedy forget to examine the play as a whole and fall into the stylistic error of seizing upon a single fashionable aspect of a subtle and delicate work and forcing it up to a point of emphasis that quite destroys the balance of production.

In 1951 it fell to my lot to produce *Twelfth Night* with a company of British actors on tour in the Antipodes. As soon as I was made aware of my fate I began to look back at the many productions I had seen of this comedy. Some had been by distinguished producers with famous companies, others by repertory theatres and touring companies like my own. Of them all, the best, it seemed to me in retrospect, had been the simplest: the least pleasing, the most pretentious; and the most pretentious, those in which producers, actors and designers had apparently exchanged glances of dismay and asked each other what they could do to put a bit of 'go' into the old show. They had done much. There had been star Malvolios and star Violas. There had been remorseless emphasis on a single character or sometimes on a single scene. The words had been trapped in the net of a fantasticated style, lost in a welter of comic goings-on, coarsened by cleverness or stifled by being forced out of their native air. I had seen Andrew wither into a palsied eld, Malvolio as a red-nosed comic and Feste, God save the mark, as bitter as coloquintida or the Fool in Lear. I had seen productions with choreographic trimmings and with constructivist back-grounds. I had, however, missed the production on ice skates.

It seemed to me that my best, indeed my only chance, was to put aside everything that I had seen, forget if possible the current fashions in *Twelfth Night* and start humbly with the play itself. It is, after all, a very good play. If I venture now to retrace this production of *Twelfth Night* it is with the hope that in doing so it may be possible to examine some of the problems of its presentation. Because it is also a very difficult play.

As I read it again I saw that in his story Shakespeare shows us the several aspects of love. He begins with Orsino's romantic absorption with the idea of loving the inaccessible Olivia and repeats this theme, burlesqued, in Malvolio's assumption that Olivia loves him. This in turn modulates into Olivia's completely unreal 'crush' on Viola. Through these three aspects of fancied passion he weaves three aspects of true devotion: Viola's for Orsino, Antonio's for Sebastian and, a delicate echo, the Fool's almost inarticulate adoration of Olivia. These variations on a dual theme are linked by the sun-dazzled flowering of Sebastian's love for Olivia, while skipping discreetly through the pattern is the buffo romance of Toby and Maria. Andrew's foolish acceptance of the role of suitor to Olivia is the final detail in an exquisitely balanced design. It is a pattern made by setting fancy against truth, dream against reality. Of course one did not hope, when one discussed the play with the actors, that an audience, in the ripeness of time, would go away muttering: "We have seen a comedy of eight variations on two aspects of love." One merely hoped that the production would be an honest one because the actors had referred their job back to their author.

As I prepared the script it seemed to me that if, following Stanislavsky's rule, one were to say in a single word what *Twelfth Night* was about, that single word would be Illyria. It chimes through the text nostalgically as if Shakespeare would make us desirous of a place we had visited only in dreams.

> *Viola.* What country, friends, is this?
> *Captain.* This is Illyria, lady.
> *Viola.* And what should I do in Illyria?
> My brother, he is in Elysium....

Andrew is "as tall a man as any's in Illyria". Maria is "as witty a piece of Eve's flesh as any in Illyria". And so it goes on. The rehearsal period was journey in search of Illyria; the performance, we dared to hope, would be our arrival there.

And what happens in Illyria? By day the sun shines with a golden richness on boscage, on palaces and on well-tended gardens. At night a full moon presides over revels that for all their robust foolery are tempered with wistfulness. The inhabitants move with a certain precision. Toby, Andrew, Maria and Fabian step across their landscape to an antic measure, now lively, now reflective but always compact and articulate. Orsino, the Renaissance man in love with love, moons in the grand manner over the young countess Olivia, whose principal attraction rests on her refusal to have anything to do with him. She, for her part, mopes with adolescent excessiveness over the death of her brother. And moving between these two strongholds of romantic nonsense are the Shakespearian girl-boy, gallant and wise, and Feste, the errant Fool. The whole most lovely play is set down in words that are so exact an expression of its aesthetic tone that one wonders how one dare meddle with them.

However, meddle we must and one of our first concerns would be the visual presentation of Illyria in terms of a touring company. How must it look and what must its inhabitants wear? After consultation with our young Australian designer, it was decided to use a Watteauesque décor. The dresses of Watteau belong to no precise historical period: they are civilized, rich and fantastic and they have an air of freshness. We had three little pavilions of striped poles and airily draped banners. There were flights of steps, dark green backgrounds, platforms and a cyclorama. A traverse turned the half-stage into the interior of Orsino's palace. A jointed screen in two sections mounted on wheels and painted with a formalized seaport design was pulled across for the front scenes. These changes, effected by two nimble pages in view of the audience, took a matter of seconds to complete. For the letter-reading scene, there was a formalized boxtree-hedge and a group of flamboyant statuary with which Toby, Andrew and Fabian associated themselves to good comic effect. A giant be-ribboned birdcage, prominent throughout the garden scenes, afterwards became Malvolio's mobile prison, being clapped over his head, leaving his legs free. The colour throughout in paint, fabrics and lighting modulated from grey and blue-pink to full Watteauesque gold and turquoise.

As I read the play again, I caught—and who could miss them?—its overtones of regret. It has a character that is, I believe, unique in English comedy, a particular tinge of sadness that is the complementary colour of aesthetic pleasure. One listens to it with the half-sigh that accompanies an experience of perfect beauty. This is an element that has much to do with music and nothing at all to do either with sentiment or with tragedy and it is the quintessence of *Twelfth Night*. The warp of regret is interlaced with a vigorous weft of foolery. The producer's job is to retain them both in their just proportion. It is because *Twelfth Night* is so gay that it is also so delicately sad.

I planned a swiftly running production with only one interval. This would come after the letter-reading scene and the coda of laughter that follows it. Toby would pick Maria up in a pother of giggles and petticoats and carry her off. Andrew and Fabian would follow arm in arm and the curtain come down. My aim at this stage of production was to catch the measure of the whole. That measure would be sustained by the occasional use of music. For this we chose Purcell's *Golden Sonata*, which seemed to me to be perfect Illyria.

It was now, when the script was plotted, the music chosen, the design in preparation and the first rehearsal called, that I was most forcibly reminded of the influence of theatrical fashion upon actors. I had in my company a number of young actors and actresses who had worked under distinguished direction and one senior actor of great talent, experience and discernment. It was among the youngest players that the fashionable attitude to *Twelfth Night* was most tenderly embraced. At least two of them were consumed with the desire to play up the regretful over-tones for all and more than they are worth. "Infinite sadness" was a phrase much bandied about during the earlier rehearsals, minor overtones were remorselessly insisted upon, the horrid ghost of *I Pagliacci* seemed to lurk behind the boxtree hedge. I had seen all this sort of thing done and very cleverly done and had felt it to be an error in taste and discernment. The Fool in *Twelfth Night* is *not* the Fool in *Lear*, Malvolio's downfall was *not* conceived as a tragic downfall. He would not, therefore, be allowed to gloom himself into a sort of cross-gartered Richard II.

No: he would be as acid as a lime and as lean as a preying mantis. He would have such an air of creaking dryness that when his transformation came about it would be as if he were galvanized into egregious gallantry. There must be no nonsense about making him sympathetic. Shakespeare disliked the fellow and so must the audience.

With Olivia I was able to air what had long been a fervent belief. There is another fashion in our theatres (stemming from who knows what forgotten managerial charms) that would make a mature woman of Olivia. For far too long, more than mature leading ladies have confronted us with the not very delectable prospect of solid worth extended in corsetted melancholy upon some comfortless *chaise-longue*, distressingly besotted on a girl-boy and finally marrying the latter's twin brother. Could anything be less Illyrian? I defy the fashionmongers to find in the text one single hint that the spoilt young countess is in fact anything but very very young. There is not a ponderable note in Olivia: the bloom of adolescence adorns every word she speaks. Viola's impatience is with a girl of her own age who is making a little silly-billy of herself. Our Olivia was as pretty and young as a rosebud, her mourning was as nonsensical as Orsino's love-lorn dumps. Having shut herself up in a charming prison she fancied herself head-over-heels in love with the first personable boy to walk into it and was exasperated beyond measure when he failed to respond. None of my cast had ever thought of Olivia being played in this key. The concept of the stricken dowager dies hard.

There are, however, no fashions in Violas. She has, as far as I know, withstood the most determined onslaughts of the modish 'fun' merchants and has neither holla-ed Olivia's name through a megaphone to the reverberant hills nor yet disguised her fair and outward character in a track-suit. Our Viola fulfilled the first requirements of a heroine in a Shakespeare comedy by being an accomplished actress, very young, intelligent and a darling. She moved through the play with charm, wit and good breeding. By the command of a certain quality in her voice she was able to alight on her lyrical passages and in so doing bring about that sudden stillness in a theatre that tells an actress she is safely home.

And Feste? It was with Feste that fashion threatened most insistently to put up her unlovely visage, for it is through him more than any other of the Illyrians that Shakespeare shows us the reverse side of the coin of comedy. I had of late seen Festes who, by plugging at the minor theme in their part, had administered a series of excruciating nudges in the ribs of their audiences. "Goodness!" in Morley's phrase, they seemed to exclaim, "Goodness, how sad! Look!" But Feste is *not* Lear's fool. He must play against his own ruefulness and if he does this his ruefulness will speak for itself. It shows most markedly in the songs. "Youth", Feste sings, "is a stuff will not endure." "What's to come", he sings, "is still unsure." Beauty, he says, is a flower, and elsewhere the Duke reflects that "women are as roses, whose fair flower Being once displayed, doth fall that very hour". Viola agrees:

> And so they are: alas, that they are so;
> To die, even when they to perfection grow!

Olivia swears by the roses of the spring. The shroud of white in the Fool's song of death is strewn with yew and "not a flower, not a flower sweet" on his coffin shall be strewn. This flower image is scattered through *Twelfth Night* like the daisies on a Botticelli lawn and it is Feste who most often expresses it. He wanders about the play mingling with its several themes. He is by turns listless and brilliant. He has an artist's resentment for Malvolio's criticism of his professional status and can be waspish. He is all things to all men and yet very much himself and very much alone. His devotion to Olivia drifts across the text with no more insistence than a breath on a looking-glass. He can be ruined by an actor who sees in him a chance to make a big thing of a light part. He sets the tone of the play.

I felt that there should be some visual expression of his function and looked for it in the flower image. On Olivia's first entrance, Feste, who has played truant from her household, sets about fooling himself back into her good graces. Our Feste mutely asked her for the rose she carried. It was refused and given to Fabian, that oddly occurring character whose sudden appearance is thought to have some reference to the departure of Kemp from Shakespeare's company and the arrival of Armin to take his place. Fabian seems to have been brought in arbitrarily to replace the Fool in the letter-reading scene and perhaps to suggest a rival to him in Olivia's favour. It was to sustain this suggestion that Fabian escorted Olivia on this first entry. Later, on his own line: "So beauty's a flower", Feste snatched the rose from Fabian and wore it on his motley for the rest of the play. At the end he was left alone to sing his wry song of the wind and the rain. At its close he laid down his lute on the stage and broke the rose between his fingers. The petals fell with a faint tinkle of sound across the strings. Feste tiptoed into the shadows and the final curtain came down on the lute and rose-petals, vignetted in a pool of light. This use of a visual symbol in the rose was the only piece of extraneous production imposed on the play and even this could be referred back to the text. There was comic 'business' enough, certainly, in the buffo scenes, but it was kept in style and played strictly to the general tempo of the production. The result, surprising to actors and audience alike, was the discovery that the comic scenes in *Twelfth Night* are funny.

It remains only to say that with the intelligent and patient co-operation of the actors this treatment of *Twelfth Night* became articulate. It was successful in performance. This, I am sure, was because we came freshly to the text and, seeking its true savour, bent all our thought and energy to serving it.

"If that this simple syllogism will serve, so: if it will not, what remedy?" None, I am sure, in any approach to the play that imposes an extrinsic fashion upon it. Whatever the style for *Twelfth Night*, it must be in grain. Only so will it endure the wind and weather of production.

F

PRODUCING THE COMEDIES

BY

SIR BARRY JACKSON

Memory plays strange tricks, and it is a somewhat hazardous undertaking to revive recollections of the course of the production of Shakespeare's comedies over a period of some sixty years. Youthful enthusiasms are responsible for much distortion, but I would never subscribe to the doctrine of "the good old days when everything was so much better than it is today". As in life itself, the changes in "the mirror of the age" have been so many and so diverse as to have been totally unbelievable half a century ago. So far as Shakespearian comedy is concerned, the diversity has naturally lain in the treatment rather than in the comedies themselves. These are firmly embedded in things elemental to humanity. To suggest "for all time", a phrase often heard, might be claiming too much, but the settling of any precise period is far beyond our understanding. In everyday parlance, "for all time" is as good a guess as any other.

Before dealing with purely personal recollection of the changes in the production of the comedies, some reference to their treatment in the nineteenth century might be considered.

I have in my possession the prompt copy of the production by Charles Kean of *The Winter's Tale* in 1856. The time and energy expended to achieve this orgiastic hash exceeds all comprehension. For some unaccountable reason—probably Apollo and the Delphic Oracle—the action was shifted from Bohemia to Bithynia. Hermione's reference to her father, the Emperor of Russia, was, of course, cut. But that was only one of the never-ending excisions. On the front page of the paper binding is a list, presumably written by the stage manager, of the works consulted, including, of all things, an atlas. Among the cast is the name of Ellen Terry—her first appearance on any stage at the age of nine—as Mamillius, and a Miss Heath as Florizel. A female Florizel appears to be a strange contradiction when so much attention was spent on verisimilitude. Charles Kean himself must have had a tough constitution for, in addition to playing Leontes, he assuredly had a hand in marshalling and grouping his actors. The magnitude of his task may be gathered from notes incorporated in the prompt copy. In Act I, scene ii, in addition to the dramatis personae demanded by the author, there are six pages, four lords, a butler, six slaves, three water-carriers, and a ballet in the form of a Pyrrhic Dance, with attendant musicians. Charles Kean believed in adding "honey a sauce to sugar". Elaborate as these directions are, they are nothing when compared with the Trial Scene where the list of 'omnes' incorporates one officer of the court, four heralds, fifteen ladies, ten sages, two officers of the guard, twenty-four guards, eight squires, one clerk to the court, twenty-four priests, eight trumpeters, and thirty-five spectators—the figure "60" is erased, and one can only surmise that the stage was full. With the principals, the number of artists was about one hundred and sixty—a somewhat prolific addition to "Enter Leontes, Lords and Officers".

In 1857 *The Tempest*, as produced by the same actor-manager, has an interesting note to the published acting edition. Charles Kean asks for "the kind indulgence of the public should any lengthy delay take place between the acts. The scenic appliances of the play are of more extensive and complicated nature than ever has been attempted in any theatre in Europe, requiring the aid of one hundred and forty operatives nightly, who, unseen by the audience, are engaged in working the machinery and carrying out the various effects".

With what topics of conversation the audience amused themselves in these presumably lengthy interims can only be left to the imagination, but it may safely be assumed that the text was not one of them.

Lengthy entr'actes in those days gave one the opportunity to see, be seen, and discuss any subject that chanced to be in the air. When touring, Sir Henry Irving's *Merchant of Venice* necessitated a pause of something in the nature of twenty minutes between the Court and Belmont scenes, about as long as the final scene took to play, perhaps even longer. The orchestra, in the meantime, played the major part of Luigini's *Egyptian Ballet* to encourage conversation, its main purport in the English theatre. The dramatic effect of the calm serenity and happy ending to the comedy, after the tense atmosphere of the Court, was entirely lost by this lack of immediacy.

The Winter's Tale, more than any other of the comedies, seems to have attracted actor-managers and latter-day producers as a fit subject for experiment: as witness Kean's excessive care for the archaeological detail of a country far removed from that named by the author; Granville-Barker's nondescript setting in 1912, though he made no effort to place the pastoral scene anywhere but near the Cotswolds; and Stratford's excursion into the Balkans in 1948, based, no doubt, on the very "Emperor of Russia" line that Kean had excised. In 1876 Edward Saker at Liverpool was determined to ensure the locality with a firm hand: how could Leontes, King of Sicilia, have lived anywhere else but in Sicily? Saker's acting edition contains a scenic note which must have given the dwellers by Merseyside considerable food for thought. Modern texts designate II, ii, quite simply as "A Prison", but Saker calls it: "One of the *Latomioe*, or prisons of Syracuse, excavated out of the rock, and known as the Ear of Dionysus."

Archaeologists and specialists of every description were called upon to give realism to such bleak directions in other plays as "A Street in Venice", "Olivia's Garden", "A Forest", "Another Part of the Forest", and so forth; which directions, after all, were added to the texts in the early eighteenth century and never imagined at all by the author. Treated as though they were as sacrosanct as the original text, they have caused unbelievable perplexities to scenic designers. Did the Banished Duke retire to Arden or the Ardennes? In the eighteenth-century operatic version of *As You Like It*, named *Rosalinda*, the latter seems to have been acceptable, but, as neither palm trees nor lions exist in either locality, speculation seems but a waste of time. Bohemia has no sea coast, and it is extremely dubious whether sailmakers ever existed in Bergamo. The traveller who embarked at Verona in order to reach Milan by water would have made the journey much quicker on foot. Faced with a proposed setting for *All's Well That Ends Well*, the painter designer would require considerable architectural skill to differentiate the rapid changes from Rousillon to Paris, and from Florence to Marseilles. Such instances are innumerable and all tend to the conclusion that in the press of telling his story, the poet gave little or no thought to time or place—the antithesis to classic pattern. His world was unbounded and knew no limitation. Yet the archaeologists, on the invitation of the actor-managers, had a good spell. To obtain what appeared to be truth, creative imagination was stretched beyond belief. A mere word of the poet's was sufficient to inspire fantastic detail and supposed actuality, trailing along until invention itself became exhausted, more a hindrance than help. In a production of *The Winter's Tale* at Manchester, a living bear on a chain was introduced. Reference to the "dappled herd", also at Manchester, was sufficient to introduce deer, one of which bit the Orlando in the seat to such effect that he was indisposed for some performances. "A wood near Athens" would be enhanced by growing ferns, the tree-pots cunningly concealed; and there was an ending to *Twelfth Night* in true pantomime tradition—a general entrance, a double marriage ceremony in the Illyrian cathedral, accompanied by every possible pomp and circumstance. To augment the romantic appeal of Orsino, Augustine Daly in 1894 thought it advisable to introduce him offering a serenade to Olivia. The song he chose was *Who is Sylvia?*, but, in order to give no offence, he merely transposed "Olivia" for "Sylvia" and relied on Schubert for the rest. I was a trifle astonished at the time, young as I was.

During these years, the texts of the comedies were larded *ad infinitum* with excrescences, inter-polations, musical accompaniments, all and everything appertaining to the producer's whims, and what in his opinion was likely to attract the multitude. Hints have frequently been made that had the poet been aware of the machinery of the modern stage, he would have approved of such devices. I wonder. His free and soaring spirit would have been fettered to canvas and timber, dress designers, electricians, and the almost limitless accessories of the stage today. He would have been sharply reminded that it was not possible to flit from one locality to another owing to technical exigencies, and he would have found that the restrictions imposed upon him must inevitably reduce dramatic tension and interest. The rather sinister atmosphere of the opening Court Scenes of *As You Like It*—and every comedy worthy of the name includes a touch of acidity—is quickly obliterated and forgotten in the magic of the forest with its mood of elemental nostalgia, yet quite unexpectedly in III, i, we are brought back to the Court for the briefest space to remind us that poetic justice hovers in the background. If Shakespeare had not had the opportunity of introducing such a scene, we might have been so lost "under the shade of melancholy boughs" that we would have become forgetful of the "perils of the envious court".

The disentangling of experiences over the course of years presents difficulties: one event merges into another and calm deference to prevailing conditions is accepted without murmur. My early experience of presentation of the comedies was coloured, somewhat overwhelmingly I fear, by the opulent theatrical treatment remaining from the period of which I have given examples. The actor-manager was in full control and, in youth, I was not a little impressed by the lavish spectacles he provided. The exception was Frank Benson, and, living in the provinces, close to Stratford, it is to him that I owe a great deal of my early Shakespearian theatregoing. Spectacle was not Benson's strong suit. Not much in that respect could be expected from a company performing six or eight plays in a week, and, in addition, changing its locale unceasingly after the season in Stratford. The comedies in his repertoire were the well-tried favourites, and, a trifle cynically it may be noted, those in which there were outstanding protagonists. The only exception was *A Midsummer Night's Dream*; otherwise it was a continuous round of *As You Like It, Twelfth Night, The Tempest, The Taming of the Shrew, Much Ado About Nothing*, and *The Merchant of Venice*. These, by the way, head the lists of productions at the Memorial Theatre since its rebuilding; portents of public taste. Here I must mention the gentleman I encountered in an interval during a performance of *Cymbeline*. Asked if he was enjoying the play, he said: "Yes. Nice change, isn't it?"

Of spectacular presentation, the comedies at His Majesty's Theatre, under Beerbohm Tree, are the outstanding memories. One extraction from Tree's acting version of *The Tempest* is of interest. As the normal size of artists makes the property ship in the first scene appear ridiculous, the passengers were doubled by children in order to attain appropriate scale. The lines in this scene were cut to about a dozen, and half of these were spoken whilst the band played the overture. In Tree's *Much Ado About Nothing*, between the end of II, i, and the opening of II, iii, there was a representation before our eyes of the passing of a night. He also augmented the cast of *Twelfth Night* with three or four lesser Malvolios, who followed the real Malvolio about. The settings were as elaborate as paint or canvas could make them, and there still exist individuals who maintain that this lavish profusion touched the high-water mark for all time, and, as stage interpretations of the poet's works, could never humanly be excelled. I must say that among the multitude, I too was dazzled—stars in the principal parts, and decoration as flamboyant as the eye could desire. With the rest, I accepted prevailing conditions, only asking that excess should better excess. Yet, beneath my youthful and fashionable enthusiasm, I was dimly aware that all was not as it should be, although I could not put my finger on the cause of my uneasiness.

The first sign of any break with prevailing conditions, in my own experience, occurred in 1903. This was Gordon Craig's production of *Much Ado About Nothing*. Here was that impressive simplicity of scenic design that is achieved only by means of impeccable taste. It consisted of three full sets and a front cloth for intermediary scenes. The Church Scene was a miracle of beauty that I have never seen surpassed. Some discussion with Paul Shelving on the subject of Craig's front cloth leads us to believe that it may have been one of the earliest experiments in projected scenery. Shelving recalls a flickering of buildings in the Pent-house Scene, and I remember a horizontal shaft of light—"The gentle day...Dapples the drowsy East with spots of grey..."— which could not possibly have emanated from the front of the auditorium as it would have caused shadows. But, apart from his scenic design, Craig was imbued with tradition. He accepted between-act waits, though clearly indicating that it was possible to attain sheer beauty of setting without recourse to precise detail of architecture or landscape. The stage photography of the day was none too good, and such reproductions as exist give no notion of the results.

The supreme awakening adventure was yet to come. This took place at the Stratford Memorial Theatre in 1908 when Miss Horniman's production of *Measure for Measure*, under the direction of William Poel, completely shattered all that had gone before. For the first time in my life I was caught up in the play's action, which, divested of all the gallimaufry on which I had been bred, rose triumphant, swift and sure. Mentally I was elevated into another world, a world towards which I had hitherto been vainly groping. In a flash all became clear. It was the text that mattered. Poel brushed aside all that interposed, and crumbled to the dust all notions of fanciful excess which for years had been strangling the poet's word. I would not say that Poel was without fault: genius is invariably inclined to be a little wayward, not infrequently overstepping the limit. For instance, when he was unable to find a Valentine for *The Two Gentlemen of Verona* with the type of voice he needed, he gave the part to an actress. Other oddities intruded into his productions, but what was as clear as daylight was his absolute insistence on the text and rapidity of action—no extraneous music and no long waits between the acts, and no raising and lowering of the tableau curtains such as had worried my sense of urgency. Poel went right back to the days of the first Elizabeth, and tried to give exact reproduction of the plays as they would then be performed—swiftly and without halt. In attempting to revive the past, an archaeologist who put all other stage archaeologists to shame, Poel built the future. Our indebtedness to his theories,

F *

though accepted everywhere, has received but paltry expression, but it is good to know that a volume devoted to his work is now in hand.

And now I may come to the Birmingham Repertory Theatre, where over the years many of the comedies have appeared on the boards. In this theatre, although we indulged in constant experimentation, from the very first there was a tendency to simplify—sometimes, I fear, for financial reasons, which is not always a bad thing. Our early settings were generally of a conventionalized character, that is a fairly heavily built full stage with traverse curtains for intervening scenes. One exception was a *Merry Wives of Windsor*, which followed the example of Oscar Asche, with sets of half-timbered houses in wintertime. We gave a *Tempest* where experiment in colour was pre-eminent, founded oddly enough on the iridescent tones of a seam of copper falling down the wet cliffs of a remote Cornish cove. The island and the characters belonging to it were of every shade of blue, from eggshell to deepest indigo, laced here and there with silver. The interlopers were in various reds and the linking character, Ferdinand, in a purple that was anything but strident. The fashions of the costumes were of the simplest cut and of no particular period beyond what might be termed 'romantic'. For two productions, *Much Ado About Nothing* and *The Merchant of Venice*, a solid loggia was built about six feet from the footlights. The centre was arched over a flight of some dozen steps; on either side of the arch were two square openings with balustrades, and beneath these two square blocks on the stage itself. The loggia was pure white and backed with a greeny-blue hemisphere. In mere words, this arouses a picture of severe starkness, but cunning lighting supplied endless variety. *Much Ado About Nothing* was produced by Conal O'Riordan, who was imbued with the idea that this comedy is of peculiarly hard and brittle quality, and who asked for costumes to suggest such an atmosphere. Consultation with the designer, Guy Kortright, resulted in the sole example I have known of period designs based on the early fourteenth century, carried out in every possible permutation of reds, yellows and their associated tints. The only exception to these was a waspish black and yellow Don John. The result gave the producer all he asked for in brilliant clarity to the eye. O'Riordan introduced Borachio as overhearing the conversation between Don Pedro and Claudio regarding Hero in I, i, and so explaining visually to the audience his later relation to Don John. I had never seen this before. *The Merchant of Venice* was played in the same set, but as the costumes for *Much Ado* had evoked a general effect of almost violent brightness, the designs for the Venetian comedy, whilst of extreme simplicity, made some attempt to recapture the opalescent tones of the lagoons and palaces as I had seen them in the bright light of the early spring. The result was obtained by using material of any colour with a glossy surface covered with multi-coloured fine net, the two together regardless of shade giving a milky appearance of the watery city. These two experiments remain in my memory as efforts to use colour to accentuate atmosphere. I need hardly add that I never heard any reference made to them by members of the audience.

Despite the pleasant satisfaction of *dressing up* a comedy, I always had a sensation that in the process the main purport of the play and the poet's words were often overwhelmed. This sensation was endorsed when I came to examine Charles Kean's prompt-book of *The Winter's Tale*. When in 1923 I decided on a production of *Cymbeline*, the fantastic directions of time and place proved, as they always do, to be most puzzling. H. K. Ayliff, who was working with me at the time, suggested that an idea I had long discussed with him should be put into operation—the using of contemporary costume. In the poet's day Elizabethan costume had been acceptable; in the eighteenth century powder and hoops; so why not adventure with modern dress in the 1920's? It is never easy, or indeed possible with any certainty, to track down the source of ideas. I have a vague notion that I read somewhere or other of a production by Reinhardt in Berlin of a *Tartuffe* in contemporary dress. But what had influenced and impressed me directly was the performance by some schoolchildren of scenes from *A Midsummer Night's Dream* when the 'mechanicals' appeared in their worn, everyday clothes, carrying the tools of their trade, their midday meals in pudding basins wrapped up in bandanna handkerchiefs, precisely as one saw their fathers in those days in the Black Country and other industrial areas throughout the land. The fairy world was cut off by an amplitude of cheap white muslin and Christmas tree ornaments. But Bottom, Quince, Starveling and party summoned up no feeling of ancient Athens: they had just walked in out of the street. I nearly leapt out of my seat, for the whole thing became startlingly alive and vibrant. To that school I owe an unrepayable debt for an idea, born perhaps of poverty, for there is a limit to the number of towels and old sheets that mothers and teachers can supply, an idea which has been acclaimed and derided with almost ferocious argument. Which was one of the purposes intended. Bricks are better than apathy, the deadliest attitude in the theatre, as indeed it is in everything else that is worthy. *Cymbeline* duly appeared to meet with a rather bewildered response, but with a result that warranted further adventure and eventually created a national and worldwide controversy. In the theatre itself we learnt a great deal about the poet himself in the midst of the simplicity of modern dress and settings. Many extraneous ornaments, live rabbits, ballets, processions and the like were drastically swept out of mind, leaving the magnificent structures splendidly bare.

Of the Shakespearian canon, only two comedies have been produced in modern dress at the Birmingham Repertory Theatre—*All's Well That Ends Well* in 1927, and *The Taming of the Shrew* in 1928. *The Shrew* proved to be a gay romp and was extremely popular in Birmingham and London. *All's Well* opened in a delightful French atmosphere with the Countess swathed in the crêpe so beloved of Gallic widows, and Helena in a very simple dress to indicate her position as a dependant. (I have seen Helena covered in theatrical gewgaws and with a velvet train three yards long, which, if the eye of the spectator works in conjunction with the mind, would suggest a peeress of the realm.)

I account myself fortunate in having witnessed very considerable changes in the approach to the production of Shakespeare's comedies—and his tragedies and histories too for that matter. As a peg upon which the producer can hang all his whims and fancies and imagination, not infrequently running riot in the process, what always emerges is the gigantic stature of their creator, the poet himself. Lesser works would never have survived the butchering treatment perpetrated by producers down the ages. In surveying these changes in scenic presentation what impresses me most is the gradual movement in our own days towards closer adherence to the texts, towards simplification of pictorial setting, and towards rapidity of action. The advising voice of the scholar has infiltrated slowly but surely so far as the texts are concerned, and has been raised in no uncertain tone when any severe mutilation has taken place. Such mutilation, however, has been more obvious in the tragedies and histories than the comedies—probably because the comedies in general are fairly short. On the whole, the comedic texts have suffered very little during the last quarter of a century—I limit myself to our own language, for what has transpired in translation is anybody's guess. To judge by the laughter I have heard in European theatres, it is very obvious that Elizabethan witticisms, which leave the general English public mystified, have been changed to become acceptable.

So far as pictorial presentation goes, the simplification of settings has evolved with the growing attention to the text and speed. There appears to be no hard and fast line where it is possible to say that at such and such a time a particular change took place, though outstanding to myself was the work of Granville-Barker and Norman Wilkinson of Four Oaks on *The Winter's Tale* (the costumes for this were by Albert Rutherston), *A Midsummer Night's Dream*, and *Twelfth Night* at the Savoy Theatre between 1912 and 1914. The effects, simple and of exquisite taste, came as a shock after the ostentation to which we had become accustomed. It is only now, after the passing of years, that their eminently satisfactory design becomes apparent. Here indeed were creative inspiration and delicacy combined. With the exception of Craig's *Much Ado About Nothing*, they were before their time, and it is dubious whether they have ever been excelled. The German theatre, too, has had some hand in the simplification of setting: examination of the various Rheinhardt productions would endorse this statement.

In thus casting my memory back over the Shakespeare productions I have seen or been associated with, it occurs to me that the seventeenth-century split between Play and Masque may be regarded as symbolic. There is general agreement that *The Tempest* was inspired by both—although even here the fiery and intense drive of the poet's imagination overwhelmed the spectacular element. In the Play, words are all-important, and usually those who know their Shakespeare are intent on having these words emphasized on the stage. In the Masque, on the other hand, spectacle is dominant, and those who are not so well acquainted with Shakespeare's works perhaps need to have scenic adornment if they are thoroughly to enjoy the production. Today, thanks to the scholars' growing acceptance of contact with the living theatre and to their influence, much closer attention is being paid to the printed word, but there still remains the possibility of a finer union of Play and Masque than Charles Kean was able to present in the nineteenth century. I think, for example, of Peter Brook's *Love's Labour's Lost* at Stratford in 1946 and 1947. There is some affinity, as he saw, between this comedy and the 'Voyage à Cythère', itself inspired by theatrical productions that Watteau had seen. The combination of Shakespeare's lines and the fragile Watteauesque atmosphere, therefore, seemed to me to be entirely right—the frail comedy of youth thus enwrapped in a delicate beauty remaining for me one of my unforgettable memories of the stage.

THE NEW WAY
WITH SHAKESPEARE'S TEXTS
II. RECENT WORK ON THE TEXT OF
ROMEO AND JULIET

BY

J. DOVER WILSON

In *Shakespeare Survey*, 7 I described how A. W. Pollard and W. W. Greg, now Sir Walter Greg, laid the foundations of a more exact method of dealing with Shakespeare's texts by basing it upon previous bibliographical inquiries into the practices of printers and publishers in the fifteenth, sixteenth and seventeenth centuries. In *Shakespeare Survey*, 9 I hope to show how our knowledge of these texts has since been deepened and extended by the study of such dramatic manuscripts as have come down to us from that period. The present article is intended to illustrate the new methods by explaining what they involve when applied to a problem of peculiar difficulty. It so happens that G. I. Duthie formerly of McGill and now of Aberdeen University, the well-known textual scholar, has for some years been engaged with me upon an edition of *Romeo and Juliet,* and the following account of the conclusions we have come to and of how we came to them is given with his permission, though since it has not been possible for him to see it in final draft, he may still have some reservations on details.

As I observed at the end of the previous article, before a modern editor can or should begin his operations on the text of an Elizabethan or Jacobean play, he is expected to decide, or at any rate to conjecture from the best evidence available, what sort of copy was used by the printers of the original editions. In this matter the text of *Romeo and Juliet* has proved unusually baffling. Various scholars have offered solutions of the problem from time to time, most of them during the last thirty years.[1] Yet none seems to have proved completely satisfactory. We ourselves made four attempts before this; the first attempt being a paper read by Duthie before the English Institute, New York, on 9 September 1950, and later published in *Studies in Bibliography*, IV (Virginia, 1951). What here follows draws freely upon this and its conclusions are not dissimilar, though they are in the main based upon other evidence, and were reached only after a lengthy and often voluminous discussion carried on across the Atlantic, into which both Sir Walter Greg and Dr Alice Walker, with their accustomed good nature, have at different times allowed themselves to be drawn. A brief statement of the main factors in the problem and of the principal solutions hitherto offered will make the issues clear.

Two only of the early texts of *Romeo and Juliet* are of primary interest to an editor, viz. the First Quarto (Q1) of 1597 and the Second Quarto (Q2) of 1599; later quartos and the text of the play in the First Folio (F1) of 1623 being derivative editions so that readings peculiar to them are at best printer's emendations and usually mere misprints. The main editorial problem, therefore, is a two-fold one of defining the character of Q1 and Q2 and determining the relation between them. That Q1 is a 'bad' quarto is now admitted on all hands. It is also generally agreed that it is a 'reported' text, that is to say a version reconstructed from memory by an actor, or actors, who had taken part in performances of the authentic play; while it was prepared for publication by some sort of unauthorized editor. In a word it is a pirated edition and H. R. Hoppe, in the latest and fullest examination of it, has shown that it exhibits all the stigmata we have learnt to associate with such texts, viz. weak synonym substitution, paraphrase, irregular metre, the transference of words or expressions belonging to one episode or situation to a similar episode or situation in another part of the play, and so on.[2] And that is practically all an editor needs to know about this text, except that it is surprisingly well 'reported' for the first two acts, after which its fidelity to the genuine play declines steeply. Unfortunately, he needs to discover a good deal more about Q2, or rather to be able to interpret the facts that have been discovered. For the main facts are actually not in dispute.

That it is on the whole what Pollard called a 'good' quarto, in other words that it is in some way derived from a Shakespearian manuscript, has long been recognized, though it was, we believe, Greg who first showed that the manuscript was in all probability Shakespeare's rough draft, or as the Elizabethans phrased it, his 'foul papers'.[3] Dependence on the 'foul papers' is suggested by Q2's varying designations for certain characters in the stage-directions or speech-headings, whether in full or abbreviation. Thus Capulet is sometimes '*Cap.*' or '*Capu.*', some-times '*Father*', '*Fat.*' or '*Fa.*'; while Lady Capulet has half a dozen different titles, viz. '*Wife*', '*Lady*', '*Old Lady*', '*Lady of the House*', '*Mother*', and abbreviations of these. Such variations would inevitably confuse a busy prompter during performance, and must therefore have been regularized in the prompt-book.[4] Again, in some places Q2 apparently preserves Shakespeare's 'first shots' side by side with his final decision; so that it seems to afford us glimpses of him in the very process of creation. At III, v, 176ff., for instance, it gives Capulet this:

> Gods bread, it makes me mad,
> Day, night, houre, tide, time, worke, play,
> Alone in companie, still my care hath bene....

The clumsy lines "Gods...play" should form a pentameter; and we get one, if we remove "houre, tide, time"—three synonyms which fit most awkwardly into the context of antitheses. The hand of Shakespeare, it seems, having written "Day, night", doodled with "houre, tide, time"; rejected each in turn; but omitted to score the rejects out, because the mind then flowed on without further difficulty. Or take the even more interesting case at III, ii, 19, where Juliet (in Q2) tells us that Romeo will "lie vpon the winges of night"

> Whiter then new snow vpon a Rauens backe—

an impossible line, which was emended in F2, and has since been read by editors, thus:

> Whiter than new snow on a raven's back.

But the Q2 "upon" is needed to balance "upon" in the previous line, while "new" must be in error, since it is absurd to suppose *old* snow on a raven's back.[5] Yet what more natural than that Shakespeare should first have written "new snow", the whitest thing that came to mind, and then, to correspond with "wings of night", have written "raven's back", the blackest thing that came to mind, but forgot to delete the now inconsistent "new", though he had done so mentally as its metrical redundance shows? Other and similar examples of probable 'first shots' will be suggested in the notes to our edition.[6]

It is certain, then, that Q2 was in some way dependent upon Shakespeare's original manuscript. But it is also certain that it was in some way dependent upon Q1. As long ago as 1879 a German critic,[7] while arguing that Shakespeare's manuscript was the principal copy for Q2, pointed out that a passage of some ninety-five lines, from about I, ii, 46 to I, iii, 36, had undoubtedly been set up from Q1, inasmuch as the two quartos are here not only identical in substance, apart from a few trivial differences, but are actually linked together by similarities of spelling, misprint and even type. The typographical link is most conspicuous in the speeches of the Nurse, which Q1 prints in italics[8] down to the end of Act I, as does Q2 down to twenty-five lines short of the end, i.e. to the foot of its sheet B. Forty-seven years after the German, and apparently in ignorance of his article, Miss Greta Hjort, observing these italics, drew the opposite conclusion, viz. that Q2 was printed throughout from a copy of Q1, which had been corrected and added to by a scribe working with Shakespeare's manuscript before him.[9] Which of those alternative theories offers the true solution? Since Miss Hjort wrote in 1926 critical opinion has veered first to one and then to the other; the most striking instance being Greg, who has entertained both on different occasions.[10] Nor are the alternatives absolute, since the printers might conceivably have used the foul papers and a corrected copy of Q1 in different parts of the book. One critic, indeed, Sidney Thomas,[11] would rule out correction altogether and maintains that Q2 was printed from the foul papers throughout, except between I, ii, 58 and I, iii, 36, when the manuscript being defective or illegible the compositor was obliged to have recourse to Q1. It is true that there is no sign of correction in this passage, but when Thomas argues that "a page-by-page comparison" of the first two sheets (the first sixteen pages) of the quartos proves it would have been "physically impossible" for Q1 to have carried all the corrections required, even with the aid of inserted slips of paper, so different are the texts in the first three opening scenes, he does not appear to have observed or envisaged the pages very clearly. The Prologue, for example, is printed on the recto of sig. A3,[12] leaving the verso a blank page, upon which it would have been easy enough for a scribe to copy out from the manuscript most, if not all, the prose dialogue between the serving men (ll. 1–60) where the texts diverge most. Thomas, moreover, fails to reckon with the fact that the outer margins in an uncut quarto, which would certainly have been available to any scribe in 1599, are two or even three times wider than those in most of our pitifully cropped extant library copies.[13] There is nothing at all "impossible" about the correction of those two sheets, and "a page-by-page comparison" even suggests its likelihood. Both Greg in 1928[14] and Duthie in 1950[15] independently noted a striking similarity between the typographical settings of the Prologue, and there are other passages in sheets A and B of Q1, apart from I, ii, 58 to I, iii, 36, which have clearly influenced the printing of Q2. That, for instance, the speech-headings in the dialogue at I, ii, 46–58 should run in both quartos thus: *Ben. Romeo. Ben. Romeo. Ben. Romeo. Ben. Rom.* can hardly be mere coincidence. Yet if a corrected sheet B was used as copy for Q2, it follows that the corrector must have been somewhat careless in his collation with the manuscript, for he appears to have overlooked three errors and a couple of abnormalities which he ought to have put right.[16]

In a British Academy lecture (1928) Greg had been prepared to entertain, if only tentatively as he makes clear, Miss Hjort's theory of a corrected or supplemented Q1 as the sole copy for

Q2. But in his *Editorial Problem in Shakespeare*, 1942, he comes down definitely on the other side and declares:

There is no doubt...that Q2 reproduces Shakespeare's foul papers.... This is clear from some confusion in the Queen Mab speech and a duplication of the Friar's opening words [II, iii] besides other indications.

Yet he admits some correction; for a little later he continues:

But Q2 was not printed throughout from manuscript: a section near the beginning (the exact extent of which is disputed) appears to have been set up from a corrected copy of the 'bad' first quarto, and there are some later passages in which Q1 was at least consulted. Presumably the manuscript was in parts defective or illegible.[17]

It is not surprising that Greg and others since should come to this general conclusion, for it cannot be denied that few if any of the 'good' quartos are so full of indications, of which only a few examples can be here given, pointing unmistakably to derivation from foul papers. What has not been appreciated is the extent and abnormality of the Q2 corruption and the weight of evidence, on the other side, which favours derivation from a corrected Q1. And but for our experience of editing the play we might not have come to appreciate these things either.

In 1928 Greg had stressed a point which proves beyond doubt that the Q2 compositor had at least consulted Q1 in one passage outside the identical ninety-five lines in I, ii and I, iii. At II, i, 13 we get the reading "*Abraham : Cupid*" in both quartos. It is possible to argue that *Abraham* is a misprint for *Adam*, which indeed most modern editors read (we think wrongly). But the colon is certainly incorrect and it is equally certain that Q2 must have copied it from Q1. Trivial as it may seem, a good deal hangs upon this coincidence—as we shall presently discover. Meanwhile, let us turn to a series of parallel passages exhibiting bibliographical links which cannot be explained on any theory of mere consultation of Q1 by those responsible for Q2.[18]

II, ii, 158–64

Q1 [D3ʳ]   *Iul: Romeo, Romeo, O for a falkners voice,*
To lure this Tassell gentle backe againe:
Bondage is hoarse and may not crie aloud,
Els would I teare the Caue where Eccho lies
And make her airie voice as hoarse as mine,
With repetition of my *Romeos* name.

Q2   *Iuli.* Hist Romeo hist, ô for a falkners voyce,
To lure this Tassel gentle back againe,
Bondage is hoarse, and may not speake aloude,
Else would I teare the Caue where Eccho lies,
And make her ayrie tongue more hoarse, then
With repetition of my *Romeo.*

Note the capitals in "Tassell", "Caue", and "Eccho"; and the spelling of "falkners", to say nothing of a possible common error in "hoarse".[19]

II, iv, 36–45

Q1 [E1ʳ]   *Ben:* Heere comes *Romeo.*

Mer: Without his Roe, like a dryed Hering. O flesh flesh how art thou fishified. Sirra now is he for the numbers that Petrarch flowdin: *Laura* to his Lady was but a kitchin drudg, yet she had a better loue to berime her: Dido a dowdy Cleopatra a Gypsie, *Hero* and *Hellen* hildings and harletries: *Thisbie* a gray eye or so, but not to the purpose. Signior *Romeo* bon iour there is a French curtesie to your French flop: yee gaue vs the counterfeit fairely yesternight.

Q2   *Ben.* Here Comes *Romeo,* here comes *Romeo.*

Mer. Without his Roe, like a dried Hering, O flesh, flesh, how art thou fishified? now is he for the numbers that Petrach flowed in: *Laura* to his Lady, was a kitchin wench, marrie she had a better loue to berime her: Dido a dowdie, Cleopatra a Gipsie, *Hellen* and *Hero,* hildings and harlots: *Thisbie* a grey eye or so, but not to the purpose. Signior *Romeo, Bonieur,* theres a French salutation to your French slop: you gaue vs the counterfeit fairly last night.

Note again the coincidence of capitals, together with the coincidence of colons, and the fact that in both texts all the names are italicized except Dido and Cleopatra.

III, v, 26–35

Q1 [G3]
> *Jul:* It is, it is, be gone, flye hence away.
> It is the Larke that sings so out of tune,
> Straining harsh Discords and vnpleasing Sharpes.
> Some say, the Larke makes sweete Diuision:
> This doth not so: for this diuideth vs.
> Some say the Larke and loathed Toad change eyes,
> I would that now they had changd voyces too:
> Since arme from arme her voyce doth vs affray,
> Hunting thee hence with Huntsvp to the day.
> So now be gone, more light and light it growes.

Q2
> *Iu.* It is, it is, hie hence be gone away:
> It is the Larke that sings so out of tune,
> Straining harsh Discords, and vnpleasing Sharpes.
> Some say, the Larke makes sweete Diuision:
> This doth not so: for she diuideth vs.
> Some say the Larke and loathed Toad change eyes,
> O now I would they had changd voyces too:
> Since arme from arme that voyce doth vs affray,
> Hunting thee hence, with Huntsup to the day.
> O now be gone, more light and light it growes.

Here once more punctuation and capitalization are so close as to make the two versions almost identical, while they, like the texts at II, ii, 158–64, are also linked by what we believe is a common error in "change eyes".[20] Furthermore, the passage in Q1, which begins on the recto and continues overleaf to the verso, is preceded by one of twenty-six lines (1–26) which is scarcely less

85

close to its parallel in Q2. It seems undeniable then that G3 as a whole served after correction as copy for Q2.

This third example has a special interest in that it occurs so late in the play. For it will be remembered that while the reporting in Q1 is strikingly good during the first two acts it deteriorates progressively from that point onwards. The Q1 leaves, therefore, would become progressively less helpful to a collator as he moved forward. Yet a close comparison of its text on pages I3ʳ, I4ʳ and on both sides of K1, with the parallels in Q2 will I think convince most students that occasionally Q1 was found of service right up to the end. It is of course impossible to quote the whole at length here. A few scraps must serve to illustrate the point, the reader's attention being directed to the numbered lines:

v, i, 6–24

Q1 [I3ʳ]

    Me thought I was this night alreadie dead:
    (Strange dreames that giue a dead man leaue to thinke)
    And that my Ladie *Iuliet* came to me,
8 And breathd such life with kisses in my lips,
9 That I reuiude and was an Emperour.
       Enter Balthasar his man booted.
12 Newes from *Verona*. How now *Balthasar*,
14 How doth my Ladie? Is my Father well?
15 How fares my *Juliet*? that I aske againe.
    If she be well, then nothing can be ill.
      Balt: Then nothing can be ill, for she is well,
18 Her bodie sleepes in *Capels* Monument,
19 And her immortall parts with Angels dwell.
    Pardon me Sir that am the Messenger of such bad tidings.
      Rom: Is it euen so? then I defie my Starres.

Q2

    I dreamt my Lady came and found me dead,
    Strange dreame that giues a deadman leaue to thinke,
8 And Breathd such life with kisses in my lips,
9 That I reuiude and was an Emperor.
      [I omit two lines]
      Enter Romeos man
12 Newes from *Verona*, how now *Balthazer*,
    Dost thou not bring me Letters from the Frier?
14 How doth my Lady, is my Father well:
15 How doth my Lady *Iuliet*? that I aske againe,
    For nothing can be ill if she be well.
      Man. Then she is well and nothing can be ill,
18 Her body sleepes in *Capels* monument,
19 And her immortall part with Angels liues.
      [I omit four lines]
    Rom. Is it in so? then I denie you starres.

v, ii, 1–13

Q1 [I4^r]

      Enter Frier Iohn

    John: What Frier *Laurence*, Brother, ho?

2 *Laur:* This same should be the voyce of Frier *Iohn*,

    What newes from *Mantua*, what will *Romeo* come?

5 *Iohn:* Going to seeke a barefoote Brother out,

6 One of our order to associate mee,

7 Here in this Cittie visiting the sick,

    Whereas the infectious pestilence remaind:

8 And being by the Searchers of the Towne

    Found and examinde, we were both shut vp.

13 *Laur:* Who bare my letters then to *Romeo*?

Q2

      Enter Frier Iohn *to Frier* Lawrence.

    Ioh. Holy *Franciscan* Frier, brother, ho.

      Enter Lawrence.

2 *Law.* This same should be the voyce of Frier *Iohn*.

    Welcome from *Mantua*, what sayes *Romeo*?

    Or if his minde be writ, giue me his Letter.

5 *Ioh.* Going to find a barefoote brother out,

6 One of our order to assotiate me,

7 Here in this Citie visiting the sicke,

8 And finding him, the Searchers of the Towne

     [I omit two lines]

    Seald vp the doores, and would not let vs forth,

    So that my speed to *Mantua* there was staid.

13 *Law.* Who bare my Letter then to *Romeo*?

Apart from the other parallels in these two illustrations, the capitalization of "Searchers of the Towne" in both texts at v, ii, 8 can hardly be accidental, while the interesting variants in v, i, 24 will be discussed below. It is not necessary to number the lines in the next illustrative scraps, since parallels occur in almost every one.

v, iii, 18–120 (extracts from)

Q1 [K1^{r&v}]

    Par: The boy giues warning, something doth approach.

    What cursed foote wanders this was to night,

    To stay my obsequies and true loues rites?

    What with a torch, muffle me night a while.

    Rom: Giue mee this mattocke, and this wrentching Iron.

    And take these letters, early in the morning,

    See thou deliuer them to my Lord and Father.

. . . . .

    Par: This is that banisht haughtie *Mountague*,

    That murderd my loues cosen, I will apprehend him.

87

Stop thy vnhallowed toyle vile *Mountague*.
Can vengeance be pursued further then death?

$\cdot \qquad \cdot \qquad \cdot \qquad \cdot$

[*Rom.*] I loue thee better then I loue my selfe:
For I come hyther armde against my selfe,
   Par: I doe defie thy coniurations:
And doe attach thee as a fellon heere.
    Rom: What dost thou tempt me, then haue at thee boy.
                They fight.
    Boy: O Lord they fight, I will goe call the watch.
    Par: Ah I am slaine, if thou be mercifull
Open the tombe, lay me with *Iuliet*.
    Rom: Yfaith I will, let me peruse this face,
Mercutios kinsman, noble County *Paris*?

$\cdot \qquad \cdot \qquad \cdot \qquad \cdot$

Death lye thou there, by a dead man interd,

$\cdot \qquad \cdot \qquad \cdot$

Come desperate Pilot now at once runne on
The dashing rockes thy sea-sicke weary barge.
Heers to my loue. O true Apothecary:
Thy drugs are swift: thus with a kisse I dye.

The Boy giues warning, something doth approach,
What cursed foote wanders this way to night,
To crosse my obsequies and true loues right?
What with a Torch? muffle me night a while.
           Enter Romeo *and* Peter.
    Ro. Giue me that mattocke and the wrenching Iron,
Hold take this Letter, early in the morning
See thou deliuer it to my Lord and Father,

$\cdot \qquad \cdot \qquad \cdot \qquad \cdot$

    Pa. This is that banisht haughtie *Mountague*,
That murdred my loues Cozin,...

$\cdot \qquad \cdot \qquad \cdot \qquad \cdot$

                ...I will apprehend him,
Stop thy vnhallowed toyle vile *Mountague:*
Can vengeance be pursued further then death?

$\cdot \qquad \cdot \qquad \cdot \qquad \cdot$

[*Rom.*] By heauen I loue thee better then my selfe,
For I come hither armde against my selfe:

$\cdot \qquad \cdot \qquad \cdot \qquad \cdot$

    Par. I do defie thy commiration,
And apprehend thee for a Fellon here.

Q2

Ro. Wilt thou prouoke me? then haue at thee boy.
  O Lord they fight, I will go call the Watch.
 Par. O I am slaine, if thou be mercifull,
Open the Tombe, lay me with *Iuliet.*
 Rom. In faith I will, let me peruse this face,
Mercutios kinsman, Noble Countie *Paris,*

  . . . . .

Death lie thou there by a dead man interd,

  . . . . .

Thou desperate Pilot, now at once run on
The dashing Rocks, thy seasick weary barke:
Heeres to my Loue. O true Appothecary:
Thy drugs are quicke. Thus with a kisse I die.

The italics in Q2 for "O Lord they fight...Watch" we take as an indication that the corrector supposed the boy's cry was meant to be a stage-direction, presumably because Shakespeare wrote this off-stage speech in the margin as he apparently did with the Nurse's off-stage cries of "Madam" at II, ii, 149, 151, though there his purpose was correctly interpreted. And if the mistake was the collator's, it shows him, as we shall later discover elsewhere, slavishly and unintelligently following the manuscript in preference to Q1, even when it is "evident to any formal capacity" that the latter must be correct.

With the foregoing evidence in hand we can now legitimately assume that the bibliographical links noted above in signatures A and B point to the use of a corrected Q1 there also. This means that seven out of the ten sheets of which Q1 consists had been corrected by a scribe to provide copy for Q2, viz. signatures A, B, D, E, G, I, K; and we shall presently find undoubted proof of his hand in signature C; while, did space allow, it would not be difficult to detect it also in portions of Q2 corresponding to the other two sheets. To express this more precisely in terms of pages, it is, we hold, possible to trace links with Q2 in thirty-one out of the seventy-five printed pages of Q1, viz. A3^r, B3^r, B3^v, B4^r, B4^v, C1^r, C1^v, C2^r, C4^v, D1^r, D1^v, D3^r, D3^v, E1^r, E1^v, E2^r, F4^r, F4^v, G1^r, G1^v, G3^r, G3^v, H2^r, H2^v, H3^r, I3^r, I4^r, K1^r, K1^v, K3^r, K4^r. Is there any reason in the nature of things, or in the character of the Q2 text, why the complete copy should not have been provided in this way, if we allow for an increasing use of inserted slips[21] as the collator proceeded with his task? Greg suggests that Q1 was resorted to only because "the manuscript was in parts defective or illegible".[22] But that involves the assumption that these defective or illegible passages happened to coincide with the better reported passages in Q1, an assumption which surely becomes quite untenable in face of all the parallels cited above.

But what of those confusions and duplications in Q2 which, Greg claims, point to the use of the foul papers? Some certainly prove that Q2 was largely derived from them, but not that it must have been printed from them, since a copyist is just as likely to be responsible for such features as a compositor. Indeed, we are inclined to think that this particular copyist was even more likely to stumble in the reproduction of foul papers than a compositor of ordinary

G

competence. Discussing the aims and accuracy of the collation of *Richard III* (Q6) with the playhouse manuscript in the preparation of copy for F1, Miss Walker writes:

Its object was clearly something better than an approximation: it represented an effort to reproduce through the medium of Q6, and therefore in everything but accidentals...what was in the manuscript.... It was clearly no part of the collator's business to act editorially and to determine whether the quarto stage directions served a reader's purpose as well. This is especially clear from the Folio's speech prefixes.[23]

The collator of *Romeo*, we suggest, worked in the same fashion: his aim was diplomatic, the aim of a professional scrivener. When, for instance, he saw "Enter Will Kemp" in the manuscript at IV, v, 99, or "Enter Romeo and Peter" at v, iii, 21, he just copied it out. On the other hand, Miss Walker estimates that the collator of *Richard III* overlooked some 44 errors which he ought to have corrected in Q6,[24] and we have no reason to suppose that our collator was any more exact. And it is, we think, pretty clear that he possessed even less understanding of the material he was handling, which would be natural enough if the collation of *Richard III* "was undertaken at Heminge and Condell's direction",[25] as Miss Walker plausibly conjectures, that is presumably by a theatre scribe, while the *Romeo* collation was carried out, as we suppose, by a scrivener from Creede's office or one employed by him. Certainly what he produced could not be described as "on the whole a very reputable piece of work" to quote Miss Walker again on the *Richard III* collator. We must recollect, moreover, that he was certainly faced with a manuscript of no ordinary difficulty and one which might have baffled or led astray even a scribe accustomed to dramatic documents. We submit that copy prepared by an apparently incompetent or inexperienced scrivener, collating a reported text like Q1 with a Shakespearian manuscript in a state of unusual disorder, is sufficient, if we make due allowance for misunderstandings on the part of the compositor, to account for all the "confusions and duplications" in Q2 and for a good deal of its other corruptions as well, though, as we shall find, the compositor himself should probably bear the blame for some of them.

But let us put the matter to the test, and consider four major examples of confusion or duplication in Q2, two of which Greg picks out for special mention as pointing to foul papers.[26] And we will begin with a textual muddle which we think can only be explained as arising from a misunderstanding by the compositor of a corrected passage in Q1.

II, ii, 38–42

Q1 [D1ᵛ]   *Iul:* Tis but thy name that is mine enemie,
Whats *Mountague*? It is nor hand nor foote,
Nor arme, nor face, nor any other part.
Whats in a name? That which we call a Rose,
By any other name would smell as sweet:
So *Romeo* would, were he not *Romeo* cald,
Retaine the diuine perfection he owes:

Q2   *Iu.* Tis but thy name that is my enemie:
Thou art thy selfe, though not a *Mountague*,
Whats *Mountague*? it is nor hand nor foote,

> Nor arme nor face, ô be some other name
> Belonging to a man.
> Whats in a name that which we call a rose,
> By any other word would smell as sweete,
> So *Romeo* would wene he not *Romeo* cald,
> Retaine that deare perfection which he owes,

Clearly a conflated text of some kind is required for the first six lines. That adopted by Malone and most later editors runs (with the conflation italicized) thus:

> *Jul.* 'Tis but thy name that is mine enemy;
> Thou art thy self, though not a Montague.
> 40 What's Montague? it is nor hand, nor foot,
> Nor arm, nor face, *nor any other part*
> *Belonging to a man. O, be some other name!*
> What's in a name? that which we call a rose

But, as noted by Miss Walker to whom we owe the solution of the puzzle, this gives an extra-metrical foot in l. 42, and an awkward repetition of "other" in ll. 41-2. She therefore conjectures:

> *Jul.* 'Tis but thy name that is my enemy;
> *Thou art thyself, though not a Montague.*
> *O, be some other name!* What's Montague?
> It is not hand, nor foot, nor arm, nor face,
> Nor any part *belonging to a man.*
> What's in a name? that which we call a rose

If this be the true text, as we believe, Q2 was here unquestionably set up from a corrected page of Q1, since it retains the incorrect lineation of the latter, while textual restoration can only be attained by conflation. Nor is it difficult to see in part what happened. The collator copied into the margin the three additions from the foul papers, which we have italicized for the reader's benefit in the restored text, but did so in such a manner that the compositor took the shorter ones to be continuous and inserted them at the wrong point, though in the right order, not topsy-turvy as Malone supposed. McKerrow, Miss Walker tells us, thought "nor any other part" was an actor's interpolation. But, she notes, some phrase corresponding to it is required, both to clarify the meaning of "dear perfection" (l. 42) and to give weight to the penultimate line of Juliet's speech:

> And for thy name, which is no part of thee.

She suggests, however, that the word "other" may well belong to the reporter, since it echoes the "other name" which he had forgotten and completes the sense and metre of his line. Yet if all this be so we must credit the collator with the absence of "any other part" from Q2. Perhaps he struck out "other" but so carelessly that the compositor imagined he had intended to delete the rest of the phrase as well.

Signature D1ᵛ of Q1 was, anyhow, indisputably a corrected page used for the printing of Q2. And it virtually carries its recto along with it inasmuch as we have only to lay the dialogue of D1ʳ beside the corresponding text of Q2 to see that the former requires very little correction to bring it into conformity with the latter. Further, if D 1ʳ be conceded as part of the Q 2 copy, what about C 4ᵛ, the next page back, which contains the *"Abraham: Cupid"* recognized bibliographical link and raises problems of peculiar interest? The Q 1 page begins with the first six lines of II, i, not quite perfectly reported, but correctly divided as verse; these are followed by Mercutio's two speeches which are once again not word perfect and this time printed as prose, with a single line of Benvolio's dividing them; finally Benvolio's three line speech, which completes the page, is printed as verse. Why the two verse speeches of Mercutio should have taken prose form is a problem for an editor of Q 1 which need not here concern us. Our problem is the corresponding text of Q 2 which is, apart from trivial irregularities perhaps due to Shakespeare himself, divided as verse throughout, but is at the same time full of the queerest possible misprints especially in the first of Mercutio's longer speeches. There is not room here to quote the whole at length, but a comparison of ll. 1–14 in the two texts provides enough for our purpose.

II, i, 1–14

Q 1 [C 4ᵛ]

Enter Romeo alone.

Ro: Shall I goe forward and my heart is here?
Turne backe dull earth and finde thy Center out.

Enter Benuolio Mercutio.

Ben: Romeo, my cosen *Romeo.*
Mer: Doest thou heare he is wise,
Vpon my life he hath stolne him home to bed.
Ben: He came this way, and leapt this Orchard wall.
Call good *Mercutio.*
Mer: Call, nay Ile coniure too.

Romeo, madman, humors, passion, liuer, appeare thou in likenes of a sigh: speak but one rime & I am satisfied, cry but ay me. Pronounce but Loue and Doue, speake to my gossip *Venus* one faire word, one nickname for her purblinde sonne and heire young *Abraham: Cupid* hee that shot so trim when young King *Cophetua* loued the begger wench....

Q 2

Enter Romeo alone.

Ro. Can I go forward when my heart is here,
Turne backe dull earth and find thy Center out.

Enter Benuolio with Mercutio.

Ben. Romeo, my Cosen *Romeo, Romeo.*
Mer. He is wise, and on my life hath stolne him home to bed.
Ben. He ran this way and leapt this Orchard wall.
Call good *Mercutio:*
Nay Ile coniure too.
Mer. Romeo, humours, madman, passion louer,
Appeare thou in the likenesse of a sigh,
Speake but on rime and I am satisfied:
Crie but ay me, prouaunt, but loue and day,
Speake to my goship *Venus* one faire word,

> One nickname for her purblind sonne and her,
> Young *Abraham: Cupid* he that shot so true,
> When King *Cophetua* lou'd the begger mayd.

At first sight the Q2 text here quoted seems a clear instance of the compositor working directly from the foul papers, seeing that its errors, strange as they look, are similar to those found in other 'good' quartos and of a character ordinarily explained as misreadings of Shakespeare's handwriting. Yet, we repeat, what a compositor might misread a copyist is likely to misread also and to misread in much the same fashion. Moreover, the presence of a corrected page of Q1 behind Q2 is at least suggested by the common stage direction "*Enter Romeo alone*", the identical capitals in "Centre" and "Orchard" and the spelling "humerous" which both Q2 and Q1 print in l. 31, though this spelling is also found in *Love's Labour's Lost*, III, i, 177. Significant also is the misplacement of the prefix "*Mer.*" in l. 7, since this can best be accounted for as a misunderstanding by the Q2 compositor of a direction by the collator. If we assume that the latter had to prepare this page for the Q2 compositor, how would he set about it? Having not merely to correct the errors and supply the omissions in Mercutio's speeches but to make certain also that they were set up as verse, his simplest plan would be to copy them out on a slip and label it "*Mer.*" to show which character it belonged to. The prose lineation of Q1 does not begin, however, until after the opening half line of the first speech, and that half line had of course its "*Mer.*" prefix. Thus if the collator proceeded in the fashion suggested, the Q2 compositor would be faced with two consecutive lines each prefixed "*Mer.*". He may even have set both prefixes up, since he preserved, it will be noticed, the Q1 division of l. 6 into two half lines. But if so, in the end one "*Mer.*" had to go and he pitched upon the wrong one.

If all this be granted, we may learn from it something more about the attitude and competence of the collator. A striking feature of the parallel passages before us is their wide divergence of reading combined with their exact correspondence in the incorrectly punctuated "*Abraham: Cupid*". As noted above, critics are now agreed,[27] the agent of transmission for this last, whether compositor or copyist, baffled by the names he saw in the manuscript, turned and consulted Q1. And we may observe in passing that proper names are surprisingly accurate in Q1 for a reported text, while they are not likely to have been particularly easy to read in the foul papers, so that this was probably by no means the only instance of such consultation. As for the striking differences of reading in the rest of the speech, they seem to show once again a slavish following of the manuscript. In other words, when the collator, as we assume the agent to have been, felt he could read the writing before him he tended to interpret it according to his lights in preference to Q1, even though the latter offered him excellent sense. It may indeed be that he found his reading of Shakespeare's lines, nonsense as it seems to us, no more incomprehensible than the, to him, abstruse banter of Q1. Yet if so, he must have been a very stupid fellow.

Turn now to the well-known duplication in Q2 of the opening four lines of the Friar's speech at the beginning of II, iii. These appear, in their now accepted position, as follows in Q1 [D3ᵛ]:

(C)
> The gray ey'd morne smiles on the frowning night,
> Checkring the Easterne clouds with streakes of light,
> And flecked darkenes like a drunkard reeles,
> From forth daies path, and *Titans* fierie wheeles:

Q2, however, not only prints them twice over but in different versions and at different points of the text: first, as part of Romeo's last speech in II, ii, thus:

(A)
> The grey eyde morne smiles on the frowning night,
> Checkring the Easterne Clouds with streaks of light,
> And darknesse fleckted like a drunkard reeles,
> From forth daies pathway, made by *Tytans* wheeles.

and second, as in Q1, at the beginning of II, iii thus:

(B)
> The grey-eyed morne smiles on the frowning night,
> Checking the Easterne clowdes with streaks of light:
> And fleckeld darknesse like a drunkard reeles,
> From forth daies path, and *Titans* burning wheeles:

There are misprints in both the Q2 versions, e.g. in (A) "fleckted" for "flecked" or "fleckled", and in (B) (probably) "checking" for "checkring" while in (B) also "burning" has been printed for "fierie" by attraction from "burning eie" in the following line. But, apart from this, which of the two is Shakespeare's and for which character did he intend it? The second question is easily answered: Romeo could not possibly speak of the "blessed blessed night" (II, ii, 139) which had just ended for him as "frowning".[28] Nor is it difficult to decide which lines are Shakespeare's. First (A)'s "fleckled [or "flecked"] like a drunkard", which recalls the flushed or blotchy face of the toper as he reels homeward, gives us a characteristically Shakespearian image; and secondly, (B)'s last line, whether emended or not

> From forth daies path, and *Titans* burning [fierie] wheeles

is nonsense, as Steevens long ago noted, whereas (A)'s

> From forth daies pathway, made by *Tytans* wheeles

is a typical piece of Elizabethan astronomy, referring as it does to the course across the sky along which Titan Phoebus drives his chariot from sunrise to sunset, a course marked according to Golding's *Ovid* (ii, 175; *Met.* ii, 133) by his "charyot rakes" or ruts. Moreover, the absurdity of (B) should rule out the notion entertained by some[29] that it represents Shakespeare's revision of (A). Where then does (B) come from? It is very close to (C) and there is little doubt in our minds that it is simply a slightly inaccurate reprint of that text. In short, we must suppose that the collator copied Shakespeare's version from the foul papers into the margin of Q1 without clearly indicating its precise position and without deleting the reporter's version (C), so that the Q2 compositor reproduced them both, inserting the marginal addition where it seemed to him convenient.[30]

A fourth extended passage in which the text of Q2 goes wrong is the Queen Mab speech (I, iv, 53–95); and this, though in some ways more puzzling than the others, may be dealt with at shorter length, since a number of its interesting points will be more conveniently discussed in the Notes to our edition. It is the question of its provenance that is here at issue, and this turns upon our interpretation of two salient and indisputable features: (i) thirty-eight lines, i.e. ll. 54–91 ("She is the fairies midwife...bodes"), are printed in Q2 as twenty-six or rather as twenty-five and two-thirds lines of prose, which occupy the lower portion of a right-hand page, though the speech reverts to verse over-leaf; (ii) ll. 59–61 ("Her chariot...coach makers") are printed after l. 69 in Q2, thus making Mercutio absurdly describe the parts of the coach before mentioning the coach itself. If Q2 was here printed from foul papers, the prose arrangement must be set down to the restoration of lines at first overlooked by the compositor. It implies, in other words, that he originally set up twenty-six lines of verse from the copy in the lower portion of the page and that, observing then Shakespeare's additional lines in the margin or on a separate slip, he managed to get these in on the same page by distributing the type of the twenty-six lines and resetting them as prose. But this involves three further assumptions: (a) a solicitude for the accuracy of the text on Creede's part for which there is little evidence elsewhere in Q2; (b) that Creede was both lucky enough to discover the omission and lucky enough to be able to accommodate the extra matter in the space available;[31] and (c) that, since 26 from 38 leaves 12, Shakespeare's hypothetical addition(s) must have totalled a dozen lines, neither more nor less. As to (c), if the speech in Q2 be examined one can point to two alternative pairs of passages and two only which might be additions, i.e. which could be omitted without serious injury to the text—namely either (i) the lines 77–81 ("Sometime...benefice") which suggest an afterthought, since "courtier's nose" is repetitious after "courtier's knees" (l. 72), and the misplaced ll. 59–61 which deals with the coach, or (ii) lines 77–81 as before and lines 62–9 ("Her waggon-spokes...maid [Q2 man]") which seem a more likely afterthought than ll. 59–61, since the whole coach would occur to a mind before its parts. Neither pair, however, fits the case, since (i) amounts to seven lines only, five too few, and (ii) to thirteen, one too many. Actually the position would be even worse, if, as we believe, the apparently repetitious "courtier's nose" should rightly read "counsellor's nose".[32]

On the other hand, suppose that Q2 was here, as elsewhere, set up from a corrected copy of Q1 (i.e. of signatures C1^v, C2^r), no insuperable difficulties seem to arise. Indeed, since ll. 59–61 form a passage omitted by the reporter their misplacement in Q2 finds an obvious explanation: the collator copied them into the margin but did not clearly indicate their correct position. As for the prose lining, that may well be accredited to the Q2 compositor. The collator could have corrected and supplemented the verse column in Q1 without going to the trouble of transcribing the whole thing easily enough, as he did, we conjecture, in II, i. But faced with the pages of Q1 thus corrected and baffled by the problem of lineation, a compositor would naturally decide that the easiest and quickest solution was to set up the bulk of it as prose. Incidentally, if this explanation be accepted, it gives us two more leaves of sheet C which served as copy for Q2.

A crucial question remains. Did the scribe have to go to the theatre to collate his Q1 with the manuscript, in which case the printer would not have seen a line of the latter; or did Shakespeare's company hand over the manuscript to Creede as they did to Roberts in 1604 for the printing of *Hamlet* Q2, in which case he, like Roberts, could have utilized both the 'bad' quarto and the manuscript? Whether or to what extent he is likely actually to have utilized the manuscript, if he got it, would probably depend upon the comparative 'badness' of the bad quarto. If, for instance, his compositors were like Jaggard's, who in 1621–3 set up the type for the First Folio, they would have preferred working from a printed text, however heavily corrected in ink, to puzzling their way through the perplexities of a Shakespearian rough draft.[33] In 1604, however, the text of *Hamlet* Q1 diverged so far from the manuscript after Act I that Roberts had no alternative but the manuscript to print from; and we might expect the same thing to have happened with *Romeo* after Act II or a little later. Nor can one be certain it did not. All one can say is, there seems to be no evidence for it, while on the other hand what evidence there is, which admittedly grows inevitably scantier in the last three acts of the play, points as we have seen in the opposite direction. In a word, there is no necessity to assume the presence of the foul papers at Creede's printing-house; and taking all the possibilities into account, we think it safer to suppose that they never left the theatre.

We incline then to believe that the copy used by Creede in 1599 was not the foul papers eked out at places from passages in Q 1, but a specimen of Q 1 itself corrected throughout and supplemented by a scribe who was given access to the foul papers of the theatre; a conclusion, be it recalled, which is virtually that already reached by Miss Hjort in 1926. The scribe, we have seen reason to think, was at once careless when collating and too exact when transcribing. On the one hand, he was liable to overlook words in Q 1 which he should have corrected and to leave passages standing which, having transcribed the corresponding authentic version from the foul papers, he should have crossed out, while he did not always indicate clearly to the compositor the point at which his additions should be inserted in the text. On the other hand, he generally followed the foul papers with a slavish and unintelligent fidelity, reproducing Shakespeare's first and second shots side by side; substituting his often defective, imprecise, or purely theatrical stage-directions for more explicit and accurate ones in Q 1;[34] sometimes mixing up a stage-direction with the dialogue; and finally, when he found the handwriting difficult, spelling it out painfully letter by letter with little or no regard to the sense of the passage.

Now printer's copy prepared in this fashion, whatever Creede may have thought of it, was not likely to afford a very sound text for a modern editor. And this is not the end of our trouble. The compositor who handled the copy was himself, it can hardly be questioned, a slovenly or overdriven craftsman. Q 2, for example, contains a number of 'literals', of words with missing or superfluous letters, of missing words and these generally short ones, of dittographs, of inattention to word-endings, and of literal assimilations. Most of these were probably due to the compositor attempting to carry too many words in his head at a time, which points to hurried workmanship.[35]

Thus Q 2, which is the only evidence we have as to Shakespeare's intentions, may at any point have been corrupted in one of four different ways: (i) by the 'first shots' or other obscurities left by Shakespeare himself; (ii) by actors' perversions overlooked by the collator when correcting Q 1; (iii) by the collator's own perversions and misunderstandings when attempting to decipher the foul papers; (iv) by the misprints or misplacements for which the compositor was mainly accountable. Confronted with a situation like this, what should be an editor's procedure? No editor can escape responsibility for his text. But the measure of his responsibility is determined to a large extent by the confidence he has in the original text or texts, and when as in the present instance his confidence is small the burden of responsibility is correspondingly heavy. Yet he is not thrown back entirely upon his own judgement as was a pre-Pollardian editor, who, having nothing to go upon but guesses about the character of the texts, selected his readings more or less indiscriminately from them according to his own fancy. The old eclectic editors undoubtedly, for example, adopted far too many readings from Q 1, knowing nothing of the provenance of that text. Aware, as we now are, that the only authority it possesses is the memory of the actor or actors who had performed it, we have no right to follow it until we have exhausted the possibilities of Q2, understanding by those of course, not logical possibilities, but readings which the editor thinks possible for Shakespeare. Nevertheless, Q1 can never be ignored, since the memorial reconstructor may often have recalled the correct word, especially in the first two acts. Nor is it even safe altogether to neglect his readings in the later and badly reported ones. Here, for example, are three instances, all of capital importance, all from near the end of the play, and in all of which we unhesitatingly prefer Q1 wholly or in part, as we believe most other students will also.

(i)   IV, iii, 58

Q1   *Romeo* I come, this doe I drinke to thee.
Q2   *Romeo, Romeo, Romeo,* heeres drinke, I drink to thee.

In this Q1 seems not only better than Q2 but to bear the stamp of authenticity, though it is not easy to see how the feeble Q2 arose.

(ii)   V, i, 24

Q1   Is it euen so? then I defie my Starres.
Q2   Is it in so? then I denie you starres.

Since "in" is a not uncommon spelling in Shakespeare for "e'en", the word "denie" is the only corruption in Q2 here; and corrupt it clearly is, though once again it is difficult to explain it.

(iii)   V, i, 76

Q1   I pay thy pouertie, but not thy will
Q2   I pray thy pouertie and not thy will.

The corruption in this case is "pray" and one not so unaccountable as the others. Yet in all three decisions, as with many others in this text, we have little but our own taste and judgement to go upon.[36]

Amid so many uncertainties and possibilities plenty of room is left of course for differences of opinion. Well over a score of the readings in the text we shall publish have, for example, been keenly debated between us, and though in the end agreement was arrived at on most, a few differences remain unresolved, as our notes will confess. For it is no easy road Shakespeare's editors have now to tread and, like his first editors, we pray the great variety of our readers not to envy us the office of our care and pain.

NOTES

1. The chief ones are: Robert Gericke, '*Romeo and Juliet* nach Shakespeare's, Manuscript', in *Shakespeare Jahrbuch*, XIV (1879), 207–73; Greta Hjort, 'The Good and Bad Quartos of *Romeo and Juliet*', in *Modern Language Review*, XXI (1926), 140–6; W. W. Greg, 'Principles of Emendation' (British Academy Lecture, 1928), reprinted in *Aspects of Shakespeare* (1933), relevant pages, 144–7, 175–81; W. W. Greg, *The Editorial Problem in Shakespeare* (The Clark Lectures, 1939), 1942, 2nd ed. 1951; Sidney Thomas, 'The Bibliographical Links between the first two quartos of *Romeo and Juliet*', in *Review of English Studies*, XXV (1949), 110–14; G. I. Duthie, 'The Text of Shakespeare's *Romeo and Juliet*' (English Institute Lecture, 1950), in *Studies in Bibliography*, IV (University of Virginia, 1951–2), 1–29; Richard Hosley, 'The Corrupting Influence of the Bad Quarto on the received text of *Romeo and Juliet*', in *Shakespeare Quarterly*, IV (1953), 11–33. A useful book for students is P. A. Daniel's *Parallel-text Edition of the Quartos* (New Shakspere Society, 1874).

2. H. R. Hoppe, *The Bad Quarto of 'Romeo and Juliet'* (Cornell, 1948).

3. Greg, *Editorial Problem*, p. 61.

4. This important point was first established by R. B. McKerrow in 'A suggestion regarding Shakespeare's manuscripts', *Review of English Studies*, XI (1935), 459.

5. Duthie first detected this 'first shot', but it was Miss Walker who decided upon "new" as the superfluous word and showed us the reason for thinking so.

6. I.e. at II, ii, 10–11; III, iii, 40–44; IV, i, 110; V, iii, 102–3, 107–8. The line numeration of the text in this article follows that of our forthcoming edition.

7. Robert Gericke, *v. supra*, note 1.

8. "The most obvious explanation" of the italics in Q1, writes Greg (*op. cit.* p. 62), "is that an actor's part, written in Italian script, had been cut up and pasted into the copy."

9. *Modern Language Review*, XXI (1926), 140 ff.

10. On the first, the British Academy Lecture 1928, he was admittedly merely stating what seemed to be the accepted doctrine at that date.

11. *Review of English Studies*, XXV (1949), 110–14.

12. I.e. on the front of the third leaf of the first sheet. "Sig." (= signature) refers to the letter or figure at the foot of the page, by which the compositor numbered or 'signed' his different sheets. The four leaves, for example, in the second sheet of Q1 were signed B, B2, B3, the last leaf not being signed; and such signatures are always found on the recto of the leaf.

13. I was fortunate enough to inspect an uncut quarto of *Troilus and Cressida* 1609 at Martin Bodmer's Library, Geneva, three years ago.

14. *Aspects of Shakespeare*, p. 176.

15. *Studies in Bibliography*, p. 15.

16. Thomas (*op. cit.* p. 113) asserts that "only the most careless editor or compositor could have failed to correct them", which puts it rather high. The errors are (i) the stage direction, "He reads the Letter" (I, ii, 63), when what he reads is a list, not a letter; (ii) "Vtruuio" (l. 67) for "Vitruuio"; (iii) a little muddle (ll. 75–6) where

"*Ser.* Vp. / *Ro.* Whither to supper? / *Ser.* To our house."

should read

"*Ser.* Vp. / *Ro.* Whither? / *Ser.* To supper, to our house."

And the apparent anomalies are (*a*) the italic type for the list and for the Nurse's speeches, (*b*) the printing of both these as prose. As to this last, editors have never been able to make anything but very rough verse out of these speeches and it is quite possible that Shakespeare intended them to be rhythmical (i.e. easily memorized) prose. The italic was the printer's affair with which a scribe concentrating upon the substance of the dialogue would not be concerned; and after following copy in signature B the Q2 compositor realized his mistake, so that in signature C and later the Nurse is dressed in roman. Finally the three errors seem commonplace enough to an editor accustomed to the misprints in thirty quarto and folio texts: we shall find our scribe guilty of much graver oversights later on.

17. *Editorial Problem*, pp. 61–2.

18. The second and third, together with the coincident colons in "*Abraham: Cupid*" at II, i, 13 (*v.* pp. 84, 92) were first pointed out by Alfred Pollard and myself in an article for the *Times Literary Supplement* in 1919. Shakespearian textual criticism was then in its salad days and we drew deductions from those bibliographical links which we thought better of a few years later.

19. P. A. Daniel conjectured "hushed". Q2 omits 'mine' after 'then'.

20. We read "changed eyes".

21. Duthie tentatively suggested in 1950 (*Studies*, pp. 5–6) that the scribe "tore out" the corrected leaves of Q1. But I feel that as Q1 would be sewn and probably cased it might be more convenient to keep it in book form and insert the transcribed slips between its pages, at any rate until the compositor got to work.

22. *Editorial Problem*, p. 62.

23. Alice Walker, *Textual Problems of the First Folio* (1953), p. 22.

24. *Ibid.* p. 24.

25. *Ibid.* p. 21.

26. See above, p. 84 (top).

27. Cf. *Aspects*, pp. 146–7, 180–1; *Studies in Bibliography*, pp. 15–17; Hosley (*op. cit.*), pp. 18–19. We believe "Abraham" to be the correct reading.

28. A point we owe to Miss Walker.

29. E.g. by Richard Hosley (*op. cit.*), pp. 30–1, who also thinks Shakespeare intended the lines for Romeo, and contends that Shakespeare's manuscript was the principal copy for Q2. Hosley's article, which is full of interesting and at times less debatable points than these, reached our hands at a late stage of this investigation, and has since been followed by an edition of the play by him (Yale, 1954), not seen before going to press.

30. Both the (B) and (C) versions became current, (B) being quoted in *England's Parnassus*, 1600, and C imitated by Drummond in *Phoebus Arise* (*Poems*, 1616).

31. Points (*a*) and (*b*) we owe once again to Miss Walker.

32. See note I, iv, 77 in our edition.

33. For Jaggard's preference for printed copy see Alice Walker (*op. cit.*), *passim*.

34. Compare, e.g. III, i, 89, Q2 "Away, Tybalt" with Q1 "Tibalt vnder Romeos arme thrusts Mercutio in and flyes"; IV, v, 95, Q2 "Exeunt manet" with Q1 "They all but the Nurse goe foorth, casting Rosemary on her and shutting the Curtens"; and IV, v, 99, Q2 "Exit omnes" ⟨error⟩ "Enter Will Kemp", with Q1 "Enter Seruingman".

35. Possible instances of dittographs are: I, iv, 45 "lights lights"; II, i, 3 "Romeo, Romeo"; III, v, 19 "the the"; IV, v, 95 "my my"; v, iii, 187 "too too"; of carelessness in respect of word-endings II, iv, 29 "phantacies" (fantasticoes); v, iii, 209 "earling" (early) and perhaps I, i, 191 "louing" (lovers'); IV, i, 94 "distilling" (distilled); while assimilation may account for the following strange misprints II, ii, 83 "*washeth* (washed)...farthest"; II, ii, 152 "*strife* (suit)...grief"; IV, i, 98 "no *breast* (breath) shall testifie thou liu*est*"; IV, v, 51 "I *did* yet *bedold* (behold)". Lastly this compositor had a tendency, not uncommon with printers of Shakespearian texts, of expanding contracted or colloquial forms, often to the ruin of the verse. We reckon there are some sixteen instances of this.

36. Conjectural explanations of the Q2 readings will be found in the Notes to our edition.

THE SIGNIFICANCE OF A DATE

BY

I. A. SHAPIRO

So long as much of the chronology of Elizabethan drama remains unknown or uncertain, the dating of any plays of that period must present problems of interest. When, as sometimes happens, the date of one play may help to fix that of others, the correct solution of the problem may be exceptionally important. A prime example is the dating of the manuscript of Anthony Mundy's *John a Kent and John a Cumber*.

John a Kent is by no means a dull play; its ingenious construction helps to explain why Meres in *Palladis Tamia* (1598) described Mundy as "our best plotter" and why he included him among "the best for comedy". But the play's intrinsic merits are likely to be overshadowed always by the relationship of the manuscript to that of *Sir Thomas More*. The latter play is also by Mundy, originally perhaps by him alone, although later others had a hand in it. The manuscript, in Mundy's writing, has revisions and alterations in five other hands (including Chettle's and Dekker's). Among these are three pages which many have argued are in Shakespeare's writing.[1] If this is so, these three pages are our only sample of Shakespeare's hand other than six signatures dated some twenty years later, during his last four years.[2]

If Shakespeare took part in the revision of *Sir Thomas More* we should naturally wish to know exactly when he was thus working with Chettle, Dekker and other playwrights, for that knowledge might ultimately lead to further and unexpected glimpses of his earlier career as a dramatist. Unfortunately there is no internal or external evidence by which we can satisfactorily date the play or its revision. The only clues seem to be the various hands in the manuscript, and especially that of Mundy. Three extended examples of Mundy's writing are known: (1) the manuscript of *John a Kent*; (2) many pages of the manuscript of *Sir Thomas More*; and (3) the first four pages of his translation of an Italian devotional work, *The Heauen of the Mynde*, of which the holograph dedication was signed and dated by Mundy on 22 December 1602.[3] In addition to these, Mundy's signature to his will, drawn up by a scrivener and dated 19 March 1628[–9], adds something to our knowledge of his penmanship; nevertheless, it has not been reproduced hitherto nor, apparently, considered in connexion with this problem.[4]

The experts agree that Mundy's writing in *Sir Thomas More* is to be dated after that in *John a Kent* and before that in *The Heauen of the Mynde*, probably much nearer to the former.[5] The manuscript of *The Heauen of the Mynde* is already dated; we need still to date that of *John a Kent*.

John a Kent contains no internal evidence of when it was composed, but the last page of the manuscript bears a contemporary inscription which, originally read as "...Decembris 1595", is now always transcribed as "...Decembris 1596".[6] Most unfortunately the last leaf is defective, more than three-quarters having been torn off. What is left of the last page contains the second half of each of the last seventeen lines of the play, followed by "[fin]is" and Anthony Mundy's signature. Below the signature, in different ink and in a different hand, is the date referred to above (Plate I). There seems little doubt that this date is *not* in Mundy's hand,[7] but who inserted it and why is unknown. There was room before it for a brief note, and A. W. Pollard suggested that the date may be all that is left of a record of the play's sale by the company for which it was originally written.[8] However, the nature of the inscription is less important than the fact that it establishes a *terminus ad quem* for the writing of the manuscript.

No one has hitherto questioned the reading "1596" and all discussions of *Sir Thomas More* have been based on the assumption that this is the correct transcription, yet it can be shown that this is not so. Elizabethan '6's' are of two kinds. Some were made much like our modern '6's', beginning at the top of the left-hand stroke and coming down and round anti-clockwise in a continuous curve back to the middle or bottom of the down-stroke, and either just short of it or touching it, very rarely crossing it. Many others were made with a movement exactly reversing that just described, beginning at the top of the loop, and curving clockwise round and up to form the tail of the '6'. This is how Mundy formed his '6' in dating his dedication of *The Heauen of the Mynde* (Plate II A). At first sight the last figure in the date at the end of *John a Kent* seems to have been formed in the same way. It is exceptional, however, for the loop of such a '6' to begin so far left that the upstroke has to cross it, as, apparently, here; the loops of such '6's' are sometimes closed, but generally they are open at the top, often so much so that the '6' resembles a modern script *b*. The unusual character of the supposed '6' led me to scrutinize it more carefully in facsimiles of the last page of *John a Kent*. Examined closely, it seemed to have the form of 'o' rather than '6'. It was noticeably lower than the top of the other three figures, as Elizabethan 'o's' usually are, whereas one would expect '6' to have a loop about the size of that of the '9', not distinctly smaller, as here. More important was the fact that under a glass the facsimile issued by Farmer indicated that the loop did not continue up to form the 'tail' of the supposed '6' and that the 'tail' was a separate stroke attached to the beginning of the loop. Enlarged photographs of the date, here reproduced, leave no room for doubt that the last figure cannot have been intended for '6' but must be 'o'. The photographs (Plate I) show that the writer began the final figure at the top left and brought his pen round until it was a little to the right of the start of the loop and just below its top; apparently he then lifted his pen back to the start and added the final flourish which has caused the figure to be misread first as '5' and later as '6'.[9]

We can thus prove that *John a Kent*, although it may have been written earlier, is certainly not later than 1590. This fact immediately assumes peculiar importance. In the last of the Marprelate tracts, *The Protestation*, issued about mid-September 1589, occurs the following passage:

Then among al the rimers and stage plaiers, which my Ll. of the cleargy had suborned against me, I remember Mar-Martin, John a Cant. his hobbie-horse, was to his reproche, newly put out of the morris, take it how he will; with a flat discharge for euer shaking his shins about a maypole againe while he liued.

As long ago as 1909 Dover Wilson, drawing attention to this passage,[10] argued that "Mar-Martin" here must allude to Anthony Mundy and his activities as the Archbishop of Canterbury's pursuivant, and, presumably, anti-Martinist playwright and pamphleteer. Evidence that Mundy was Whitgift's leading hunter of Martinists is plentiful; for example, in the mock "oration of Iohn Canturburie to the pursuivants", in *The Reproof of Martin Junior* (printed about 29 July 1589), the first to be harangued is "Maister Munday".[11] We can therefore understand why Mundy should be described as Whitgift's "hobbie-horse"; but why is the Archbishop here called "John *a* Cant." rather than "John Canterbury", "John Cant.", or "John of Cant." as the

Marprelate tracts elsewhere style him? Wilson made no comment on this, nor any reference to Mundy's authorship of *John a Kent*, which I believe is alluded to here. Although John a Kent was a well-known legendary figure before Mundy wrote a play about his exploits, it seems pointless, for the sake of an idle pun, to identify with this merry magician the grim and humourless Whitgift. But if Mundy's play had been acted before September 1589 the allusion to "John a Cant. his hobbie-horse" gives us a typical and skilful double pun, of the kind so loved by the Elizabethans, involving both "John Cant." (i.e. John Whitgift, Archbishop of Canterbury) and his agent Mundy, author of *John a Kent*: since playwrights were to many Martinists as hateful as pursuivants, the pun is both an amusing identification of Mundy and a shrewd dig also at the Archbishop who employed such a reprobate. If this interpretation of the "John a Cant." allusion is correct we shall have to date Mundy's play as not later than August 1589; but again we should have to note that this allusion would fix only a *terminus ad quem*, and that the play might be months, even a year or more, earlier than the allusion.

Even if the foregoing interpretation of the "John a Cant." allusion be rejected, the discovery that the manuscript of *John a Kent* was written by December 1590 upsets several assumptions about other plays of the period. In the first place, of course, it reopens the whole problem of *Sir Thomas More*. If the experts are right in their view of the sequence of these two manuscripts and the interval between their writing, Mundy must have written *Sir Thomas More* by 1593 at latest, and possibly earlier. If my interpretation of the "John a Cant." allusion be accepted also, *More* would have to be dated not later than 1591 and again possibly earlier. Whichever of these alternatives is accepted, those who believe Shakespeare joined in the revision of *Sir Thomas More* may have to consider more seriously the suggestion that the revision occurred about 1593, when Lord Strange's men, who then included Shakespeare, were temporarily associated with the Admiral's company.[12] In a subsequent article I hope to discuss in greater detail the redating of the *More* manuscript and its implications.

Since any new information about *Sir Thomas More* must be exceptionally exciting to students of Elizabethan drama, other consequences of redating *John a Kent* may seem comparatively insignificant. They have nevertheless an important bearing on our picture of dramatic development in the 1580's, the decade that saw the rise of Marlowe and probably of Shakespeare. For example, the new date of 1589 for *John a Kent* is that usually assigned to Greene's *Friar Bacon and Friar Bungay*, a play obviously closely related to Mundy's. Unfortunately the data available are insufficient to determine their sequence. Clearly, however, about 1589 there was a demand for plays introducing magicians and 'magical' effects, a demand created perhaps by the success of such a play. It seems necessary therefore to reconsider the occasion and date of Marlowe's *Dr Faustus*. Some scholars have assumed that Marlowe would not have followed fashions set by others, and that *Faustus* must therefore have preceded *Friar Bacon*; such reasoning (if that is the right word) would now require them to date *Faustus* before *John a Kent*, i.e. before the middle of 1589, perhaps in 1588. Those who maintain that *Dr Faustus* set this fashion for plays about magicians may like to be reminded that Greene's reference to Marlowe in the preface to *Perimedes* (entered in S.R. 29 March 1588) contains a phrase much more applicable to *Dr Faustus* than to any other Marlowe play:

Such mad and scoffing poets that have poetical spirits, as bred of Merlin's race....[13]

PLATE I

A. Mundy's signature, and date added subsequently by another hand

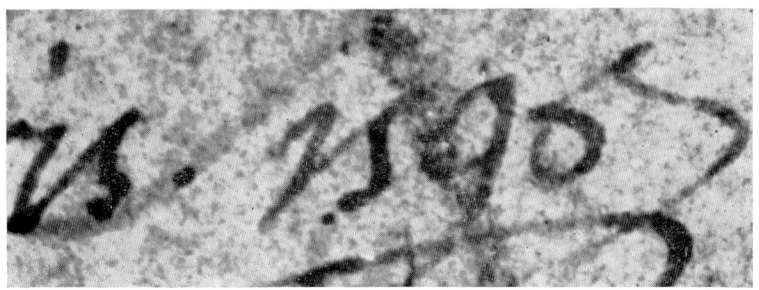

B. Detail

PART OF LAST PAGE (ENLARGED) OF MS. OF
John a Kent and John a Cumber

PLATE II

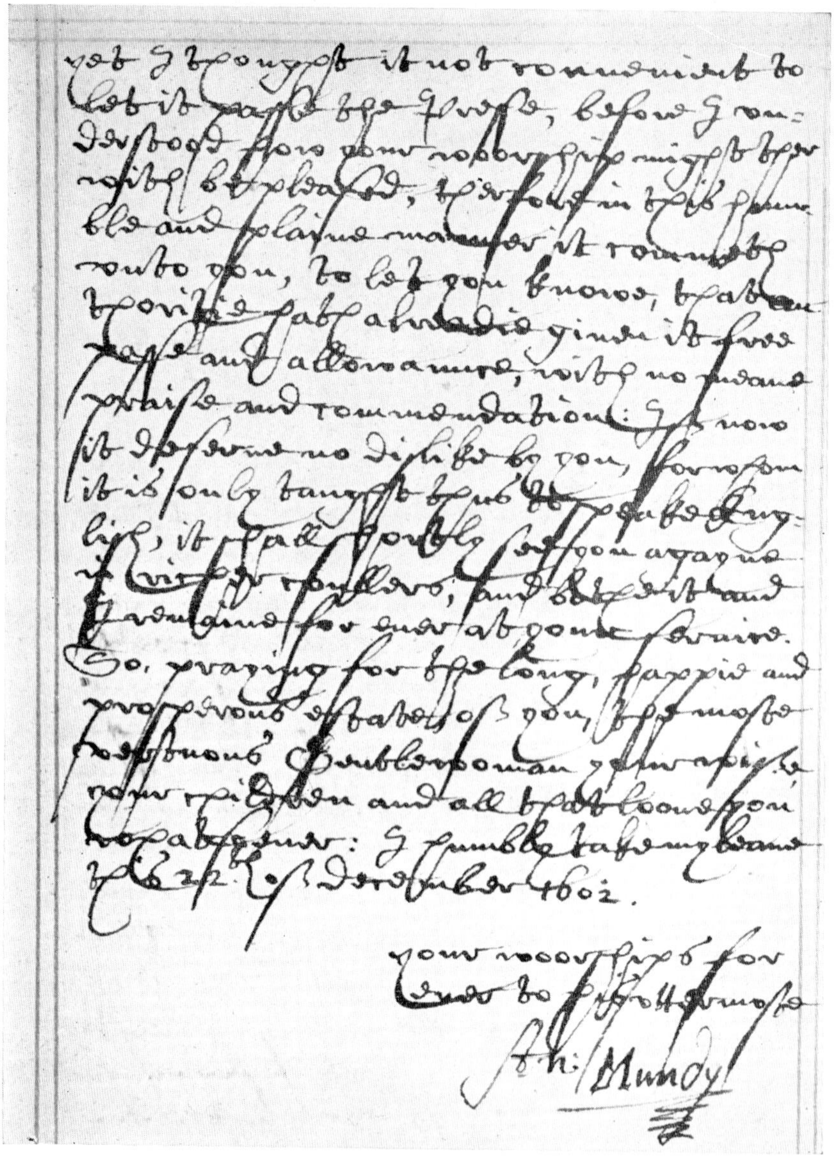

A. Second Page of Mundy's Holograph Dedication of
The Heauen of the Mynde

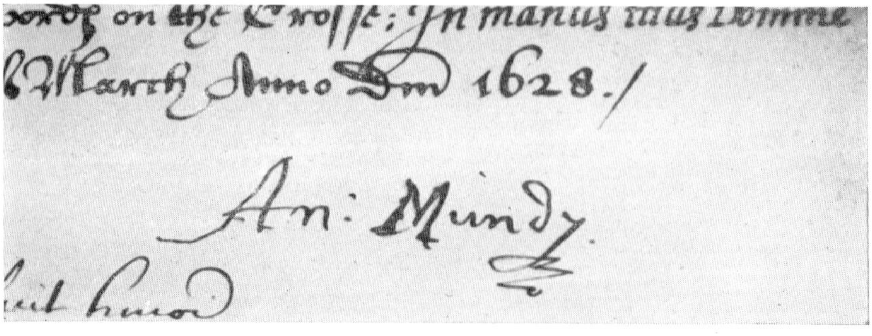

B. Mundy's Signature to his Will, 19 March 1628–9

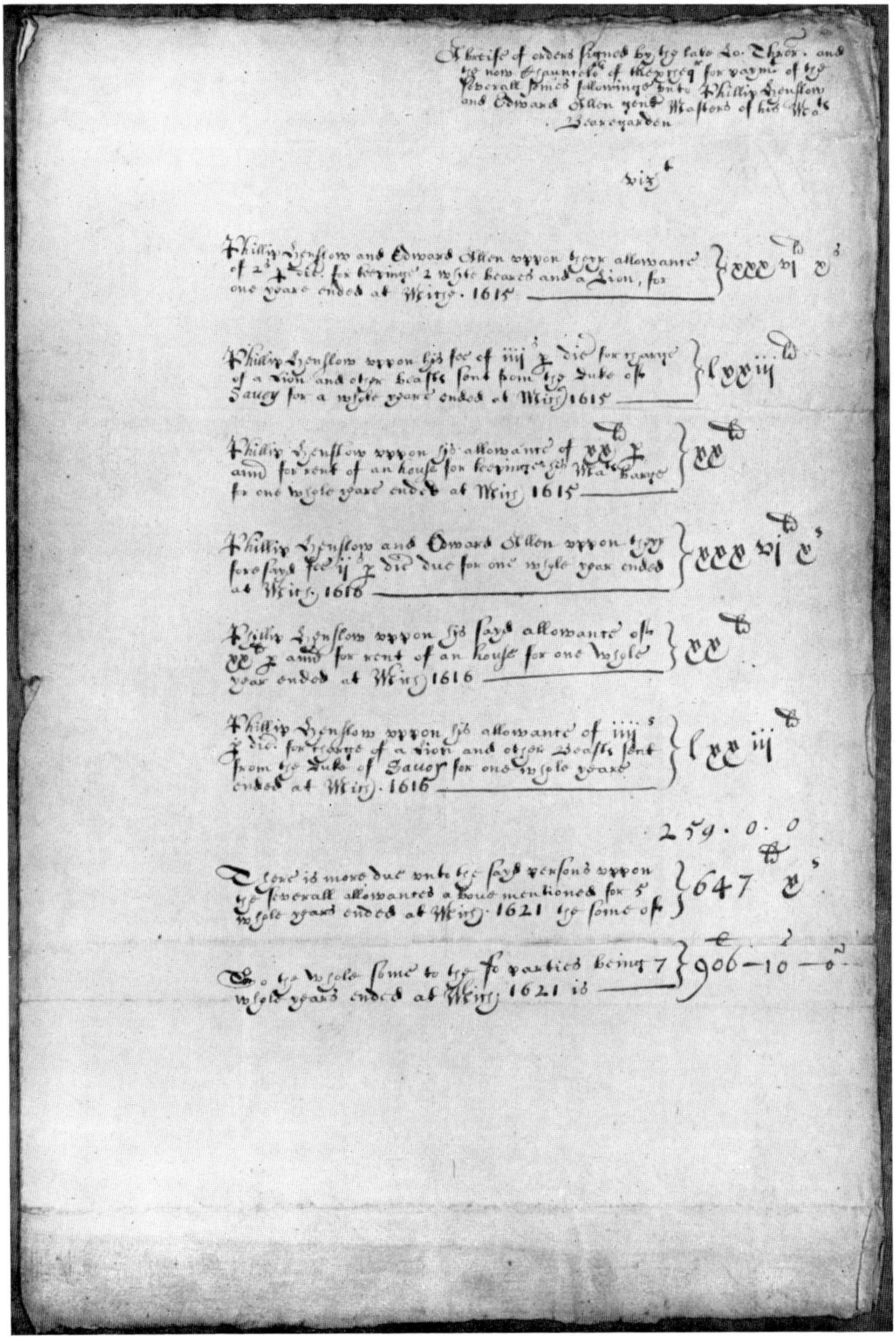

PLATE III

ACCOUNT OF EXPENSES INCURRED BY PHILIP HENSLOWE AND EDWARD
ALLEYN AS MASTERS OF THE BEARGARDEN, 1615–21

PLATE IV

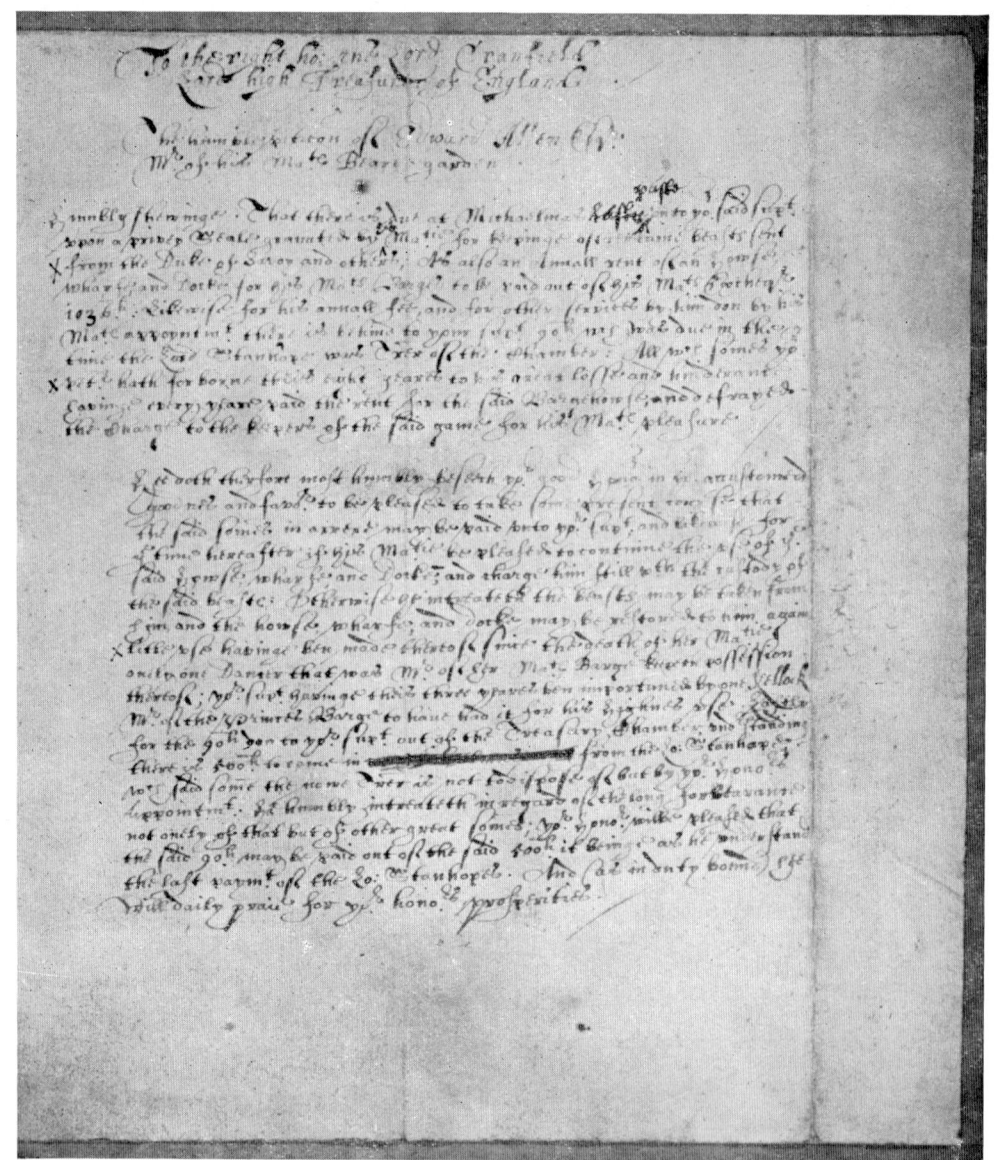

PETITION OF EDWARD ALLEYN AS MASTER OF
HIS MAJESTY'S BEARGARDEN, 1622

The assumption that Marlowe would not have followed Greene's or Mundy's fashion is probably as unsafe as a similar assumption about the parallels between *A Midsummer Night's Dream* and *John a Kent*. Because the antics and malapropisms of Turnop and his companions in *John a Kent* resemble those of Bottom and his fellow-"mechanicals", because the malicious humour of Shrimp seems to reflect that of Puck, and because both plays are primarily concerned with the difficulties and misadventures of two pairs of lovers, it has been argued that *John a Kent* is influenced by, and later than, *A Midsummer Night's Dream*.[14] Unless the date of the latter play is to be pushed back earlier than has hitherto been suggested, we shall have to suppose either that the parallels between the plays are fortuitous, or that Shakespeare may have taken hints from Mundy, as perhaps Greene or Marlowe did.

Finally, we have to note that the redating of *John a Kent* requires us to revise our estimate of both the duration and the contemporary prominence of Mundy's activity as dramatist. Since we have hitherto lacked certainty that his playwriting had begun by 1589, there has been doubt whether the dramatist Post-haste (clearly intended for Mundy) in the anonymous *Histriomastix* could belong to that play's original version, which is usually assigned to 1589. There is now no reason to suspect that Post-haste's part owes anything to later revision, for *John a Kent* is manifestly the work of an experienced writer for the theatre and, whether we date it 1589 or 1590, indicates that Mundy must have commenced dramatist several years earlier at least. When *Histriomastix* was written Mundy was so well-known to playgoers as to be immediately identifiable by the name Post-haste; evidently his dual activities as pursuivant and playwright were widely known.[15] This is indicated again when another character, admiring Post-haste's extemporizing, asks "Is't not pity this fellow's not employd in matters of State?"[16]—a shaft that would have been otherwise pointless. We may be certain that other characteristics of Post-haste, as well as ballad-making, had recognizable relation to Mundy; for example, in the assertion "that I Post-haste the poet extempore can sing"[17] there is confirmation that Mundy was well-known as an extemporizer, a form of Elizabethan theatrical entertainment about which we know too little. If the assertions of the anonymous *True Reporte of the Death...of M. Campion* (1582) are correct, and there is no reason to question them, Mundy "did play extempore" as early as 1579 or 1580 but was "hissed...from his stage"; nevertheless, before March 1582 he had begun "again to ruffle upon the stage".[18] *Histriomastix* proves that as late as 1589 Mundy's extemporizing was still as well-known as his playwriting, and that he continued to pride himself on it. If we consider how short and easy is the step from extemporizing to playwriting, and that from 1579 onwards Mundy was a facile and prolific writer in verse and prose, it seems impossible to doubt that he must have commenced formal playwright early in the 1580's. Thus Mundy was probably writing for the popular theatre, and with success, before any of the "university wits" except perhaps Lyly and Peele. Almost certainly he was a predecessor of Marlowe, Greene, Kyd and, of course, Shakespeare. We have already had occasion to glance at possible reflections of *John a Kent's* success in plays by Marlowe, Greene and Shakespeare. How can we even guess at what they and later dramatists learnt from his lost plays, or from refashioning others as well as *Sir Thomas More*? If *More* was written by 1591, it is even possible that the patriotic and zealously anti-Catholic Mundy was a pioneer of the English history play, for his known plays, and the titles of many now lost, show a marked liking for this genre. Nor was he merely a lucky prospector whose discoveries were put to better use by his successors.

The references in Meres's *Palladis Tamia* prove that Mundy was a busy and popular dramatist down to 1598; that this remained true later we know through the accidents that from 1597 to 1602 Mundy wrote for Henslowe's companies and that Henslowe's *Diary* for that period survives. Most probably Mundy went on writing plays after 1602. As far as we can tell he was the only pre-Shakespearian dramatist who continued to write for the theatre after the rise of Shakespeare in the mid-1590's. Unless he had understood and supplied what playgoers demanded even while Shakespeare's success was reaching its height, that shrewd business man Henslowe would not have continued to employ him. Jonson's gibes at him in *The Case is Altered* and in *Every Man in his Humour* (1601) no more necessarily reflect contemporary general opinion than do his sneers at "York and Lancaster's long jars"; if anything, they prove that Mundy's plays still held the stage while Jonson was trying to introduce comedy of a different and, to Jonson, better kind.

Yet of all the plays Mundy wrote or collaborated in, we know only five; of these *Kent* and *More* remained in manuscript until last century, and Mundy's authorship of the latter was unsuspected until forty years ago. Much of our knowledge of this dramatist would have been lost if the manuscripts of *Kent* and *More* had perished, as might easily have happened; nearly all the rest comes from Henslowe's *Diary*. Although it is now evident that Mundy was much more active as dramatist, and much earlier, than we had supposed, we cannot tell whether his surviving plays were among his best or his worst, or are even representative, and we can only wonder if any of the surviving anonymous Elizabethan plays come, wholly or partly, from his pen. It may be salutary to insist on this, for we may be in similar or worse ignorance of other of Shakespeare's immediate predecessors and contemporaries in the theatre.

Even more chastening is it to reflect that our assumptions about the development of Elizabethan drama in the 1580's are so precarious that they can be seriously upset by correction of the date of a single play. In the long run our new estimate of the period of Mundy's playwriting may seem more important than the redating of *Sir Thomas More*.

NOTES

1. See A. W. Pollard, W. W. Greg and others, *Shakespeare's Hand in 'The Play of Sir Thomas More'*, 1923, esp. 41 *seq.*; and R. C. Bald's survey of '*Sir Thomas More* and its Problems' in *Shakespeare Survey*, 2 (1949), 44 *seq.*

2. Without more extended authentic examples of Shakespeare's handwriting, it seems impossible to hope to establish on palaeographical evidence that he wrote the three pages in 'hand D' in *Sir Thomas More*. The other arguments assembled in *Shakespeare's Hand*... show that in style and content the three pages are not demonstrably un-Shakespearian, but offer nothing more positive. My own opinion is that the case is not proven.

3. The manuscript of *John a Kent* is now in the Huntington Library, California. A facsimile of the whole was published by J. S. Farmer in 1912, in his *Tudor Facsimile Texts*. The last leaf is also facsimiled in Sir E. M. Thompson's article on 'The Autograph Manuscripts of Anthony Mundy', *Transactions of the Bibliographical Society*, XIV, 325-53, and (less satisfactorily) in the Malone Society reprint of *John a Kent* (1923).

The manuscript of *Sir Thomas More* was included by Farmer in his *Tudor Facsimile Texts* (1910). Facsimiles of the various hands, including Mundy's (fo. 22a), are given in W. W. Greg's edition in the Malone Society reprints (1911). Part of a page in Mundy's handwriting is facsimiled in E. M. Thompson's article, *ut supra*.

The Heauen of the Mynde is in the British Museum (MS. Add. 33, 384). Of the four pages in Mundy's handwriting one (the least characteristic) is facsimiled in E. M. Thompson's article. I do not understand why Greg (*Shakespeare's Hand*..., p. 50) thought these pages "afford rather poor evidence of the general character of Munday's hand" in 1602. They seem on the contrary a more useful and varied sample of Mundy's writing than either of his other surviving manuscripts. Greg's *English Literary Autographs*, Part I, Plate XI, gives facsimiles of parts of two of these pages, as well as samples of Mundy's hand in *Kent* and *More*.

4. Mundy's will was proved in the Commissary Court of London on 14 August 1633. It consists of one folio double sheet; only the signature is by Mundy.

5. Cf. E. M. Thompson's article (cited in n. 3), pp. 334, 352; and Greg in *Shakespeare's Hand...*, pp. 49–51.

6. J. P. Collier and J. S. Farmer both thought the last figure was a '5'; E. M. Thompson and Greg, and following them all later scholars, make it a '6'.

7. E. M. Thompson, *op. cit.* pp. 326, 333, 348, was emphatic that the date is not in Mundy's handwriting; his analysis of the differences between Mundy's "pseudo-Italian" letter-forms and those in "Decembris" seems to me conclusive. Greg seems once to have favoured the possibility that the date is in Mundy's hand (cf. *Shakespeare's Hand...*, pp. 49 and 50 n.), but in *English Literary Autographs* (*loc. cit.* in n. 3) he says "the date is added in quite another hand".

8. E. M. Thompson, *op. cit.* p. 335; cf. also Pollard and Greg in *Shakespeare's Hand...*, pp. 10, 29, 52 n.

9. Godfrey Davies, of the Huntington Library, California, to whom we are indebted for these enlarged photographs, kindly examined the figure in the manuscript and reports as follows:

"Mr H. C. Schulz, Curator of Manuscripts, and I examined the original signature of Anthony Mundy and the date. It looked to us clear that the author wrote an 'o' starting from the left. As the photograph shows, there is a slight gap between the top left side of the 'o' and the terminal loop when it comes round to the left again. After that the writer seems to have made a flourish which happens to resemble the modern 5 but is not at all like the 5 in the date 1590. The ink of the text and signature is of a pronounced brown colour while the date is in a different ink of a grayish brown colour.

"Unfortunately, the ultra-violet rays reveal nothing additional. In fact, I think one can see better with the enlarged photograph than with the rays. As regards the signature I am afraid nothing more can be done than our photographer accomplished. Before the manuscript came to the Library an apparent attempt was made to remove a stain on the signature which lightened the ink and destroyed a little of it."

10. *Modern Language Review*, IV (1909), 488–90. I reprint Wilson's text, as that in William Pierce's edition of *The Marprelate Tracts* (1911), p. 412, has modernized spelling and expanded contractions.

11. Wilson, *loc. cit.*; Pierce's *Marprelate Tracts*, pp. 352–4. Further evidence of Mundy's activity as pursuivant before this time and later is collected in Celeste Turner's *Anthony Mundy* (Berkeley, 1928), pp. 77, 89, 93.

12. Cf. Pollard and Greg, *Shakespeare's Hand...*, pp. 27–8, 56.

13. My attention was drawn to this by Professor Allardyce Nicoll.

14. Cf. J. W. Ashton in *PMLA*, XLIX (1934), 755–60.

15. This incidentally supports my interpretation of Martin Marprelate's allusion to "John a Cant. his hobbie-horse". Since that allusion was made in September 1589, it adds to the grounds for dating *Histriomastix* in the same year.

16. II, 130 (as in Richard Simpson's *School of Shakespeare* (1878), vol. II).

17. II, 297; cf. also II, 121, 126.

18. The relevant passage is quoted by Turner, *op. cit.* p. 59.

H

OF STAKE AND STAGE

BY

JOHN BRILEY

> When I'se come there, I was in a rage,
> I rayl'd on him that kept the Beares,
> Instead of a Stake was suffered a Stage
> And in Hunkes his house a crue of Players.   *A North Country Song* [1]

So goes the lament of a North Country balladeer describing his disappointment when, on visiting the Bear Garden (the popular cognomen for both Paris Garden and its successor the Hope Theatre), he was cheated of his expected entertainment and shown a play instead. All through the reigns of Elizabeth and James bear-baiting competed vigorously with the drama for the purse and applause of both prince and people, and a pre-eminent symbol of that competition may be found in the building, set on the Bankside near the Globe, formally titled the Hope Theatre, but

commonly called the Beare Garden, a Play House for Stage Playes on Mundayes, Wedensdayes, Fridayes, and Saterdayes, and for the baiting of the Beares on Tuesdayes and Thursdayes, the stage being made to take vp and downe when they please. [2]

So closely were the two entertainments linked that an investigation into the financing of the theatre in Shakespeare's time inevitably becomes involved with an inquiry into the finances of bear-baiting. Peculiarly significant is the fact that the man responsible for the tormenting of the ballad-writer's bear Hunkes was none other than the great Edward Alleyn, who won early fame as Kyd's Hieronimo and Marlowe's Tamburlaine and who later made a considerable fortune in property dealings on the Bankside where he financed the building of both the Fortune Theatre and the 'Bear Garden'-Hope.

Unfortunately precise information concerning the economics of bear-baiting is slim in the extreme. Indeed, Sir Walter Greg has been forced to state that our knowledge "is meagre beyond Alleyn's statement that he derived an income of £60 a year from the business". [3] Thus any new documentary evidence on the subject has a real value.

The two papers presented herewith [4] do not, it is true, shed any light on the takings at public baitings at the Bear Garden itself. The 'sport', however, was a royal entertainment as well as a popular spectacle, and Alleyn himself frequently baited before the King. [5] He and his father-in-law, Philip Henslowe, were able to secure the court appointment of Masters of the Royal Game of Bears, Bulls, and Mastiff Dogs, which gave them charge of the royal animals and sole right to give public performances of baiting. It is significant that in both documents Alleyn is referred to as Master of "his Majesty's Bear Garden". This makes it clear that the bear-baiting enterprise at the Hope was dependent on royal grant and implies that, at least in theory, it was intended to be partially subsidized by payments for maintenance of the royal beasts. The documents in question refer only to the sums due from the King's treasury—and they show that, while Alleyn's office may have been ultimately lucrative, he made no easy gains from that side of his activities.

The first paper is a summary of orders signed for payment to Alleyn and Henslowe of £906. 10s. and covers a period from 1615 to 1621, Henslowe's share of the office evidently falling to Alleyn on Henslowe's death in 1616. The account includes expenses for the "rent" of the King's barge house and for the keeping of two white bears, a lion,[6] and "other beaste sent from the Duke of Sauoy". This list of expenses that had already been approved for payment probably accompanied the other document, which is a formal petition[7] addressed by Alleyn to the Lord High Treasurer —a somewhat impatient reminder that the money due by the first paper, in addition to other expenses for the use of a "wharfe and docke" by the royal barge, was long since overdue. Whether Alleyn ever was reimbursed is uncertain, but the conclusion of his petition suggests he was not very hopeful and would probably have been glad to settle for much less than the full sum.[8]

NOTES

1. *Wit and Drollery* (1656). Hunks was a well-known bear. The young Inns-of-Court student satirized by Sir John Davies is made to forsake his lawbooks "for filthy sports...to see old Harry Hunks and Sacerson" (*Epigrammes and Elegies* (1590) sig. D2 verso).

2. Quoted from a manuscript continuation of Stow's *Annales* (1631) by Sir Edmund Chambers, *Elizabethan Stage* (1923), II, 374–5.

3. Henslowe's *Diary* (1904), II, 38.

4. Sackville-Knole MSS. I, old numbers 5200 and 6994.

5. See Stow's *Annales* (1631), pp. 835–6, for an account of one such occasion. Alleyn's diary, transcribed in William Young's *History of Dulwich College* (1889), refers to others; e.g. the entry for 11 June 1622: "I baighted before y[e] king & my men washt my shep & pd 2[d] a skore ...o. 1. o."

6. The original warrant for paying Henslowe and Alleyn for keeping the two white bears and a lion is dated 20 March 1610/11 (*Calendar of State Papers, Domestic, 1611–18*, p. 17). There the allowance is given as 12s. a day, but this would seem to be an error.

7. The difference in the total figures—£906. 10s. in the order for payment and £1036 in Alleyn's petition—is, of course, largely accounted for by the addition of a further year's expenses to the earlier sum.

8. In the petition a certain Kellock is referred to: a "Kellocke" "of Rederesse", is recorded in Henslowe's *Diary* (II, 291) and among the papers at Dulwich is a statement (7 August 1607) prepared by Thomas Kellocke of "wronge and iniuries" done to him and his wife (George F. Warner, *Catalogue of Manuscripts and Muniments at Dulwich College* (1881) MS. IV, 63, p. 132).

ALLEYN'S PETITION TO LORD CRANFIELD

[This petition is written on one side of a large piece of paper which has been divided by a fold down the middle like the centre sheet of a folio book. The half-sheet to the left of the fold is again divided into two columns. Of these the column on the left has not been reproduced since it simply bears a modern summary of the petition. The other column, which appears as the left third of this reproduction, is written in secretary hand. It reads: "...A. Octobr: *1622* / Mr Allen M[r] of the / Beare Garden. / To sende for Dancer who was / M[r] of Q. Annes Barge. / [Master of the / Bearegarden] /–/ [1622] / [...]".]

> To the right ho: the Lord Cranfield
> Lord high Treasurer of England./
> The humble peticoñ of Edward Allen Esqr:
> M[r] of his Ma[te] Bearegarden: /

Humbly shewinge· That there is due at Michaelmas laste ⌜paste⌝ vnto yor said sup[t] vpon a privey Seale graunted by ⌜his⌝ Matie for keepinge of certaine beaste sent from the Duke of Savoy and others; As also an Anuall rent of an Howse, wharfe, and Docke for his Ma[te] Barges to be paid out of his Ma[te] Excheq[r] io36ˡⁱ: Likewise for his anuall fee, and for other services by him don by his Maᵗᵉ appoyntmᵗ there is behind to your supᵗ 90ˡⁱ wᶜʰ was due in the time the Lord Stanhope was Trēr of the Chamber: All wᶜʰ soɱes yoʳ petʳ hath forborne theis eight yeares to his great losse and hinderance havinge every yeare paid the rent for the said Bargehowse, and defrayed the Charge to the keepers of the said game for his Maᵗᵉ pleasure:/.

Hee doth therfore most humbly beseech yoʳ good Honoʳ in yoʳ accustomed goodnes and favoʳ to be pleased to take some present course that the said soɱes in arrere may be paid vnto yoʳ supᵗ, and likewise for yᵉ time hereafter if his Maᵗⁱᵉ be pleased to continue the vse of yᵉ said Howse, wharfe, and Docke, and charge him still wᵗʰ the custody of the said beaste: Otherwise he intreateth the beaste may be taken from him and the howse, wharfe, and docke may be restored to him again litle vse havinge ben made thereof since the death of her Maᵗⁱᵉ onely one Dancer that was Mʳ of her Maᵗᵉ Barge keepeth possession thereof; yoʳ supᵗ havinge theis three yeares ben importuned by one Kellock Mʳ of the Princes Barge to haue had it for his Highnes vse. Lastly for the 90ˡⁱ dow to yoʳ supᵗ out of the Treasury, Chamber, vndʳstanding there is 500ˡⁱ to come in ⌐...Michaelmas...⌐ from the Lo: Stanhope—wᶜʰ said soɱe the nowe Trēr is not to dispose of but by yoʳ Honoʳˢ appointmᵗ: He humbly intreateth in regard of the long forbearance not onely of that but of other great soɱes; yoʳ Honoʳ wilbe pleased that the said 90ˡⁱ may be paid out of the said 500ˡⁱ it beinge as he vnderstand the last paymᵗ of the Lo: Stanhopes. And (as in duty bound) hee Will daily praie for yoʳ honoʳˢ prosperities./

AN ACCOUNT OF EXPENSES AT THE BEAR-GARDEN, 1615–1621

[This account is written on one sheet of paper. On the back of the sheet there appears a note: "Expence of / the / Bear Garden / 1615-1621 / – / James 1st."]

A breife of orders signed by the late Lo˙ Thrēr˙ and the now Chaunceloʳ of thexcheqʳ for paymᵗ of the severall soɱes followinge vnto Phillip Henslow and Edward Allen gent Masters of his Maᵗᵉ Bearegarden

Vizᵗ

Phillip Henslow and Edward Allen vppon theyr allowance of 2ˢ ₱ diē for keepinge 2 white beares and a Lion, for one yeare ended at Miche˙ 1615	xxxvjˡⁱ xˢ
Phillip Henslow vppon his fee of iiijˢ ₱ diē for charge of a Lion and other beastₑ sent from the Duke of Sauoy for a whole yeare ended at Mich 1615	lxxiijˡⁱ
Phillip Henslow vppon his allowance of xxˡⁱ ₱ anñ for rent of an house for keepinge his Maᵗᵉ barge for one whole yeare ended at Mich 1615	xxˡⁱ
Phillip Henslow and Edward Allen vppon theyr foresayd fee ijˢ ₱ diē due for one whole year ended at Mich˙ 1616	xxxvjˡⁱ xˢ
Phillip Henslow vppon his sayd allowance of xxˡⁱ ₱ anñ for rent of an house for one Whole year ended at Mich 1616	xxˡⁱ
Phillip Henslow vppon his allowance of iiijˢ ₱ diē for charge of a Lion and other Beastₑ sent from the Duke of Sauoy for one whole yeare ended at Mich. 1616	lxxiijˡⁱ
	˙259˙ 0˙ 0
There is more due vnto the sayd persons vppon the severall allowances aboue mentioned for 5 whole years ended at Mich˙ 1621 the some of	647ˡⁱ xˢ
	l s
So the Whole some to the sd parties being 7 whole years ended at Mich˙ 1621 is	906–10–0ᵈ

THE CELESTIAL PLANE IN SHAKESPEARE

BY

ROY WALKER

The heavens have always played a dramatic role in the works of poets and playwrights, both Christian and pagan, and, notwithstanding the impersonal cosmology of modern science, they still do so. Thunder and lightning, as interpreted by Oedipus[1] and the chorus, is as portentous as it is in *King Lear*. In the *Paradiso*[2] souls shine among the stars as in Juliet's vision of Romeo transfigured after death. It has been well said that the fundamental divergence between Chaucer's[3] world and our own is the shift of attitude towards the starry heavens. Yet a T. S. Eliot[4] hero prays for a hearth under the protection of the stars, a Christopher Fry[5] heroine believes in man's ordeal by star, and Claudel's[6] curtain falls on lovers making star-signs with their hands in token that their souls will be henceforward intertwined like a two-fold star. Even in the masterless night of modern science, Maxwell Anderson[7] hears a heart cry towards something dim in distance.

If, as J. Q. Adams[8] supposes, Shakespeare as a boy saw the Mystery Plays at Coventry, he may have seen the star in the east that blazoned forth the birth of Jesus. He was probably taught that the sun stood still and the moon stayed for Joshua and that the stars in their courses fought against Sisera. When he came to man's estate and to the London playhouses he found even the supposedly atheistical Marlowe[9] drawing on the Prophetical Books to give a sort of cosmic grandeur to Tamburlaine, much as in later ages Napoleon believed in his star and Hitler trusted astrologers. John Lyly[10] might write a comedy in which the seven planets are personified and mortal temperament is transformed as each is ascendant in turn. At the time when Shakespeare was writing his last plays in retirement at Stratford, Thomas Heywood[11] made a dramatic climax of Jupiter's destruction of Hercules with a thunderbolt, after which

his body sinkes, and from the heauens discends a hand in a cloud, that from the place where Hercules was burnt, brings vp a starre, and fixeth it in the firmament

to signify, as the closing lines of the play put it, that his soul is made a star and has mounted heaven.

The Elizabethan public playhouses had as a permanent feature a roof over part of the stage, called the heavens and probably[12] decorated as such. The heavens were likewise part of the drama, as natural a part as the skies to which these theatres were open in all weathers. The names of the planets were also names of classical gods and goddesses. The name of the heavens did not dissociate the habitation of God and his angels from the region of the stars. The celestial globes[13] of the time give us vivid hints of what the stars might signify to the popular imagination.

What its author claimed to be the first work on Shakespeare's astronomical references was written by a pious resident of Stratford, Thomas Lowe,[14] and published in 1887. Lowe characterizes Calphurnia's apprehension that the heavens themselves blaze forth the death of princes as splendid poetry but unsound philosophy, and, firmly bowdlerizing Edmund, he invites us to note with what force Shakespeare explodes the doctrine of fatalism and the delusions of astrology. In this, however, Lowe was unconsciously echoing the opinion of a more illustrious star-gazer.

H*

Coleridge[15] too had admitted that astrological predictions sometimes possessed Shakespeare's mind, but "it was a transient folly merely of the time, and therefore it did not belong to Shakespeare". Much virtue in "therefore".

Forty years after Lowe's book, Cumberland Clark[16] also claimed to be the first to treat comprehensively of Shakespeare's astronomical references. Clark likewise concluded that although Shakespeare used astrology for poetic and dramatic purposes he did not believe in it. In another book he divided the poet and working dramatist who wrote of such superstitions from the progressive, practical philosopher and thinker that Shakespeare "really" was. A third book by Clark recognizes uneasily that "it is the bad characters like Edmund and Iago...who pronounce the more reasonable, sane and scientific opinions" and that "Shakespeare seems to justify superstition by following dreams and unusual meteorological phenomena with tragedy and disaster", but clings to the schizophrenic explanation, bolstered with the vague assurance that Shakespeare always had some higher dramatic purpose in mind.

It was not until 1941 that a special study of this subject appeared which drew the obvious conclusions from the poetic evidence. "Since the Renaissance believed in astrology", wrote D. C. Allen,[17] "we should not be shocked, as some have been, to discover that Shakespeare...inclined to the side of 'the superstitious'." Although "the philosophy of the literary men of the English Renaissance was in many ways that of the moderate astrologers", Shakespeare himself "was more given to speaking about the stars and their services and disservices to men than most of his literary fellows".

Nineteenth-century idealization of Shakespeare had, however, lingered on to prejudice selection and distort judgement in ways less obvious than the rather naive contradictions of Clark. Dover Wilson's *Life in Shakespeare's England*[18] treats astrology at the tail end of the section on superstition. The three items under this head are a two-line quotation about the Ides of March, the short passage from *King Lear* in which Edgar shows amused surprise at finding his half-brother playing the "sectary astronomical", and two pages of a mock prognostication by Nashe. Elsewhere[19] Dover Wilson gives pride of place to cosmology in his account of the Elizabethan scene and observes that Shakespeare's "very language is full of astronomical notions now long forgotten". Five years after Dover Wilson's anthology, *Shakespeare's England*[20] raised astrology from the superstitions to the sciences, of which the first section, by E. B. Knobel, was devoted to *Astronomy and Astrology*. Since it was still segregated from religious beliefs and imaginative dramatic use of common assumptions, the promotion was more apparent than real. "The fault, dear Brutus, is not in our stars..." is alleged to show that Shakespeare, like Stubbes, "tilted with equal frankness against the astrological principle of starry domination" and the argument is clinched with Edmund's "excellent foppery o' the world". The general resemblance to Dover Wilson's choice of quotations is completed by something that parallels his passage from Nashe, the reproduction of the loquacious title-page of Melton's *Astrologaster, or The Figure-Caster. Rather the Arraignment of Artlesse Astrologers*, etc. Knobel deals with a number of references in the plays that can be made more or less astronomically respectable, without discussing their significance in the poetic context. But he remarks that

the technical language of astrology was familiar to the Elizabethan playgoer, and the forgotten knowledge must needs be studied afresh before the meaning of many passages in Elizabethan drama grows intelligible.

The general attitude of these background studies, it may be considered, is to make the most of anything in Shakespeare that can be reconciled with modern science and to show little interest in the poetic use that is made in the plays of contemporary beliefs about the heavens.

Insight into the Elizabethan outlook reached a new depth with the publication of Hardin Craig's *The Enchanted Glass* [21] of which the preface is dated 1935. Craig criticizes such factual compilations grouped by community of subject as had been produced by Clark and others and emphasizes the need for synthesis. He commences with a reconstruction of Elizabethan cosmology, the poetic image of a universe that spoke to man in a thousand ways that seem strange to our own impersonally scientific conception of the universe. Divine will was believed to produce marvellous motions in the heavens, corresponding to strange perturbations on earth. As the virtues of the terrene orb and its inhabitants proceeded from the celestial, there was not only correspondence but also influence and causation spreading downwards through the great hierarchy of being. Havoc in nature's order wrought by the stars was within the scheme of God's providence because, as E. M. W. Tillyard [22] explains, God, prompted by the Fall, set the celestial bodies against each other in their influence on the sublunary universe, though their opposition was so tempered as to preserve a sort of balance of power. Astrology was consequently tolerated if not sanctioned by the Church, and Craig characterizes Shakespeare's treatment of it as respectful and considerate.

But astrology was itself hybrid and therein Moriz Sondheim [23] recognized the difficulty of defining Shakespeare's attitude towards it. It was a union of religion and so-called science. Sondheim argues that Shakespeare rejected horoscopy and mathematical calculation of the fatal hour whose coming was signalled in the skies, and inasmuch as that would reduce dramatic characters to automata this is what we might expect. He asserts that Shakespeare believed in the general influence of the heavenly bodies upon life on earth, but not in any influence of the stars on the destiny of individuals, of nations, or of their rulers. That statement, however, is immediately qualified by the admission that Shakespeare believed in a providence in which the power of Fortuna becomes an astral fate. This would seem to be a distinction between powers and portents, between astral causes and correspondences, but if so the rejection of the former is surely too absolute. But scholarship does seem to have reached a point where we might hope to evolve a comprehensive concept that should be more serviceable in interpreting Shakespeare's poetic drama than the limited ones that have so far been given extensive critical application.

Wilson Knight's *The Shakespearian Tempest* [24] first appeared in 1932. It is hard to grasp the limits of his nuclear conception of 'tempest' which, as opposed to 'music', is presented as the central value of Shakespeare's works. 'Tempest', we learn, is related to all weather thoughts, it is a thread in a wider pattern of disorder thoughts that includes comets and meteors, it cannot be finally abstracted from the totality of Shakespearian imagery, which includes that of sun, moon, stars, light and dark, nor from the passions and plots of human and social upheavals. 'Music' can, of course, also be a cosmic image, as in allusions to the music of the spheres. Knight's conception clearly comprehends both influences and correspondences, but it is a vertical division of warring opposites at all levels, no doubt suggested by the nature of drama as conflict and resolution. A horizontal division into corresponding and interacting planes might reduce a chaos of related images to a recognizably Elizabethan order. This impression is rather strengthened by the chart incorporated in the recent reissue of *The Shakespearian Tempest* where 'London Crowd' is exalted to the company of gods and angels and 'New Order' is down among the dead men.

Weather images are more numerous than those of all the celestial bodies together in Caroline Spurgeon's[25] tabulation, but she treats them as of lesser poetic importance. She says that the conception of the stars moving in their spheres, and straying from them only as a sign or result of great disturbance or disaster, seems to be the most constant of astronomical images in Shakespeare's mind. But her major observation on astral references in a single play is that "the idea... of being born under good or evil stars, and so being subject to their influence, and to that extent the plaything of fortune," runs through a great part of *All's Well That Ends Well*. Miss Spurgeon counted less than forty star images altogether, and twice as many of the sun. Although she found less than ten moon images in the plays, she notes that the word 'moon' occurs twenty-eight times in *A Midsummer Night's Dream*, and "the influence and presence of the moon are felt throughout, largely through the imagery, from the opening lines...to the end". Thus two of her three main examples of astronomical images dominating the whole or a great part of a Shakespeare play are found among the comedies, where man's engagement with social order is less serious than in the histories and his encounter with the universe less crucial than in the tragedies. Miss Spurgeon's only substantial astronomical example from the histories is from the first two scenes of *1 Henry VI*, though the fact that "the conception of the king as sun is fairly constant with Shakespeare" is well illustrated. The universal imagery of *Antony and Cleopatra* is noticed, but the only tragedy treated as comparable in astronomical imagery to the two comedies mentioned is *Romeo and Juliet*.

Miss Spurgeon treated imagery largely as atmosphere and background. W. H. Clemen,[26] the original edition of whose book was contemporary with hers, took a more dramatic view of the cosmic element in the tragedies. In the following passage citations of the four major tragedies are omitted:

Almost all the heroes of Shakespeare's tragedies stand in close relationship to the cosmos, the celestial bodies and the elements. This is a characteristic feature of the tragedies, lacking in the histories. Not only do the cosmic forces accompany the action of the tragedies; the characters feel themselves to be closely related to them and to the elements. When in the histories, the people turned their eyes to the sun, taking its dull gleam for a foreboding of evil, this was in the tradition of omen. But in the tragedies, the characters apostrophize the sun and stars directly.... Sorrow reaching even up to heaven and forcing entrance there is a motif frequently expressed in the imagery.... Moreover, in the dramatic structure of the individual tragedies the appeal to the elements makes its appearance at definite turning-points. Not until they begin to despair of men and earth do the tragic heroes turn to the heavens. When their firmest beliefs have been shaken, when they stand alone and forsaken, they renounce the earth and call upon the cosmic powers.

But will they come when you do call to them? Clemen does not answer any more directly than Glendower. He does not commit himself beyond correspondences to influences and still less to causation, and the reservation comes out in his comment on *Romeo and Juliet*. He accepts Miss Spurgeon's characterization of the atmosphere of that tragedy, with its light-images of sun, moon and stars, as "spreading over the whole play an intensive atmosphere of free nature". As

Theodore Spencer[27] says Romeo's tragedy is caused by the stars above him, and this aspect of 'The Imagery of *Romeo and Juliet*' has been further developed by E. C. Pettet.[28]

To illustrate the pervasiveness of the celestial plane in Shakespeare's works, the intimate ties that connect it with the terrestrial action through the correspondences, and something of the range of variations on a single poetic theme, it is proposed to consider here the following limited basic pattern:

> Stars (light).
> Candles and torches (light and/or heat).
> Eyes (light and/or heat).   Passions (heat and/or light).

In this pattern light and heat are, of course, metaphorical as well as literal. The 'light' of the stars is also a manifestation of divine radiance, and that of the pure human eye reflects the kindred 'inner light'. There is less decoration than divinity in the identification of the eyes of a Shakespearian heroine with the stars. If both hero and villain, Romeo and Edmund, find it fatal to defy the stars it is because to do so is to sin against the 'light'. Consequently it is less profoundly true to say that Shakespeare portrays enforced obedience to planetary influence than that through the correspondences he reveals as participants in the drama spiritual forces that are often first manifest in the heavens, though cruder astrological propositions are undoubtedly also present on occasion. This metaphysical position at any rate makes Shakespeare as remote from the figure-casters as from philosophers who seek to sum up deity in mathematical formulae.

The simple scheme outlined above, which glances from heaven to earth and from earth to heaven, will now be summarily illustrated from *The Rape of Lucrece*, the early tragedy of *Romeo and Juliet*, the four major tragedies of *Hamlet*, *Othello*, *Lear* and *Macbeth*, and *The Tempest*. All the terms of the series occur in significant and usually explicit relationship in these works, and many of them also occur together elsewhere in Shakespeare, including the comedies and histories.[29] These summaries do not, of course, purport to give a complete account of the celestial plane in the poem or play concerned, but are deliberately confined to the essential pattern we are attempting to trace, and to bringing out the Shakespearian variations on that theme. To do this it is necessary to separate phrases from their context and bring them together for comparison, a process that does considerable outrage to the poetry. But when these fish out of water are restored to their native element they will swim as well as ever and we may find it easier to recognize the families among the larger shoals with which they mingle.

In *The Rape of Lucrece*, each item of our series is linked to others in poetic phrases apt to the immediate context. Thus the eye of heaven is out on the dark night of the outrage, when no comfortable star did lend his light. The smoking waxen torch in Tarquin's hand must therefore be lode-star to his lustful eye. Though temporarily blinded with a greater light by her awakening gaze, that burning eye fixes upon Lucrece. The opening stanza of the poem had pictured Tarquin's lust as lightless fire and the second made Lucrece's eyes mortal stars, as bright as heaven's beauties, with pure aspect. After the rape the action is referred back to the skies:

> Were Tarquin Night, as he is but Night's child,
> The silver-shining queen he would distain;
> Her twinkling hand-maids too, by him defiled,
> Through Night's black bosom should not peep again.

Night will not muster mists to meet the sun and hide her shame from the piercing light of day, so Lucrece resolves to commit her soul and body to the skies and ground.

Like Lucrece, Juliet has changed eyes with two of the fairest stars in heaven, and so she teaches the torches to burn bright. Romeo is the torch-bearer and candle-holder whose flame she purifies, so that after his death he would be worthy to adorn the face of heaven with little stars, the opposite of the image applied to Tarquin in the verse just quoted. These earth-treading stars make dark heaven bright, but all too soon night's candles are burnt out and the torch is sunk in the Capulet tomb where the star-crossed lovers lie self-slaughtered. On that dismal morning the sun for sorrow will not show his head.

The ghost of Hamlet's father appears when a star has reached a certain point, or breaks in upon an account of the celestial convulsions that presage fierce events in Elsinore as formerly in Rome. Hamlet has just spoken of the fault that may be fortune's star when the Ghost interrupts him, and it could a tale unfold that would make his two eyes, like stars, start from their spheres. When the Ghost has gone the Prince calls in agony upon all the host of heaven. Later, when he doubts the revelation, this "majestical roof fretted with golden fire" appears to him no other thing than "a foul and pestilential congregation of vapours". The player's declamation of the murder of King Priam stirs him to fright Claudius with false fire. The frantic cries for lights at the end of the play scene must bring on flaming torches, emblems of royal lust brought to light. Hamlet tells his mother that at her sin "heaven's face doth glow" and a word-picture of the smoky waxen torch of lust precedes the last entrance of the Ghost:

> Rebellious hell,
> If thou canst mutine in a matron's bones,
> To flaming youth let virtue be as wax,
> And melt in her own fire.

As the star moves not but in his sphere, nor could Claudius without Gertrude, or so he says to Laertes. Laertes conjures the wandering stars and makes them stand to hear his sorrow for his sister, and Hamlet, innocent of Laertes' treachery, likens his skill with the shining foil to a star in the darkest night stuck fiery off. This time the heavens do not re-echo the thunder of the King's cannon and the earthly stars fall with dews of blood.[30]

Desdemona was the sweetest innocent that e'er did lift up eye, but like Juliet she was an ill-starr'd wench. As she voyages to Cyprus the tempest rises and

> Seems to cast water on the burning bear,
> And quench the guards of the ever-fixed pole.

Hell and night are hatching Iago's fiendish plot. Othello, like Tarquin, must put out a flaming torch in the chamber and act his violence in the dark. He recognizes the symbolic warning that once Desdemona's light is put out he knows not where is that Promethean heat, that fire from heaven, that can her light relume. But he is fatal when his eyes roll and point on her as portents. He stifles the pure flame and chaos is come again:

> Methinks it should be now a huge eclipse
> Of sun and moon, and that the affrighted globe
> Should yawn at alteration.

The moon has come too near the earth and made men mad. Desdemona will not go to burning hell, her purity outprizes a world new-made from one entire and perfect chrysolite, and her pure aspect will hurl from heaven Othello's soul, rash as fire, to roast in sulphur and be washed in "steep-down gulfs of liquid fire".

King Lear banishes the innocent Cordelia from his sight:

> by the sacred radiance of the sun,
> The mysteries of Hecate, and the night;
> By all the operations of the orbs
> From whom we do exist, and cease to be.

For this disordered judgement, and for the untimely abdication that leaves his realm in chaos, he must endure in hell-black night a storm which, like that in *Othello*, would buoy the sea itself to quench the "stelled fires". Gloucester follows his royal master into this tempest, bearing a torch (his fire of lust brightening to a flame of loyal love) and, striving to prevent Regan and Goneril from plucking out their father's poor old eyes, he loses his own. Lear's ordeal in the storm draws holy water from the heavenly eyes of Cordelia. Nothing less than a brand from heaven could part them again. But it is the stars above us govern our condition. This judgement of the heavens lights upon Regan and Goneril, whom the King arraigned in the storm, and upon Edmund who scorned all heavenly portents, but not before their malevolence has destroyed Cordelia, over whose body Lear's old eyes close for the last time.

Certain parallels have been noted [31] between *Lucrece* and *Macbeth*, where the murderer moves with Tarquin's ravishing stride, but although the correspondences here considered spring from *Lucrece* and reach their fullest development in *Macbeth*, they seem to have escaped notice hitherto. The eye of heaven is out here also. Macbeth bids the stars hide their fires, and his Lady summons the dunnest smoke of hell to hide their crime from the eye of heaven. When heaven's candles are all out, the last torch is struck from the hand of the royal child as his father is murdered. Those who have light can no longer find their way by it. Lady Macbeth walks with a lighted taper, but though her eyes are open their sense is shut. Macbeth's eyes, which his hangman's hands would pluck out, will not close in sleep and are dazzled by the sun-like radiance of the crowns of phantasmal kings. The night is long that never finds the day, and as a new dawn breaks at last over Scotland Macbeth begins to be aweary of the sun and his brief candle is snuffed out. [32]

Prospero and Miranda, such another pair as Lear and Cordelia, are happier in fortune. Miranda is affrighted by the tempest in which (as in the storms of *Lear* and *Othello*):

> The sky, it seems, would pour down stinking pitch,
> But that the sea, mounting to the welkin's cheek,
> Dashes the fire out

and she wrings her eyes again to hear how her father and herself were once hurried from Milan in the dead of darkness. Prospero, however, has now the power to raise and calm the tempest and to cause and cure her tears:

> and by my prescience
> I find my zenith doth depend upon
> A most auspicious star, whose influence
> If now I court not but omit, my fortunes
> Will ever after droop.

He may punish the lustful Caliban by sending spirits, like a firebrand in the dark, to lead him out of his way. But he can likewise summon the queen of the sky and her troop to see that the fires of passion in the young lovers are controlled till Hymen's torch be lighted. This is not hard to bring about, for when Miranda and Ferdinand first gazed upon each other she saw a spirit and he a goddess.

Other patterns engaging the celestial plane in terrestrial affairs could be followed through a number of plays. Star-destiny haunts the five Roman and half-Roman plays.[33] The sun-king theme may be traced through the English Histories, which also contain important star-references. But once the general presence of the celestial plane has been established the important task is to recognize it in the full interpretation of each play. In some cases where the correct Shakespearian interpretation of terrestrial action is in dispute—the character of Cassius is a case in point—reference to the celestial action may help us to appreciate the Elizabethan emphasis. In a much larger number of instances where correspondences are poetically handled as we have seen them treated in the star–torch–eye series it is possible to obtain new insight into the imaginative precision of Shakespeare's poetry and of the visual correlatives for which his stage-directions call.

NOTES

1. *Oedipus at Colonus.*

2. Cf. J. A. Stewart, *The Myths of Plato* (1905), pp. 358–9.

3. Cf. J. L. Lowes, *Geoffrey Chaucer* (1944), p. 21.

4. *The Cocktail Party* (1950), p. 132.

5. *Venus Observed* (1950), p. 61.

6. *Partage de Midi.* The interpretation is quoted from the programme of the Renaud-Barrault performance at the St James's Theatre, London, in 1951.

7. *Winterset* (1938), p. 133.

8. *Chief Pre-Shakespearian Dramas* (1924), p. 158 n.

9. Cf. L. and E. Feasey, 'Marlowe and the Prophetic Dooms', in *Notes and Queries*, 19 August 1950, etc.

10. *The Woman in the Moon.*

11. *The Brazen Age.*

12. Cf. C. Walter Hodges, 'A Seventeenth-Century Heaven', in *Theatre Notebook*, April–June 1950, pp. 59–60.

13. Among the celestial globes in the National Maritime Museum at Greenwich are globes by Mercator, 1551, Florentius, 1589, Hondius, 1613, Van Langeren, 1624 and Gerhard Valk, 1750, on all of which Zodiac symbols are vividly depicted.

14. *Shakespeare Under the Stars* (1887), pp. 40, 64.

15. *Lectures on Shakespeare* (1883), p. 179; the lectures were given in 1818.

16. *Astronomy in the Poets* (n.d.), pp. x, 33; *Shakespeare and Science* (1929), p. 59; *Shakespeare and the Supernatural* (1931), pp. 40–3.

17. *The Star-Crossed Renaissance* (1941), pp. 149, 169, 165.

18. *Op. cit.* (1911), pp. 46–8.

19. *The Essential Shakespeare* (1932), p. 15.

20. *Op. cit.* vol. I (1916), pp. 444–61. 'The Stars Above Us' will be a prominent subject in Allardyce Nicoll's forthcoming anthology *The Elizabethans.*

21. *Op. cit.* (1950 ed.), pp. 14, 17, 30, 33, 36–7, 41, 238.

22. *The Elizabethan World Picture* (1943), pp. 49–50.

23. 'Shakespeare and the Astrology of his Time', *Journal of the Warburg Institute*, vol. II, no. 3 (January 1939), 258, 247.

24. *Op. cit.* pp. 17–18; 1953 ed. pp. xvi–xvii. Wilson Knight is, of course, conscious of the presence and even of the predominance of horizontal order in Shakespeare's imagery. For instance, in *The Crown of Life* (1947), p. 251, he writes, "Nor must we be forced towards any mind-pictures of the vertical: *The Tempest* is...throughout horizontal...." But this does not affect my judgement that his primary principle of classification in the earlier volume is accurately described as vertical.

25. *Shakespeare's Imagery* (1935), Chart v, pp. 22, 225–6, 235–8, 259, 260, 274, 310–11. Star references in *Macbeth* are classified as 'Light', pp. 329–31.

26. *The Development of Shakespeare's Imagery* (1951), pp. 93–4, 72.

27. *Shakespeare and the Nature of Man* (1945), pp. 90–1.

28. 'The Imagery of *Romeo and Juliet*', *English*, Autumn 1950, 121–6. Comment by Roy Walker, *English*, Spring 1951, 217–18.

29. Cf. the last Belmont Scene of *The Merchant of Venice* which so exquisitely harmonizes the stars—"those blessed candles of the night"—the burning light in Portia's mansion and the light within her. Eyes as the source of true love are sung in the earlier Belmont scene of Bassanio's choice. Lewis, in a single sentence of *King John* (v, ii, 50–3) associates a tempest in the soul with weeping eyes and burning meteors in the top of heaven.

30. Since the appearance of the Ghost in *Hamlet* is associated with the stars, and the purpose of the play-scene is to test his revelation by Claudius's reaction, it is tempting to interpret "That's wormwood, wormwood" as meaning not only a bitter draught for the King, but also as referring to the star in *Revelation* called Wormwood which, by falling from heaven, made the waters bitter and fatal to man. Hooker's remarks on that text are quoted by S. L. Bethell, *The Cultural Revolution of the Seventeenth Century* (1951), p. 36.

31. Cf. Kenneth Muir, Arden Edition of *Macbeth* (1951), Appendix C, p. 195.

32. In my commentary on *Macbeth* I have drawn attention to a number of Biblical texts, some of which are probably echoed in the lines on the inner light, eyes and candles. Cf. *The Time is Free* (1949), pp. 179–80. Cf. also *Julius Caesar*, i, iii, 6–8. The star-torch-eye series is extensively employed in that play, and would require fuller discussion than is possible within the limits of this article. I hope to offer comments on the celestial plane in *Julius Caesar* and the other plays and poems of Shakespeare in a book provisionally entitled *Star of Poets*.

33. Cf. Roy Walker, 'The Northern Star: An Essay on the Roman Plays', *Shakespeare Quarterly*, ii (October 1951).

INTERNATIONAL NOTES

A selection has here been made from the reports received from our correspondents, those which present material of a particularly interesting kind being printed wholly or largely in their entirety. It should be emphasized that the choice of countries to be thus represented has depended on the nature of the information presented in the reports, not upon either the importance of the countries concerned or upon the character of the reports themselves.

Austria

The second volume of Richard Flatter's translations (see *Shakespeare Survey*, 7, p. 107) appeared in 1953. The third and last volume is promised for 1954. Parts of another translation finished by Theodor von Zeyneck before his death in 1948 have been published in the series *Stifterbibliothek* (München, Salzburg and Vienna). It professes to be more faithful to the original than Schlegel-Tieck, but in many respects the old translation is to be preferred.

Austrian productions of Shakespeare between 1945 and 1951 are faithfully recorded by Doris Eisner in *Shakespeare-Jahrbuch* (1951/2, LXXXVII/LXXXVIII, 180–97).

Of productions in 1953–4 it is worth mentioning that *Julius Caesar* was included among the plays given at the Salzburg Festival in the summer 1953, played by a cast from the Vienna Burgtheater on the large stage in the Felsenreitschule. It was later taken into the repertory of the Vienna Burgtheater itself, which, in the spring of 1953, presented also a production of *Antony and Cleopatra*. Several private theatres in Vienna tried their hands with *King Lear*, *Romeo and Juliet* and *The Taming of the Shrew*, while the Stadttheater in Klagenfurt opened its 1953–4 season with a good performance of *Twelfth Night*.

KARL BRUNNER

Belgium

In June 1953, the company of the 'Théâtre Royal du Parc' played a translation by Jacques Copeau and Suzanne Bing of *A Midsummer Night's Dream* (Director: Oscar Lejeune). The whole company scored a success, with particular acclaim for Jean-Pierre Roussillon as Puck.

At about the same time, the actors of 'la Compagnie des Galeries' (Managers: Aimé Declercq and Jean-Pierre Rey) gave beautiful performances of *Richard II* in

the fortified castle of Beersel. The French text was the romantic translation of François Victor Hugo. To my knowledge the play had never previously been presented in Belgium. Later in the summer, they revived *Hamlet* (adapted by Romain Sanvic) with Ivan Dominique in the title role, and in the early autumn they started their season in their town theatre with *Julius Caesar* in a French text by Edmond Fleg, Raoul Demanez being Brutus and Paul Anrieu Antony. The three Shakespearian plays were all brilliantly directed by Louis Boxus.

During the winter of 1953–4, Claude Etienne's daring company 'le Rideau de Bruxelles' played *Macbeth* at le Palais des Beaux-Arts. A member of the company, André Berger, scored a triple success as translator, producer and actor (in the title-role).

On 27 April 1954 a gala performance of *A Midsummer Night's Dream* was given to celebrate the centenary of the 'Koninklijke Nederlandse Toneel' (Royal Flemish Theatre) in Antwerp. The King was present and the success was great. There were huge decorations, 120 actors on the stage, and a full orchestra for Mendelssohn's music.

ROBERT DE SMET

Canada

1953 was a significant year for Shakespeare in Canada since it saw the beginning of the Stratford (Ontario) Shakespearian Festival (see the article by Tyrone Guthrie, pp. 127–31). The standard of the Festival was high, and surprisingly enough it ended its first year only slightly in debt, thus ensuring that it will become an annual event. Already for 1954 James Mason has been engaged as the leading actor, and Tyrone Guthrie is returning to direct. A unique record of the whole Festival has been published by Clarke, Irwin Limited of Toronto entitled *Renown at Stratford*.

In Trinity College, Toronto, Earle Grey and his Company celebrated their fifth season of open-air Shakespeare with a seven-week programme which included *Much Ado About Nothing*, *As You Like It* and *The Winter's Tale*.

When one adds to this list the usual Shakespearian activities in the highly organized drama schools at the universities across Canada, and also the whole sequence of the History Plays done by the Canadian Broadcasting Corporation throughout the winter 1953–4, one begins to feel that at last Canada is becoming aware of Shakespeare, and that Canadian productions of his work are beginning to have real distinction. The magnitude of this development is not to be underestimated in a country whose theatrical tradition has not hitherto been its strongest point.   A. EDINBOROUGH

Czechoslovakia

Shakespeare's plays still grow in popularity in Czechoslovakia. With several broadcasts and plays on television and a whole cycle by amateur groups, they gain always wider and wider audiences. An exhibition on 'Shakespeare in Czechoslovakia' was held in the Prague National Museum, with regular lectures on the various aspects of the trends in our bardolatry. Thanks to the inexhaustible enthusiasm of the lovers of Shakespeare, the knowledge of the fruitful influence exercised by Shakespeare on our culture is spreading widely and all Shakespearian activities are followed with great interest.   BŘETISLAV HODEK

Finland

The oldest and leading theatre in Finland, the Finnish National Theatre, boasts of a remarkable Shakespeare tradition, which dates back to the time of its foundation. No less than twenty-two plays by Shakespeare have figured in its repertory. Last year, when the theatre celebrated its eightieth year of existence, *A Midsummer Night's Dream* was chosen as the festival production. This play has been in the repertory of the National Theatre since 1891.

The producer was Arvi Kivimaa, General Director of the theatre. The production aimed at a true Shakespearian tempo: the scenes followed one another in uninterrupted succession, which gave rapidity and coherence to the entire performance. Only two different sets were required, which rendered the use of the rotating stage unnecessary. The action took place in a highly stylized enchanted forest and in Theseus's palace, a few scenes being acted in front of the curtain. Instead of a forest of the conventional type, an enormous single tree in the centre, with a huge branch extending across the stage, was a dominant feature in the setting. This helped to create the atmosphere of a fairy-tale. The production turned out to be a remarkable success and ran for many performances.   RAFAEL KOSKIMIES

Germany

As in every year, Shakespeare continued to be one of the most popular and most frequently performed dramatists on the German stage. A survey of the repertory of the German theatres during the last few years shows that there appears to be a tradition whereby certain plays are given annually, and others—after an interval of half a dozen or even more years—are suddenly revived and are then put on by several theatres at the same time. To the first class belong such plays as *Hamlet*, *Macbeth*, *Othello*, *Twelfth Night*, *Taming of the Shrew*, *As You Like It* and *The Winter's Tale*; this year there figured in the second category *Richard III*, which was produced at Bochum, Berlin and Cologne. The inauguration of Bochum's newly built theatre with this production, under the direction of Hans Schalla, was a major event.

Shakespeare festivals also took place at Göttingen (where Heinz Hilpert produced five comedies during the celebration of the thousandth anniversary of the town) and at Hanover (where four Shakespeare plays were performed on the occasion of his birthday).

A remarkable feature of the stage-managing in Western Germany is an ever-increasing tendency towards 'stylization' and a pronounced attempt to cut out mass scenes and suppress historical pageantry. In obvious contrast, the Soviet Zone shows a distinct emphasis on realism: scenery, masks, costumes often are genuine historical copies down to the minutest details. A characteristic instance of symbolic staging appeared in a production of *Macbeth* at Hamburg, where the 'magic circle' of the walls drew nearer together from act to act until eventually, at the end, they are seen pressing closely upon the haunted hero.

Open-air performances of Shakespeare plays are gaining in popularity. Good examples of students' performances were those of *The Taming of the Shrew* and *All's Well That Ends Well* during the 'International Week of the Students' Theatres' at Erlangen. An interesting instance of Shakespeare's adaptation to ballet purposes is the ballet pantomime *Hamlet* with music by Boris Blacher, which was successfully performed at several leading opera houses.   WOLFGANG CLEMEN

Israel

Shortly after my translation of *Antony and Cleopatra* had appeared, two others were published—one by Hillel Bavli and the other by I. Libes. *The Taming of the Shrew*, translated by R. Eliaz (the production of which was reported in *Shakespeare Survey*, 6) is just off the press.

Preliminary preparations are now being made by the Habima and the Chamber Theatre for their forthcoming productions of *Macbeth* and *As You Like It* respectively.

REUBEN AVINOAM

Italy

After Vittorio Gassman's interpretation of *Hamlet* (see *Shakespeare Survey*, 7), the greatest Shakespearian production an Italian audience has seen has been Jean Vilar's *Richard II*, which was given at the Venice Festival in September 1953: in fact the performances of the Théâtre National Populaire can be considered among the best in contemporary Europe. A film of *The Merchant of Venice*, with a few Italian actors in the same cast with Michel Simon, has been severely criticized, while *Julius Caesar* (which counted among the technical advisers a distinguished Italian novelist and professor of comparative literature, P. M. Pasinetti), has met with good success in the translation of C. V. Ludovici. This play has also found two other translators—A. Obertello and the poet Eugenio Montale. A well-known Italian novelist, Elio Vittorini, appeared in the role of Paris in Castellani's film *Romeo and Juliet*, under the assumed name of Giovanni Rota (the very name he had while fighting in the *maquis*).

A remarkable essay of about 200 pages by Ada Sabbadini (the first wife of the well-known classical scholar and prominent communist M.P., Concetto Marchesi) deals with *Hamlet*, *Macbeth*, *Othello*, *King Lear*, under a typical title, *Umanità e favola nell' arte di Shakespeare*. It is curious to see how popular this kind of double-barrelled title has been with authors of books on Shakespeare in Italy; 1943 saw Cellini's *Vita e arte nei sonetti di Shakespeare*, 1950 Valentina Capocci's *Genio e mestiere*, *Shakespeare e la commedia dell' arte*. Ada Sabbadini's book is more the record of personal reactions than a critical essay in the proper sense of the word. Her attitude is in a way the opposite of Signora Capocci's; while the latter suspected any but the greatest passages as un-Shakespearian, Signora Sabbadini is ready to accept everything, even Hecate's speech in *Macbeth*, as genuine. Her book could be contemporary with Schlegel, and she is so much out of sympathy with the trend of modern thought that she finds that the relation of Hamlet with his mother "from whatever side you look at it, shows no ambiguity" ("Così il rapporto tra questa madre e questo figlio, guardato da ogni lato, non mostra alcuna ambiguità"). Both Signora Capocci and Signora Sabbadini are in the wake of the Croce tradition, though they mirror different aspects of it. Descending as they do from the editor of *La Critica*, it is remarkable how uncritical they are. But Signora Sabbadini's book is charmingly written.

Shakespeare's ten histories were broadcast in the Third Programme of the R.A.I. (the Italian radio) during the latter part of 1953, in eight transmissions, the three parts of *Henry VI* having been compressed into one. Except for *1* and *2 Henry VI*, translated by Giorgio Brunacci, the translations and adaptations were made by Gabriele Baldini.

MARIO PRAZ

Norway

Two plays have been staged in 1953: *As You Like It* at the National Theatre in Oslo and *Hamlet* at the National Stage in Bergen and at the New Theatre in Oslo.

As You Like It was presented in the Watteau style: a performance graceful, carefully balanced, subdued, without the fine exuberance of the genuine Shakespeare.

During the last two years a kind of *Hamlet* fever has gripped this country: the play was staged in Trondhjem and in Bergen in October 1952, again in Bergen in October 1953, and in Oslo in September 1953; in the two former places with Lökkeberg as Hamlet; in Oslo with a very young actor, Espen Skjönberg. The critics praised the way in which Lökkeberg united the impetuosity of youth with the meditative serenity of mature manhood. Espen Skjönberg prepared for us a very fascinating surprise. Most actors *play* the youth of Hamlet; Skjönberg *was* young, and somehow this rare quality made his Hamlet unusually convincing.

LORENTZ ECKHOFF

South Africa

Early in 1953 the National Theatre Organization took on tour to the principal towns of South Africa, and afterwards to the Rhodesian Centenary Celebrations, a polished *Twelfth Night*, produced by Leonard Schach, with a dignified Watteau setting designed by Frank Graves. This with the earlier, and similar, production of *Volpone* provided the basis of a repertory that had appreciative audiences everywhere.

During the year two more plays from a dismembered Second Folio of Shakespeare came to light in Pretoria. They are *Much Ado* and *Love's Labour's Lost*, owned by M. Buxton Forman, bibliophile and editor of Keats's *Letters*.

In *Theoria* (1953) Mrs S. K. King of Natal University wrote an interesting account of 'virtus' as the source of poetic inspiration in "Eliot, Yeats and Shakespeare". In discussing *Pericles* and Eliot's *Marina*, *The Winter's Tale* and Yeats's *Lapis Lazuli*, she offers valuable comment on the spirit that impelled the composition of Shakespeare's last plays.   A. C. PARTRIDGE

Sweden

With six productions recorded on the Scandinavian stages last autumn, Hamlet seemed to have settled down in his native country. Sweden's share was two presentations of the drama, one in Stockholm (Boulevardteatern) and one in Gothenburg (Göteborgs stadsteater). The last mentioned, with Per Oscarsson in the title-role, developed into an overwhelming success with packed houses. An uncommon Hamlet it certainly was. Some critics saw in him the primitive Hamlet of the old Northern tale; others discerned a modern desperate youth. This was, first and foremost, a very young Hamlet, rude and ruthless—an inspired interpretation throughout, abounding in touching and thrilling details. Oscarsson was always tense, like a spring, never relaxed, and so gave not much room to the melancholy hero. The scenery was splendid, the Ghost Scene and the duel in the last act very impressive. The comic scenes passed without being much noticed and on the whole the staging was in a certain sense devoid of humour.

The Old Town Theatre in Stockholm has, in spite of its small stage resources, produced a very fine *Macbeth*. A production of *Romeo and Juliet* at the Dramatiska teatern, Stockholm, was to a great extent characterized by its experiments with the scenery. Another *Romeo and Juliet*, and a successful one, was presented by Riksteatern (our national travelling company). The *As You Like It* in Malmö may be mentioned as a notable performance. The open air stages have now got Shakespeare on their regular repertory. All told, 1953 was a rich year for Shakespeare in Sweden.   NILS MOLIN

Switzerland

Heinrich Straumann, of Zurich University, has attempted to solve the riddle of Shakespeare's contribution to Chester's *Loves Martyr* in a pleasant little book published at Zurich (*Phönix und Taube von William Shakespeare*, 63 pp., Artemis-Verlag, 1953). He shows that the divergent interpretations that have been given of the famous little poem may be to some extent at least reconciled by assuming that the poet was writing at three different levels at the same time, paying homage to two persons well-known in public life, playing with the traditions and conventions of the age, singing the union of two ultimate values, beauty and truth. Rudolf Stamm, of the St Gall Handelshochschule, has just published his paper on *Shakespeare's Word-Scenery*; it is a plea in favour of a criticism of the plays regarded as performances essentially, as spectacles to be seen, not as books to be read, as against the present day return to a kind of neo-romantic position.

Several plays were produced in the course of last year (1953) at Bâle (*The Two Gentlemen of Verona, A Midsummer Night's Dream, Julius Caesar*), Berne (*The Comedy of Errors, A Midsummer Night's Dream, Hamlet*) and Zurich (*Measure for Measure*). None of these performances seems to have been in any way out of the ordinary. They were all in German. *The Comedy of Errors* at Berne and *A Midsummer Night's Dream* at Bâle were open-air performances and owed their popular success partly at least to the fine parks where they were staged.

In Piachaud's French translation, *The Merchant of Venice* was acted no less than three times, and each time with tremendous success, in the schoolroom of a small village, Saubraz, at the foot of the Jura range, half-way between Lausanne and Geneva. Trained by an enthusiastic village teacher, who is a born and highly gifted actor himself, and who took the part of Shylock, a group of peasants succeeded in giving a highly creditable performance of the play to their own delight and the delight of crowded audiences flocking from all the villages round.   GEORGES A. BONNARD

Turkey

By far the most important Shakespearian event was the performance of *Romeo and Juliet*, presented on 19 April 1953, in the ancient theatre at Aspendus. The players came from the State Conservatoire of Ankara and played before an audience of over twenty thousand people, most of whom were simple peasants of southern Turkey who flocked in from their distant farms and villages.

As actors appeared at the central doorway they were introduced to the audience one by one, the central doorway being explained as the entrance to the palace of the Prince, while those on the right and left led to the dwellings of Juliet and Romeo respectively.

Twenty thousand pairs of eyes were firmly fixed on the stage. At times not a single sound was heard from the rows, as though all were afraid of breathing, lest they might lose the illusion of the dreamland in which they found themselves. When the Nurse came in, followed by the sleepy Peter with his huge fan, the vast ocean of human faces waved, and Mercutio's puns caused a roar of laughter like the peal of many guns. And once again, when Tybalt appeared in defiance and rapiers were drawn, a dead silence filled the place: when the merry Mercutio was stabbed a furious roar cursed the fray. As Juliet fell down motionless upon her bed and the Nurse began to cry, a group of peasant girls burst into tears and a lady could hardly succeed in calming them down; and when she woke up in the last scene there was a unanimous sigh of relief and an applause that pealed through the rows. When she stabbed herself, innocent tears once again rolled down the cheeks of many a face both young and old. NUREDDIN SEVIN

U.S.A.

The New York City Center which produced all the Shakespeare New York had last winter again came forward with one of the two professional offerings seen during the 1953–4 season. José Ferrer presented a *Richard III* that followed tradition without adding to it. The production was staged by Margaret Webster, who moved her hastily recruited and not very experienced Shakespearian forces with all her usual authority and effectiveness. The production was designed by Richard Whorf.

The other professional production of the season was interesting from several points of view. It was presented by a new group calling itself The Phoenix Theatre, which has set up its permanent home well off the beaten Broadway track in the hope of developing a centre for the unusual play, the unhackneyed classic, the experimental and original in theatre writing and production. The Phoenix, under the management of T. Edward Hambleton and Norris Houghton, opened its doors with *Madame, Will You Walk*, a fantasy by the late Sidney Howard which had never been seen in New York. Its

second production was *Coriolanus*, vigorously directed by John Houseman. Houseman selected a young screen actor, Robert Ryan, for the title role and managed, by the resourcefulness of his direction and the vigour and immediacy with which he interpreted the play, to please critics and interest playgoers in what to almost everyone was a new Shakespearian experience. Donald Oenslager's permanent set, and Alvin Colt's costumes were exceptionally effective and John Emery and Mildred Natwick, who co-starred with Ryan, threw themselves into this rarely acted play with enthusiasm.

Though all too infrequently seen on Broadway, off that highway and across the country Shakespeare remains a favourite. In New York itself, in a settlement house on the east side, a young professional group presented *Othello* with an exceptionally fine Negro actor in the title role. The Shakespeare Festivals in Oregon and Antioch repeated their success last summer and are planning their new seasons. The 'American Shakespeare Festival Theatre and Academy', launched by Lawrence Langner, has secured land in Stratford, Connecticut, where a summer season of Shakespeare-under-canvas is projected. A unique event in Shakespeare annals was the presentation, as the opening event of the Yale Shakespeare Festival, of a production of *The Merry Wives of Windsor* in the language of Shakespeare's day. Helge Kökeritz, who coached the actors in this unusual effort, has been working for years on the reconstruction of Elizabethan speech and has recently published a book on the subject. *The Merry Wives* was spoken throughout in this reconstructed language, which has something of the richness and musical qualities of Irish speech today. Produced by the Yale Department of Drama under Frank McMullan's direction, Brooks Atkinson reports that it was "well-set, well-lighted and well-imagined" and that the strange speech, in the hands of the better actors among the student group, had "force, humor and flavor and seemed also curiously familiar".

ROSAMOND GILDER

SHAKESPEARE PRODUCTIONS IN THE UNITED KINGDOM: 1953

A LIST COMPILED FROM ITS RECORDS BY THE
SHAKESPEARE MEMORIAL LIBRARY, BIRMINGHAM

JANUARY

6   *The Merchant of Venice:* The Old Vic Company, at The Old Vic Theatre, London. *Producer:* HUGH HUNT.

19   *The Tempest:* The Playhouse, Nottingham. *Producer:* JOHN HARRISON.

FEBRUARY

2   *Twelfth Night:* Theatre Workshop, at Theatre Royal, Stratford, London, E. 15. *Producer:* JOAN LITTLEWOOD.

10   *Romeo and Juliet:* The Library Theatre, Manchester. *Producer:* STUART LATHAM.

14   *Julius Caesar:* Eton College. *Producers:* R. J. G. PAYNE, C. J. F. TROTT and N. J. MONCK.

14   *Measure for Measure:* The Norwich Players, at The Maddermarket Theatre, Norwich. *Producer:* LIONEL DUNN.

16   *As You Like It:* The King's Theatre, Hammersmith. *Producer:* DONALD WOLFIT.

16   *The Taming of the Shrew:* The Marlowe Theatre, Canterbury. *Producer:* DOUGLAS EMERY.

23   *King Lear:* The King's Theatre, Hammersmith. *Producer:* NUGENT MONCK.

23   *Henry the Fifth:* Guildford Repertory Theatre. *Producer:* ROGER WINTON.

24   *Julius Caesar:* The Old Vic Company, at The Old Vic Theatre, London. *Producer:* HUGH HUNT.

25   *Twelfth Night:* The King's Theatre, Hammersmith. *Producer:* DONALD WOLFIT.

MARCH

2   *The Taming of the Shrew:* The Midland Theatre Company, Coventry. *Producer:* PAUL LEE.

3   *Richard the Third:* Oxford University Dramatic Society. *Producers:* JOHN WOOD and DAVID THOMPSON.

7   *Hamlet:* Donal Hodson's Company, Skipton, Yorkshire. *Producer:* DONAL HODSON.

9   *The Merchant of Venice:* The King's Theatre, Hammersmith. *Producer:* DONALD WOLFIT.

9   *Romeo and Juliet:* Perth Theatre Company. *Producer:* JOHN BLATCHLEY.

9   *Titus Andronicus:* The Marlowe Society, Cambridge University. Producer and actors are anonymous in these productions.

17   *The Merchant of Venice:* Shakespeare Memorial Theatre, Stratford-upon-Avon. *Producer:* DENIS CAREY.

19   *Macbeth:* The King's Theatre, Hammersmith. *Producer:* DONALD WOLFIT.

24   *Richard the Third:* Shakespeare Memorial Theatre, Stratford-upon-Avon. *Producer:* GLEN BYAM SHAW.

APRIL

27   *The Tempest:* Dundee Repertory Theatre. *Producer:* HERBERT WISE

27   *The Two Gentlemen of Verona:* Nottingham Playhouse. *Producer:* JOHN HARRISON.

27   *The Taming of the Shrew:* The King's Theatre, Hammersmith. *Producer:* DONALD WOLFIT.

APRIL

28   *Antony and Cleopatra:* Shakespeare Memorial Theatre, Stratford-upon-Avon. *Producer:* GLEN BYAM SHAW (4 November at The Princes Theatre, London, and afterwards abroad).

28   *Twelfth Night:* Theatre Royal, Huddersfield. *Producer:* LESLIE FRENCH.

MAY

4   *As You Like It:* The Mermaid Theatre (at The Royal Exchange, London). *Producer:* BERNARD MILES.

6   *Henry VIII:* The Old Vic Company, at The Old Vic Theatre, London. *Producer:* TYRONE GUTHRIE.

11   *Henry V:* The Elizabethan Theatre Company, at The Marlowe Theatre, Canterbury. *Producer:* JOHN BARTON. (On tour, opening at The Marlowe Theatre.)

18   *The Merchant of Venice:* The Wilson Barrett Company, at The Lyceum Theatre, Edinburgh. *Producer:* RICHARD MATHEWS.

18   *The Comedy of Errors:* The Taverners (Poetry and Plays in Pubs). *Producer:* IAN SMYTHE. (On tour, opening at The Master Robert, Hounslow, Middlesex.)

20   *Twelfth Night:* Renée R. Soskin for Hampstead Theatre, Ltd., at The Embassy Theatre, London. *Producer:* LAURENCE PAYNE.

26   *Hamlet:* Renée R. Soskin for Hampstead Theatre, Ltd., at The Embassy Theatre, London. *Producer:* RENÉE R. SOSKIN.

27   *Twelfth Night:* The Bankside Players, at Regent's Park Open-Air Theatre, London. *Producer:* ROBERT ATKINS.

JUNE

1   *Twelfth Night:* The Alexandra Theatre, Birmingham. *Producer:* PETER POWELL.

2   *Henry the Fifth:* The Bristol Old Vic Company, at The Theatre Royal, Bristol. *Producer:* DENIS CAREY. (June 30 at The Old Vic Theatre, London.)

2   *The Two Gentlemen of Verona:* New College Dramatic Society, in New College Gardens, Oxford.

3   *Love's Labour's Lost:* Cambridge University Amateur Dramatic Company at The A.D.C. Theatre, Cambridge. *Producer:* PETER HALL.

5   *King John:* Harrow School. *Producer:* RONALD WATKINS.

9   *King Henry the Sixth, Part I:* The Repertory Theatre, Birmingham. *Producer:* DOUGLAS SEALE. (13 July at The Old Vic Theatre, London.)

9   *The Taming of the Shrew:* Shakespeare Memorial Theatre, Stratford-upon-Avon. *Producer:* GEORGE DEVINE.

10   *Troilus and Cressida:* Oxford University Dramatic Society, in the gardens of St John's College.

13   *Hamlet:* The Norwich Players, at The Maddermarket Theatre, Norwich. *Producer:* LIONEL DUNN.

23   *The Merchant of Venice:* The Gateway Theatre Club. *Producer:* OLAVE MARCH.

29   *Julius Caesar:* The Elizabethan Theatre Company, at The Westminster Theatre. *Producer:* MICHAEL MACOWAN.

JUNE

29   *Love's Labour's Lost:* The Bankside Players, at Regent's Park Open-Air Theatre, London. *Producer:* HUGH GOLDIE.

29   *King Henry the Sixth, Part II:* The Repertory Theatre, Birmingham. *Producer:* DOUGLAS SEALE. (14 July at The Old Vic Theatre, London.)

JULY

1   *Macbeth:* The Mermaid Theatre (on The Royal Exchange, London). *Producer:* JOAN SWINSTEAD.

2   *King Henry the Sixth, Part III:* The Repertory Theatre, Birmingham. *Producer:* DOUGLAS SEALE. (15 July at The Old Vic Theatre, London.)

13   *Twelfth Night:* The Gaiety Theatre, Ilfracombe. The John Gay Players. *Producer:* ANTONY MASSIE. (20 July at Taw and Torridge Festival, Barnstaple.)

14   *King Lear:* The Shakespeare Memorial Theatre, Stratford-upon-Avon. *Producer:* GEORGE DEVINE.

AUGUST

24   *Hamlet:* The Old Vic Company at The Edinburgh Festival. *Producer:* MICHAEL BENTHALL.

SEPTEMBER

7   *A Midsummer Night's Dream:* The Norwich Players, in the Palace Garden, Norwich. *Producer:* NUGENT MONCK.

7   *As You Like It:* The Nottingham Playhouse. *Producer:* JOHN HARRISON.

8   *Richard II:* Le Théâtre National Populaire, Paris, at The Edinburgh Festival. *Producer:* JEAN VILAR.

14   *The Merchant of Venice:* The Arts Council. *Producer:* PETER POTTER. (On tour, opening at The Little Theatre, Newport.)

14   *Henry IV, Part I:* The King's Theatre, Hammersmith. *Producer:* DONALD WOLFIT.

15   *All's Well that Ends Well:* The Old Vic Company, at The Old Vic Theatre, London. *Producer:* MICHAEL BENTHALL.

21   *The Merchant of Venice:* The Playhouse, Kidderminster. *Producer:* ROBERT GASTON.

22   *Romeo and Juliet:* The Caryl Jenner Mobile Theatre. *Producers:* CARYL JENNER and SALLY LATIMER. (On tour, opening at Sleaford, Lincs.)

28   *Macbeth:* The King's Theatre, Hammersmith. *Producer:* DONALD WOLFIT.

28   *Romeo and Juliet:* Guildford Theatre Company. *Producer:* ROGER WINTON.

30   *As You Like It:* The King's Theatre, Hammersmith. *Producer:* DONALD WOLFIT.

OCTOBER

12   *Twelfth Night:* The Elizabethan Theatre Company. *Producer:* PETER HALL. (On tour, opening at the Theatre Royal, Exeter.)

20   *Antony and Cleopatra:* Bristol Old Vic Company, at The Theatre Royal, Bristol. *Producer:* DENIS CAREY.

22   *King Lear:* The King's Theatre, Hammersmith. *Producer:* NUGENT MONCK.

I*

OCTOBER

23   *Twelfth Night:* The King's Theatre, Hammersmith. *Producer:* DONALD WOLFIT.

27   *King John:* The Old Vic Company, at The Old Vic Theatre, London. *Producer:* GEORGE DEVINE.

NOVEMBER

4   *Cymbeline:* The Playhouse, Liverpool. *Producer:* WILLARD STOKER.

13   *Twelfth Night:* The Norwich Players, at The Maddermarket Theatre, Norwich. *Producer:* LIONEL DUNN.

24   *A Midsummer Night's Dream:* The Library Theatre, Manchester. *Producer:* STUART LATHAM.

DECEMBER

1   *The Comedy of Errors:* Bristol Old Vic Company, at The Theatre Royal, Bristol. *Producer:* DENIS CAREY.

SHAKESPEARE AT STRATFORD, ONTARIO

BY

TYRONE GUTHRIE

The first Shakespearian Festival at Stratford, Ontario, is worth attention from two points of view: first as an enterprise, a feat of courage, faith and vision by the community of this little Ontario city; secondly because, so far as I know, this is the first time for many years that a stage and auditorium have been specially constructed for the presentation of Shakespearian plays.

Stratford is a town of 19,000 inhabitants, it is a railway junction, the site of a railway engine repair works, there are some furniture factories; but it is principally a market town for a very prosperous agricultural country-side, old-established by Canadian standards. It was settled over 100 years ago. The present population is some three or four generations removed from the Pioneers, who were mostly Scottish and German, although the actual township was named by a group who came from Stratford, Warwickshire, and a little willow-edged creek flowing nearby is spelt Avon, though pronounced Avvon. This creek has been dammed up to form a series of lakes and islands—very pretty, and the one feature which distinguishes Stratford visually from any one of many similar little towns in Ontario.

The idea of the Festival was conceived by a young journalist called Tom Patterson. On war-service in Italy he had encountered grand opera for the first time and been bowled over. Then, still as a soldier, in London he saw his first professional productions of 'straight' plays. Then he went to the Old Vic. The result was to make him feel that the entertainment hitherto available in Stratford, Ontario, was rather insufficient. He set to work to mobilize local interest in a Shakespearian Festival and after three years had raised a considerable head of steam. There was plenty of enthusiasm, but very little experience. So I was asked to go out and give advice. The plan we evolved was as follows:

(1) A stage that would realize the physical relation between actor and audience which prevailed in the Elizabethan Playhouse; and that would have the practical features of an Elizabethan stage, as far as we can deduce them from the evidence available.

(2) This stage to be placed in a temporary auditorium under canvas, designed to hold about 1500 people, this figure being the largest that I thought could adequately see and hear under these conditions.

(3) Two plays to be given in repertory.

(4) The services of a small group of experienced and, if possible, celebrated actors to be sought in Great Britain—the project, however, to be demonstrably an effort for and by Canadians, with some outside assistance, but not much.

This project was then 'budgetted' and it was believed that, if a subscription fund of $150,000 (£50,000) were raised, then takings of 60% of capacity for four weeks would make ends meet.

On this basis the committee went ahead. Imagine a British community of approximately similar size—Ballymena, for example, or Truro, or Tonbridge, or Skipton, or Galashiels—embarking on a similar project with no outside backing whatsoever, with no influential 'names' on the committee. This was just a group of small-town citizens, doctors, lawyers, a clergyman, business men and women prepared to back an idea with not a hope of making money—indeed, with every likelihood of a considerable financial loss and very red faces into the bargain. In the end, I am glad to say, the enthusiasm and faith were justified; the plays were given for an extended season, played to the remarkable figure of 96% capacity, were considered an artistic event of national importance, attracted a flattering amount of favourable notice from the leading American as well as Canadian critics and, by no means least important, were the cause of a considerable fillip to the business of the little town. A weekly influx of ten thousand souls on pleasure bent is not to be sneezed at by local tradesmen. The municipality, lukewarm last year, is now heart and soul 'for' the Festival. It is hoped that this will have been the first of a long annual series. Plans are already well advanced for the second Stratford Festival.

Now for the more 'Shakespearian' aspect: the two plays chosen were *Richard III* and *All's Well That Ends Well*; the first as a 'vehicle' for Alec Guinness, who headed the cast; the second as a bold contrast and because it offered a number of good parts which we thought we could cast suitably.

The acting of Guinness in *Richard III* was highly and justly admired. But it was interesting to find that the booking for *Richard* was no better than for *All's Well*, an unfamiliar and supposedly 'difficult' play; and that of the two plays *All's Well*, certainly in my opinion, and I think in that of most of the audience, emerged as much the better bit of work.

The stage, designed by Tanya Moiseiwitsch, with a certain amount of suggestion from myself, presented a balcony supported by slender pillars above a main stage thirty foot square. The balcony was accessible, in sight of the audience, by two staircases from each side of the stage, as well as from a central entrance at the back. The main stage was accessible directly from the dressing-rooms, through the pillars supporting the balcony, from the aisles of the auditorium, and from two tunnels beneath the auditorium. There was also a trap-door cut in the floor of the stage, to serve as grave, entrance to dungeons and so on.

The designer's aim was to offer the facilities of an Elizabethan stage, but not to attempt an Elizabethan pseudo-antique style. The floor was of oak, polished—about as shiny as a dance-floor; the pillars, balcony and partition wall were stained a rather darker colour, appreciably darker than the actors' faces. The general visual effect we aimed at was to be strictly 'functional'; neither aggressively modern nor antique; a structure that unobtrusively offered to the actors standing-places, seats, and things to lean against, where they needed them; a platform that offered neither too much space nor too little, and which was so placed as to be the focal point of the nearly circular auditorium.

There was no curtained alcove under the balcony, partly because I did not think either of these two plays required its use (and I am not convinced that this practicality is, in fact, a necessity), partly because we did not like the look of drapery in this position.

Because we played at night, artificial light was a necessity. But there were no illusionary 'effects' of light. We permitted ourselves an unobtrusive 'dim' at what seemed appropriate times, not without a feeling that this was a weak concession to current theatrical convention and a departure from the method and style we had adopted.

Scenic austerity was offset by extremely rich and handsome clothes. I do not think audiences felt that they had been cheated of 'spectacle' in either play; and I do not think there was any loss of 'illusion' because there were no naturalistic indications of whereabouts. It is not for me to assess how successful these performances were. I can only say that, in my opinion, they had, owing to the nature of the stage, a number of advantages, which the proscenium stage, by its very nature, can never offer.

First, because there was no picture-frame and obviously no possibility of scenery, there was no need to attempt scenic illusion. In a proscenium one *has* to create a 'picture'; even the most negative background to the actors—black curtains for instance—makes a visual statement that cannot be ignored. And if in a proscenium, with all the paraphernalia for creating 'pictures' and all the weight of pictorial tradition associated with such buildings, one gives a whole play against some carefully and monotonously negative background, it is clear that the mechanism is being denied. This denial cannot but seem emphatic and self-conscious, cannot but draw attention.

Scenic statements, even negative statements, are obviously malapropos in a Shakespearian production. The plays were written for a stage that did not offer scenery. Therefore, if it is necessary for the audience to know the whereabouts of the characters, an indication is given *in the text*. If it is important that the audience's attention be drawn to facts about the weather, time of day, season of the year, its attention is drawn *in the text*; usually in language so apt, so memorable and so timely that to make another statement in visual terms, whether in paintwork, carpentry or lighting, is not merely superfluous but impertinent.

Our stage, trying to provide the facilities which the plays do require but no others, offered a merely functional background: anything that was visible had a practical purpose and was not there just to look pretty. Even its colour and proportions were functional. They may not, in the event, have fulfilled all their purposes adequately but there was at least a sensible reason for everything being as it was. Freed from scenery, scene could follow scene without the slightest interruption of continuity. I realize that this absolute continuity can be achieved in a proscenium—Motley did so brilliantly in a recent *Antony and Cleopatra*: Moiseiwitsch in a recent *Henry VIII*—but it is achieved only by toiling and spinning, by prodigies of technique. If there can be no scenery, it is merely wilful to break the continuity of the play's flow except to give the audience a rest. I need not enlarge on the advantages of continuity.

If the audience sits, as ours did, *around* the stage, certain choreographic problems are posed. But, on balance, the grouping and flow of movement are infinitely easier to arrange. The chief difficulty arises, I think, in long soliloquies, especially meditative soliloquies where movement 'feels' wrong to an actor and tends to disturb the concentration of the audience. I think the solution is for the actor to keep turning slowly, facing now this, now that, part of the house. With a little practice this soon feels, and looks, perfectly natural. Both Alec Guinness in *Richard III* and Irene Worth in *All's Well* managed long passages of psychological monologue in a way that felt comfortable and natural to themselves and entirely held their audience.

Conversational scenes are infinitely easier to arrange if the participants do not have to conform to the highly conventional groupings that rule the proscenium stage, where 'masking' or 'upstaging' one's interlocutor are rightly crimes. On an 'open' stage masking is inevitable. It is the producer's duty to see that all parts of the house get fair do's—that if Mr X faced East at one important moment, he must face West at the next; or better still must contrive to scatter the favour of his countenance over a wide radius. In practice two things emerge: the naturalness and expressiveness of the group is more important than the face of any single member of the group; a good actor's behind is often just as expressive as his face. Finally on the 'open' stage choreography can be much more fluid and varied than in a proscenium; first, because there is no question of avoiding masking; second because the picture must all the time be planned to be expressive from all angles, not just from 'the front'; thirdly because entrances and exits can be available in *all* directions, not just left, right and centre. This is especially helpful in those scenes, so frequent in Shakespeare, when a group pauses *en route* from X to Y. In the proscenium the progress of My Lords of Norfolk, Suffolk and Rutland from X to Y occurs parallel to the footlights, from right to left; and the progress of My Lords of Kent, Sussex and Surrey from Y to X occurs, parallel to the footlights from left to right. On the 'open' stage a far greater variety both of direction and pace can be achieved, because there is a wider choice of exit and entrance and a greater variety of distance to traverse.

But the great and basic practical advantage of the 'open' stage is that an equivalent number of people can be put into a smaller space than if they are all arranged to face a proscenium. Shakespeare's plays, with large casts, involve a large number of salaries, and shoes and hats and swords and so on. They are inevitably more costly to put on than a nice little modern comedy involving from six to sixteen actors, including understudies. As a result the modern comedies occupy the small intimate theatres where the actors can play with great finesse and still make their points. Shakespeare, in order to recoup the expense, has to be played in large theatres. Most of Shakespeare's plays, but especially the comedies, are interesting only if they are played with great intimacy, great finesse; above all if they are beautifully spoken. It is all but impossible to speak beautifully if you are only audible either when you speak loudly or when you speak slowly. The wonder is that actors do as well as they do. Top-ranking performers like Olivier or Sybil Thorndike or Edith Evans can make vast auditoria seem intimate by sheer force of magnetism. A great rhetorician, like Gielgud, can, by sheer virtuosity, conceal the fact that he is able only to use a fraction of the vocal variety which he could employ in more favourable circumstances.

Finally, it may be argued that an open stage is less conducive to 'illusion' than the comparatively realistic 'pictures' created behind a proscenium. This point I must immediately concede. But is 'illusion' the true aim of a theatrical performance? I do not think so. I do not believe that anyone beyond the mental age of twelve can believe that actors in a play are 'really' the characters they are pretending to be, or that the events which are being enacted are 'really' taking place. I do not believe that an adult public has ever swallowed the 'illusion' of the theatre; and certainly not in this epoch when dramatic entertainment is squirting out of machines at every minute of the day or night, when the features of leading players are more familiar than those of Prime Ministers and Archbishops. Who in this age is really taken in when Sir Laurence Olivier makes believe to be King Lear? We admire the artifice of his disguise, the emotional force of his feeling and the intellectual acumen of his comment—for every performance is a comment by the actor upon the part, the play, upon his own personality and the collective personality of the audience. Such admiration can be so tinged with sympathy that we do actually 'feel' with the actor, are moved to laughter and to tears and to feelings deeper than laughter and tears can express. But such sympathy does not, in my opinion, proceed from 'illusion'. Exactly analogous reactions can be evoked by music or paintings, by great works of architecture or literature, where there is no question of illusion.

I suggest that theatrical performance is a form of ritual, that the audience is not asked to subscribe to an illusion but to participate in the ritual. If the performance is sufficiently expert it is not hard for the audience to participate with great fervour; for each member of the audience to lose a great deal of his own identity; to allow his personality to become fused with that of other participants, to become lost, rapt, in a collective act of participation.

The attraction for me of the 'open' stage, as opposed to the proscenium, is primarily this: that it stresses the ritual as opposed to the illusionary quality of performance. Next there is the important practical advantage that an auditorium built *around* a stage, instead of facing it, accommodates a larger number of spectators in the same cubic space (at Stratford we could seat 1500 people in great comfort and the back row was only the same distance from the stage as Row M in the stalls of the Old Vic; the Old Vic holds fewer than 1400 people packed closer in its three tiers). Thirdly, it seems to me incontrovertible that it is more sensible to attempt to produce Shakespeare's plays in something that approximates as closely as circumstances will permit to the conditions for which they were written.

This is not to say that I am for putting all sorts and conditions of plays onto an 'open' stage. Far from it. The plays of Congreve or Sheridan, for instance, of Wilde, Pinero or Barrie were written for the proscenium stage and should be so produced. Nor am I suggesting that the Memorial Theatre at Stratford, Warwickshire, or the Old Vic should straightway be torn down and replaced by more 'Shakespearian' edifices. For some time to come the open stage will still be in the experimental phase. Ours in Canada was only one of many experiments that must, and will, be made. Detailed modifications and improvements will be made to our stage and particularly to our auditorium. We were all aware, I know, of deficiencies. In my opinion the auditorium embraced too wide an arc; the nearest spectators were too near to the actors, the farthest off too far—defects only curable either by a cut in capacity, which is economically unthinkable, or by building galleries which is, for the present, economically unthinkable. All in all, however, the results achieved were very encouraging.[1]

1. Since the foregoing was written, the second Shakespearian Festival has taken place at Stratford, Ontario. *Measure for Measure, The Taming of the Shrew* and *King Œdipus* of Sophocles were produced, with James Mason, Frances Hyland and Douglas Campbell leading a company that included most of the first year's players. The season lasted for eight weeks, played to even larger business than the year before, so that the position is now strong enough both financially and in reputation for long-term plans to be made for an annual Festival.

PLAYS PLEASANT AND PLAYS UNPLEASANT

[A review of Shakespeare productions during the winter of 1953–4, with special reference to *All's Well That Ends Well* at the Old Vic and *A Midsummer Night's Dream* at the Shakespeare Memorial Theatre, Stratford-upon-Avon.]

BY

RICHARD DAVID

For the collector of Shakespearian performances the winter of 1953–4 was a disappointing season. There were workmanlike productions in plenty, faithful, coherent, agreeable, but quite without the power to engender that exaltation, that spirit of delight, that comes so rarely but repays all when it does. Such a workmanlike job was the *Othello* that opened the Stratford season, nobly mounted by Tanya Moiseiwitsch, with a great yellow and red awning (Plate V A) to give a sultry siroccan air to Iago's temptation of the Moor. Such were *Coriolanus* and *Twelfth Night* at the Vic, the routine *bonhomie* of the latter relieved by the (perhaps excessive) violence of Claire Bloom's Viola, a tigress rather than the usual mouse. Less successful was the Old Vic's first production, *Hamlet*, taken at a hissing and whispering prestissimo appropriate perhaps to the assassination scene in *Macbeth* but not to a play that both dramatically and linguistically demands space and time in which to develop and round out itself. The director, Michael Benthall, presumably hoped to achieve continuous tension by this speed; but *Hamlet* does not acquire its momentum by steady acceleration, as *Othello* and *Macbeth*; it is rather a series of increasing surges with a period of rest or recoil after each while power is gathered for the next. Confined within the director's plan, Richard Burton could make no more than a lightweight of the Prince (still further dwarfed by the reduction of his 'fell and mighty opposite' to a bibulous buffoon); he was already at his wits' end when the play began and never had time to settle into the steadiness and weight required of a tragic hero, and this hero in particular.

On the plus side of the account must go three productions that had at least moments of much more than average quality. The new production of *Henry IV, Part 1*, added by Donald Wolfit to his repertory at the King's Theatre, Hammersmith, was an appropriate vehicle for an actor excelling in bravura. Few men can bring off, as Wolfit can, the great set pieces such as the Honour speech, the story of the men in buckram, or the play extempore, with so nice a balance of control and abandon; few can pack such a concentration of mirth into a single phrase— "I knew you", delivered with equal emphasis on each word. But the waves of personality are so strong that they overwhelm the play as a whole and demolish any shape it may have. This, with a play as shapely as *Henry IV, Part 1*, is a pity. The magnification of Falstaff, too, only sentimentalizes him and in the end diminishes his force. The children in the audience love this great cuddly teddy-bear, but that is not quite what Shakespeare intended.

Nothing, not even a Bastard less oddly lackadaisical and unsympathetic than Richard Burton's, can give unity to that play of shreds and patches, *King John*, but George Devine's production at the Vic at least brought out how powerful some of the individual scenes are, and incidentally exploded the often repeated cliché of criticism to the effect that the introduction of the papal legate is a propagandist's irrelevance: we can now see that Pandulph is there to give the last turn of the screw to the highly dramatic scene of the French king's shifting allegiance. John's incitement of Hubert to the murder of Arthur had all the grip expected of it, and Fay Compton proved that in the hands of an actress of her calibre the railings of Constance can be not only rhetorically effective but deeply moving. But it is a tiresome, gritty play.

More rewarding was *The Tempest*, produced by Robert Helpmann at the same theatre. In much it did not rise above the well-carpentered class, and the masque was positively arty-crafty; but it was redeemed by Leslie Hurry's imaginative setting and by the most admirable Prospero of Michael Hordern. The play opened with the stage bare, save for the permanent set, a broad arch flanked by two narrower ones. In front of this Prospero appeared, the controller of the action; at his gesture trailing foliage, the luxuriance of the isle, crept down over the pillars of the set, and the stage filled with dimly seen spirits suggesting, by their swaying motion, the encircling sea. Then, in a sudden pool of light at the centre of the dusky stage appeared the deck of the endangered ship, its confusion and wild motion perfectly conveyed by the swinging of a lantern in contrary motion to the now almost invisible spirits, and by the crazy spinning of the wheel after the helmsman had abandoned it. As the hurly-burly died, a slow dawn spread over the backcloth behind the arches and grew to a rain-washed sky, against which a few details of the island landscape, the wispy plumes and filaments of exotic plants, showed faintly. It was an underwater world, as if Prospero's retreat had been one of those magic caverns in the ocean bed so beloved of the early romancers, and the characters had all suffered a sea-change as soon as they set foot in it. It was the perfect setting for this Prospero, whose grave calm did not altogether hide the storm of bitterness through which he has passed. Some critics found Hordern a 'prose Prospero', but they must have come to the theatre with preconceived ideas of his quality and left their ears at home. With Robert Hardy (whose ivory-painted Ariel also shocked the critics) he gave us one deeply memorable scene (Plate VIIB) and that the climax of the play. Ariel reports the plight of the prisoners:

> Your charm so strongly works 'em,
> That if you now beheld them, your affections
> Would become tender.

"Dost thou think so, spirit?" cries Prospero in a voice that carries the burning memory of his wrongs. "Mine would, sir, were I human", replies Ariel, his strained, high, level tones emphasizing his distance from humanity, and his head falls in wondering submission on his breast. Prospero turns away abruptly, pauses, turns more slowly up stage, and walks a few paces. Another pause, and he turns back to Ariel—"And mine shall", very quietly, with a slow expiration of relief. Though there is still more than a trace of fire in "Though with their high wrongs I am struck to the quick", the rest of the speech in which the wronged man renounces revenge was quiet—though delivered with exquisite modulation within the narrow range of tone—and sadly smiling. And then the farewell to magic, beginning softly, affectionately with the elves, the voice curling round the "demi-puppets" with caressing fondness, but soon growing strong, resonantly strong, for the mutinous winds and the rifting of Jove's stout oak. "But this" (wryly) "rough magic I here abjure", and the speech ends slow and deep as the drowned book itself. The whole of this movement was without a flaw, and so was Prospero's epilogue; but, alas, even such buoyant sailing, such auspicious gales as we had here, could not carry us through the doldrums of certain other scenes in this *Tempest*.

To the Old Vic also goes the credit for the one production of the season that was full of interest and excitement throughout—*All's Well That Ends Well*. By every test it should have been a thoroughly bad one, and I have heard that a young actor-producer of talent walked out half-way through the performance declaring that he had never seen a worse. Faced with a difficult play to put over, Michael Benthall resorted to all the most disreputable tricks of the trade—drastic cutting, transposing, the masking of awkward speeches with music or outrageous buffoonery. Yet it was not only in spite of these tricks but partly because of them that the producer was able to offer a coherent, convincing, and, as far as I know, a new view of Shakespeare's play, at least to those who are prepared to allow that in theatrical affairs the end may justify the means.

The difficulties of the play are rather conceptual than verbal. We have had it drummed into us by every commentator that this is a problem play, and that its subject is 'unpleasant'—in Shaw's sense or worse. No modern audience, we are told, can stomach a hero as priggish and as caddish as Bertram, or sympathize with a heroine who like Helena is determined that a man who does not love her shall accept her as his wife, and who resorts to the most ignoble tricks to cheat him into doing so. The comic sub-plot of the Braggart Parolles is despicable in its barrenness, and the only characters in the play that deserve attention and respect are the King of France and the Countess Rousillon, who both possess a wise nobility worthy of a better play.

Benthall's first step was to take the King and the Countess down a peg. The King became a figure of fun and the affairs of his court pure farce. He was attended by a couple of comic doctors, one fat, one thin, and by a friar who kept up a running Paternoster in a high monotone. His speeches were punctuated by sudden grimaces and yowling cries as his ailment griped him. Even his lucid intervals were diversified by similar 'business'. During the long speech to Bertram in which the King recalls his youth, the courtiers began to chatter among themselves, growing louder and louder until he was driven to shout them down. When he made a joke he would pause until the court had duly acknowledged it with forced laughter. After his cure at Helena's hands he still remained something of a caricature, with the tetchiness of Old Capulet and the blether of Polonius. The Countess was not ragged to this degree, but Fay Compton played the part not as the aristocratic paragon of tradition but as a very human old woman whose nobility appeared rather in what she did than in the doing of it. She was bent and crabbed, her gestures had an arthritic awkwardness, her utterance was creaky, abrupt, arbitrary. By such treatment both King and Countess became more homely, nearer to earth, and their judgements on the action more humanly convincing from their being more than a little touched with human frailty.

To this roughly individual and 'de-idealized' Chorus was added a powerful reinforcement in the shape of Michael Hordern's Parolles, which should have utterly shattered the theory that Shakespeare's Braggart is a more than usually inept version of the dullest of all stock figures. This Parolles was brimful of vitality, and a masterpiece of comic invention. As befits one who is to be found a sheep in wolf's clothing, he began by looking the opposite, his long hungry face in itself a comic contrast to the gay Florentine doublet with its huge hanging sleeves. The wolf soon begins to look a good deal sillier, and Hordern was brilliant in inventing a series of mimes to express Parolles's attempts to maintain his dignity in face of Lord Lafeu's quizzing—hurt, and chilling at the first suspicion, a scraggy cockerel when trying to outface his tormentor, at last

PLATE V

A. *Othello*, Shakespeare Memorial Theatre, 1954. Produced by ANTONY QUALE; designed by TANYA MOISEIWITSCH. UNDER THE AWNING

B. *A Midsummer Night's Dream*, Shakespeare Memorial Theatre, 1954. Produced by GEORGE DEVINE; designed by MOTLEY. THE RUDE MECHANICALS

PLATE VI

A. *All's Well That Ends Well*, Old Vic Theatre. Produced by
MICHAEL BENTHALL; designed by ROGER FURSE. LAFEU
AND PAROLLES—"SIMPLY THE THING I AM"

B. *All's Well That Ends Well*.
THE KING MARRIES BERTRAM TO HELENA

PLATE VII

A. *A Midsummer Night's Dream.* OBERON AND PUCK

B. *The Tempest*, Old Vic Theatre.
Produced by ROBERT HELPMANN; designed by
LESLIE HURRY. PROSPERO AND ARIEL

PLATE VIII

A. *Romeo and Juliet*. Performed by the drama students of the State Conservatoire of Ankara at the ancient theatre of Aspendus, April 1953. THE DANCE (I, v)

B. "CAN YOU TELL ME WHERE I MAY FIND THE YOUNG ROMEO?" (XI, iv)

swallowing with anguish the sour plum of his inability to answer back without calling down retribution. His gait was as expressive as his face. His entry in procession with the victorious Florentine army, himself in dudgeon over the disgrace of the lost drum, brought down the house—a jobbling, unco-ordinated motion, head bobbing forward between limp shoulders from which the arms dangled, feet flapping carelessly down in the abandonment of utter disgust. Equally satisfying was his return, in apparent eagerness to recapture the drum single-handed, the beaky nose uplifted and seeming to draw the rigid, gawky body after it in over-acted determination. And in the climax to this sub-plot, the interrogation of Parolles by the practical jokers who have ambushed and blindfolded him, every move and every tone was deft and delightful: the anxious gabbling of the numbers as he tumbles over himself to betray the military strength of his own side, the confidential becking of his interrogator in order to impart one extra titbit of lying scandal about his superior officers, the self-hugging satisfaction at getting through the interview, he thinks, so adroitly. When Parolles is finally unblindfolded, and discovers his captors to be his own comrades, Hordern managed an immediate and breath-taking transition from farce to deadly earnest. At the discovery he closed his eyes and fell straight backward into the arms of his attendants; then, as with taunts they prepare to leave him, he slithered to the ground, becoming wizened and sly on the instant, and with "simply the thing I am shall make me live" revealed an essential meanness not only in Parolles but in human nature as a whole. For effect the moment is akin to Lear's "unaccommodated man is no more but such a poor, bare, forked animal as thou art"; but whereas it is the physical insignificance of man that Poor Tom shows us in a flash, Parolles gives us his spiritual degradation. (Plate VI A.)

Having provided a rough and realistic framework to the drama, the producer could afford to play down the awkward facts of life in its main argument. Accordingly the story of Helena and Bertram was given the remoteness of a fairy-tale, or at least of the medieval fabliau from which Shakespeare took it. The sets immediately suggested the sense in which the story was to be read. Behind the three arches of the permanent facade a backcloth with a country scene that might have come from an illuminated manuscript created Rousillon; an equally stylized view of Florence transported us to Italy. When the action shifted to Paris, sliding panels of Notre Dame quickly blotted out the country, while in Florence the undisguised manipulation of hinged screens composed the Capilet interior. Against such ingenious and delicate stage-contraptions it was appropriate that Claire Bloom should play Helena as Cinderella. Opinions about this actress differ, and I was prepared to find no more than a beginner of talent whom youth, beauty, and an appearance in a notable film had magnified into a star. I am still in two minds about her. She moved with admirable grace, she had an appealing and ingenuous charm, and—except for a few tiresome mannerisms—she spoke musically and with authority, even managing the awkward couplet soliloquy in her first scene with a skill that made an insult of the instrumental accompaniment officiously provided by the producer. And yet her performance made no coherent impression, and the spectator was left in irritated puzzlement as to what exactly the actress had been driving at. Her vehemence in the early soliloquies—was it impulsiveness and the sudden abandon of passion long pent up? Her almost hysterical reaction when trapped by the Countess into revealing her secret love for Bertram (a scene to which Fay Compton's motherly shrewdness gave a rare tenderness)—was this violence the index of a gentle nature torn between love and loyalty, or of a wayward obstinacy? Did the aggressiveness of her rejoinders to Parolles's innuendoes come from the self-confidence of innocence or the hardness of a worldly-wise little bourgeoise? No doubt some of these conundrums are implicit in Shakespeare's lines, but it is the business of the actress to resolve them; and slowly the conviction dawned that Claire Bloom was not even attempting the task, that her emphasis came of nothing more than an eagerness to inject the maximum of feeling into every phrase and word. To be blunt, I think she was ranting —and yet she ranted distinctly, there was music if not meaning in her rant; and again what should have been a blemish turned out to be a positive contribution to the total effect of the play. A fairy-tale princess should not be too closely accountable for her actions, and the wildness of this Helena's regrets, even that trick of making her exit lines trail off on a rising intonation, like a great bird taking wing, gave an other-worldly quality to her story.

Bertram's task was easier. He had only to look like Prince Charming (which John Neville did) and to speak handsomely (which he did also). Such distinction, even unaided, might have overborne all our scruples as to the decency of Bertram's conduct, even to the shameless shifts of excuse to which he betakes himself in the last scene. This Bertram, however, was given every assistance by the producer who, taking a hint from Lafeu's "No, no, no, your son was misled with a snipt-taffeta fellow there", made Parolles responsible for all Rousillon's misbehaviour. Bertram, too much a schoolboy still to be allowed by the French King to go to the wars, was shown taking his cue at every step from his unsavoury pedagogue. It was Parolles whose nods and becks strengthened Bertram in his first resistance to the King's command that he should marry a commoner. Having married her, he appeared to soften towards her, and would have given her the kiss she so pathetically begs at parting had not a "Psst!" from Parolles recalled him to his previous resolution. Shakespeare makes Parolles the factotum in Bertram's arrangements for the disposal of his wife; Benthall made him the prime mover as well.

King and Countess as Disney dwarfs, the hero and heroine reduced to decorative pasteboard (Plate VIB), Parolles taking over the play as a sort of amateurish Mephistopheles—no wonder the orthodox were disapproving. Yet to me at least this lightening and de-personalizing of the story, this removal of the play into the half-world of pantomime and Grimms' Fairy Tales, suddenly revealed its kinship not, as is usually supposed, with *Measure for Measure* and *Troilus*, but with the last romances. With these it shares the theme of paradise lost and paradise regained: the penitent Bertram recovers the wife he has cast off as surely as do Leontes and Posthumus, and his restoration to Helena makes her as much amends as the meeting of Ferdinand and Miranda does to Prospero. Here, however, it is themselves that the losers lose and find, and their redemption is their own and not the work of another more innocent generation. The pattern in this condensed form does not perhaps make so good a play as in its extended shape, where the processes are more clear-cut; but it does make a play, a much better play when seen as a first sketch for *Winter's Tale* than as a botched *Measure*.

If the Vic succeeded in removing *All's Well* from the accepted canon of Shakespeare's Plays Unpleasant, Stratford (if we are to believe the critics) redressed the balance by corrupting *A Midsummer Night's Dream*. The producer, George Devine, had evidently decided that the conventional prettinesses were to be avoided at all costs. Motley's set was severely formal, the decoration consisting of more or less balanced groups of stylized metallic trees like the leaden cypresses in a toy farmyard. The backcloth showed the night sky, or the distant Parthenon outlined as if in neon lights. On the stage proper a low platform with sloping, banked sides had been superimposed, leaving a narrow playing space at front and sides. At the back this platform was carried up into a higher platform or narrow terrace, and at the junction of the two levels, back centre, an ingenious hollow or burrow had been constructed in which Puck could lurk or evade pursuit. These different 'stations' provided ample scope for the multifarious action of the play: the lovers might be sleeping on the forestage, with their heads pillowed on the bank of the raised platform on which Oberon and his train disported themselves, while Titania reclined with Bottom on the terrace and Puck watched the proceedings from his hidey-hole. On such a stage, too, the hide and seek between Lysander, Demetrius and Puck became both convincing and hilarious.

It should be clear already that in this production more emphasis was to be given to comic action than to poetry, and it is not therefore surprising that the centre of gravity lay with Bottom and his friends. The comedy of the rude mechanicals (Plate V B) was played for all it was worth, yet never for a moment overplayed. Teamwork was excellent, and it is only because their parts are the more important that special praise must be given to Leo McKern for his eagerly dogmatic Quince and to the engaging Bottom of Anthony Quayle, button-nosed and with red hair crew cut, as delightedly surprised by his own prowess as an actor as by his adventures among the fairies. The play of Pyramus and Thisbe was as usual overlaid with a great deal of business, but for once it was strictly relevant and in character. No less than three of the players, for instance, were shown battling desperately with their own accoutrements, yet each of these battles was quite distinct and entirely appropriate to the man engaged. The scroll that refused to remain unrolled was the aptest cross for the impatient Quince and gave a series of neat cues for the mis-placed stops in his prologue. Pyramus's flamboyant turban gradually unwinding itself as the play proceeded gave Bottom ideal scope to demonstrate the power of the Innocent to rise, with a bewildered resilience, above any disaster that fate could put upon him; while the obstinate Wall was perfectly exhibited in his determination to discharge his part conscientiously in despite of the unyielding lime and roughcast that sought to blindfold him and overbalance him at every step. It is a measure of the faithfulness shown by these clowns to themselves (and so to Shake-speare) that their two funniest moments were unscripted. When the difficulty of introducing moonshine into their theatre first strikes them, their mute consternation, sustained without a blink by all six actors through minutes of vociferous applause from the audience, gave us the men themselves; and so did the Bergamask dance into which they threw themselves with hair-raising zeal and a plugging rhythm maintained through every conceivable contretemps.

The comedy of the four lovers was naturally enough conducted on a higher level of elegance, but this too was characterized by skilled management and the well-drilled execution of com-plicated evolutions. Helena's pursuit of Demetrius was almost an exercise in ballet, the pursuer arresting her victim each time at the last possible moment by catching the extreme of his gar-ments just as he turns to fly, and finally laying hold of the naked sword with which he threatens her. Equally artificial were the losings and refindings in the wood: the distraught Helena wanders, unsuspecting, to the very point at which Demetrius lies asleep, and with a petulant stamp within an inch of his nose startles him (and herself) back into dialogue. This is all very well, but such schematized playing means that the dialogue must have an artificiality in keeping with the action and any hint of colour must be excluded from the lines. Lysander and Demetrius were vigorous enough, but in them there is little depth at the best of times. Something of value, on the other hand, does go out of the play when Zena Walker is constrained to make no more of Hermia than a pouting bobby-soxer and Barbara Jefford's natural richness of intonation must be flattened into the mincing goosiness of this Restoration Helena.

It was the fairies, however, that caused the real trouble with the critics. Devine sought, very properly, to emphasize their distinction from human kind, their strangeness, their remoteness from normality, and, with his designers, had seen as the symbol of this quality not the dainty midget, the tutu fairy, the decorative butterfly of recent tradition, but a bird, creature of freaks and passions that sometimes appear very like our own, and yet closer akin to the reptiles than to man. Accordingly the fairies were beaked and feathered (Plate VII A), Titania with broad white eye-streaks from crown to bill that gave her the air, light, bright and ferocious, of a falcon. Moth, Mustard-seed and the rest kept up a constant flirting and fluttering (an irritation this) each having a distinctive movement and gesture, just as each species of bird has its own characteristic courting display. The song "Ye spotted snakes" began as the screech of an owl and ended as the cooing of a dove.

Puck alone could not be fitted into this scheme, and for him a different symbol of the human and non-human had to be found—the ape, the wombat whose very ungainliness endeared him to Christina Rossetti, the hedgehog so captivating in his strangeness. Puck had something of all these in him, walking with the bow-legged jut-bottomed gracelessness of a chimpanzee, yet with an instant swiftness and nimbleness when required, regarding human affairs with a quick, bright, alien eye that made his observation, "Lord, what fools these mortals be!" all the more forceful as coming from one so obviously outside and distant from the thing observed.

Here again it was necessary that in the interests of consistency poetry should go by the board, and in this play such a sacrifice cannot be accepted. I am very ready to believe that Devine's fairies are much nearer to Shakespeare's than are the dream-children on which most of us were brought up; but *A Midsummer Night's Dream*—far more certainly than even the *All's Well* discovered by Benthall—is a romantic and not a realistic comedy, and at the time Shakespeare wrote it he was not consistent. He was quite prepared to digress, to write for the sake of writing or of decoration. "Ye spotted snakes" and "I know a bank" are there for their own sakes and for the colour they give to the play as a whole; they are not 'in character' and, though their speakers be bird-fairies, to scream or pipe or warble them is strictly a *non sequitur* and an admission that the producer is unaware of what his author is at.

One great virtue this business-like production did possess, in that it brought out the contrasting strands in the play and so Shakespeare's skill in weaving them together. With the lovers deliberately dehydrated it was even possible to make a clear distinction between them and the Assyrian sumptuousness of Theseus and his court, so that, with the rustic clowns and the inhuman fairies, the action plainly moved on four levels. We should be grateful for such intellectual treats, but they are not enough; the spirit of delight hovered more surely over the fitful brilliances of Wolfit, the lone authenticity of Hordern's Prospero, than over Devine's streamlined job.

THE YEAR'S CONTRIBUTIONS TO
SHAKESPEARIAN STUDY

1. CRITICAL STUDIES

reviewed by CLIFFORD LEECH

E. E. Stoll[1] has directed strong words to interpreters of Shakespeare. He attacks those who would separate the writer's 'meaning' from his intention, though he admits that the original intention may not have been fully carried out and that the 'meaning' is not to be simply abstracted. If Stoll blurs his case by confusing the merely whimsical commentators with those who may not win universal assent to their views but honestly believe that they are approaching the significance of the works they examine, there is yet no doubt that the warning here given is salutary. It is easy to grow impatient with the dramatist's complexity, to offer as his 'meaning' some part of his total utterance, or indeed unconsciously to adjust a play to fit our own inclinations. We should recognize that a creative writer's intention may develop during composition, that all of it may never come into his full consciousness, that our perception of his intention can never be sure. The interpreter's primary duties are to know his own fallibility, to be sceptical of his own simplifications, and yet to strive towards a convincing exposition of what he believes to be true. René Taupin,[2] noting the way in which Hamlet became a starting-point for romantic reverie in nineteenth-century France, observes: 'What Shakespeare wanted him to be interests only the pedants.' That is engaging, but it is not criticism.

In the period under review there have been several books and many articles devoted to individual plays. Though many of these are useful in adding to our understanding of detail, there is a smaller group where the critic seems to have come to grips with his chosen play as a totality or has explored a particular aspect of the work without distorting its whole structure. Allan Gilbert[3] has brought out the contrasted attitudes to the King and his war suggested in *Henry V*: patriotism and its often grim parody and the demonstration of kingly duty are all to be recognized in the play's substance. Hermann Heuer,[4] usefully noting the contrast presented by Dryden's simplification, has looked steadily at *Troilus and Cressida* and sees that its satiric element, evident at times even in the handling of Hector, coexists with a deep concernment with moral principle. D. J. Enright[5] has shown how in *Coriolanus* the behaviour of both patricians and plebeians is scrutinized with something of cold justice, and how limitations are imposed on our sympathy with the hero. A sensitive study of *Love's Labour's Lost* has come from Miss Bobbyann Roesen,[6] who particularly observes how the notions of mutability and death, so marked in the

---

[1] 'Intentions and Instinct', *Modern Language Quarterly*, XIV (December 1953), 375–412.

[2] 'The Myth of Hamlet in France in Mallarmé's Generation', *ibid.* pp. 432–47.

[3] 'Patriotism and Satire in Henry V', *Studies in Shakespeare*, edited by A. D. Matthews and C. M. Emery (Coral Gables, Florida: University of Miami Press, 1953), pp. 40–64.

[4] 'Troilus und Cressida in neuerer Sicht', *Shakespeare-Jahrbuch*, LXXXIX (1953), 106–27.

[5] '*Coriolanus*: Tragedy or Debate?', *Essays in Criticism*, IV (January 1954), 1–19.

[6] '*Love's Labour's Lost*', *Shakespeare Quarterly*, IV (October 1953), 411–26.

play's ending, are given recurrent expression throughout. There is balanced judgement in D. A. Traversi's[1] continuation of his study of *Lear*: he sees positive values emerging from the experience of suffering, without finding in the play an easy consolation. Francis Fergusson[2] has compared *The Comedy of Errors* with *Much Ado*, noting that we are brought close to Beatrice and Benedick not by what they say but by the impressions we have of their natures. While, moreover, the earlier comedy is constructed out of a series of farcical events, *Much Ado* derives unity from being written round an occasion of rejoicing. Arthur Colby Sprague[3] has said what should perhaps be the last word on Maurice Morgann, while fully realizing that Sir John knew his own cowardice, saw its comedy, and enjoyed it.

Three plays—*Measure for Measure*, *Hamlet* and *Othello*—have had books wholly devoted to them. In her study of the first of these, Miss Mary Lascelles[4] has considered the play's sources, the state of its text, the responses we make to its characters. She sees the Duke as a Renaissance Governor rather than an embodied Providence. She tries to present the play as a unity, where perhaps not every reader will follow her, but towards the end of her book she suggests not only that we today experience difficulty in appreciating tragi-comedy but that Shakespeare was under constraint in the form. Many things in the play leave her ill-content: Act IV, she believes, must be textually corrupt; the Duke's octosyllabics may, she suggests, have originally functioned as a Prologue to the second half of the play when it was acted, perhaps at Court, with an interval; she brushes aside the question how long the Duke had known of Angelo's treatment of Mariana. The unity that she attempts to find is no easy simplification, and one feels that it is offered with an awareness of its fragility. The book should do good if its caution and its dubieties are emulated by subsequent critics. Recent articles have often demonstrated the need for care in the handling of this play. Harold S. Wilson[5] sees a resemblance between *Measure for Measure* and *The Tempest*, with Fletcherian affinities in both. *The Tempest*, he suggests, is a more formal, less oblique statement of the ideas of guidance and forgiveness that underlie *Measure for Measure*. He assumes, it appears, a unity of manner in the earlier play. Paul N. Siegel[6] finds that each guilty figure in the drama receives treatment appropriate to him within the bounds of comedy, so that in one sense measure is indeed given for measure. John L. Harrison[7] believes that 'the meaning of the play' is to be found in the commonplace that heart and tongue should but often do not function in harmony. S. Nagarajan[8] accepts the notion of the Duke as a figure of divine proportions, with all that customarily goes along with that view.

Diverse views of *Hamlet* are taken by Bertram Joseph[9] and Jean Paris.[10] Joseph would pluck

---

[1] '*King Lear* (III)', *Scrutiny*, XIX (Spring 1953), 206–30. The first two parts of this article were noted in *Shakespeare Survey*, 7.

[2] '*The Comedy of Errors* and *Much Ado About Nothing*', *Sewanee Review*, LXII (Winter 1954), 24–37.

[3] 'Gadshill Revisited', *Shakespeare Quarterly*, IV (April 1953), 125–37.

[4] *Shakespeare's Measure for Measure* (University of London, Athlone Press, 1953).

[5] 'Action and Symbol in *Measure for Measure* and *The Tempest*', *Shakespeare Quarterly*, IV (October 1953), 375–84.

[6] '*Measure for Measure*: The Significance of the Title', *ibid.* IV (July 1953), 317–20.

[7] 'The Convention of "Heart and Tongue" and the Meaning of *Measure for Measure*', *ibid.* V (January 1954), 1–10.

[8] 'A Note on the Duke in *Measure for Measure*', *Half-yearly Journal of the Mysore University*, XIII (March 1953), 1–9.

[9] *Conscience and the King. A Study of Hamlet* (Chatto and Windus, 1953).

[10] *Hamlet ou Les Personnages du Fils* (Paris: Éditions du Seuil, 1953).

out the heart of the mystery and present it on the smallest available salver. Here Hamlet's delay is due to his fear of the damnation that will ensue if he obeys a Ghost from hell. Joseph does not consider the contradictory Elizabethan notions of revenge; he has no explanation for the play's concern with complex human relationships or for its frequent grossness of speech; without warrant in the Ghost's words, he insists that Hamlet's duty is not only to kill Claudius but to unmask him before the Danes. Ghosts in Elizabethan drama, however, were not deceitful: the audience for *Hamlet* in 1601 would credit the Ghost's words and surely feel surprise when, after the arrival of the players, Hamlet explains his behaviour by a fear of hell. Joseph is probably right in his insistence on the vague meaning of 'adulterate' in the Ghost's words, but the book suffers more than usually from the desire to make all plain. Paris's book, however, delights in complication. He sees Hamlet, Laertes and Fortinbras as representatives of different aspects of the Avenging Son: all the dramatic events stem from the wrong done by the elder Hamlet to the elder Fortinbras, with a working out of a consequent doom on the house. Shakespeare may well have had such a Senecan idea echoing faintly in his mind, and it is interesting that we learn of Fortinbras in I, i before the Danish Prince is mentioned. But the Ghost nowhere refers to the Fortinbras affair. This critic sees *Hamlet* as a clash of forces rather than characters: in every tragedy abstract forces are in conflict, but in *Hamlet* our attention is much more given to the characters and the presented incidents than to the suggested cosmic background. Again, in the result, we are here offered a simplified version of the play. Among recent articles on *Hamlet* the most interesting is I. J. Semper's[1] reply to R. W. Battenhouse[2] on the pagan or Christian nature of the Ghost. Semper rightly emphasizes the Christian colouring of the figure, but it is difficult for him to meet Battenhouse's argument that a soul from Purgatory should not demand revenge: he has to interpret "Taint not thy mind" as constituting Hamlet "an executioner akin to the hangman appointed by the State": this not only strains credulity but reminds us that Shakespeare was not much later to give odd pictures of public executioners in Abhorson and Pompey. The Ghost seems to remain a composite figure. William Empson[3] has assembled some curious observations, including the statement that Polonius and Laertes were manifestly anxious to have a royal marriage in the family. J. Max Patrick[4] considers what he calls the *erotic estimate* of Ophelia's character as opposed to the *sentimental estimate*. He thinks that Shakespeare left the interpretation, like so much in *Hamlet*, open to conjecture and thus enriched the play's effect: this, however, is to miss the distinction between the sense of contradictions in a character which we feel is nevertheless a unity and the sense that Shakespeare has withheld information, which Patrick here implies. Like Joseph, Andrew J. Green[5] feels the mouse-trap to be a necessary testing of the Ghost's words: he is sure that every detail of the play-scene has been carefully planned by Hamlet, that the players perform their parts brilliantly (despite "pox, leave thy damnable faces"), and that Hamlet must be a Man of Action, for otherwise he would be "a psychopathic case well outside of humanity". In contrast to this quaint idealizing, we find Richard Paul Janaro[6]

---

[1] 'The Ghost in *Hamlet*: Pagan or Christian?', *The Month*, n.s., IX (April 1953), 222-34.

[2] Noted in *Shakespeare Survey*, 6.

[3] '*Hamlet* When New (Part II)', *Sewanee Review*, LXI (Spring 1953), 185-205. Part I of this article was noted in *Shakespeare Survey*, 7. [4] 'The Problem of Ophelia', *Studies in Shakespeare*, pp. 139-44.

[5] 'The Cunning of the Scene', *Shakespeare Quarterly*, IV (October 1953), 395-404.

[6] 'Dramatic Significance in *Hamlet*', *Studies in Shakespeare*, pp. 107-15.

K*

presenting the view that Hamlet is not one man but five, all used as appropriate in different dramatic situations, which apparently exist each for the sake of its momentary thrill: this is deduced from the general proposition that the Elizabethans, having no concept of 'evolution', could not imagine 'growth' or 'development' in character.

We are on firmer ground in G. R. Elliott's[1] full study of *Othello*. He goes through the play scene by scene, perhaps over-elaborately paraphrasing the play's content, but with a shrewd eye for human imperfections. Pride he sees as the root of Othello's disaster, and he has good observations to make on Desdemona and Cassio. It is more difficult to follow him in his notion of a true 'wedding' for Othello and Desdemona at the end of the play. He brusquely disposes of the hazardous consequences of Othello's suicide, and joins with those critics who find that this tragedy has peace at its close. In remarkable contrast to Elliott's view is Paul N. Siegel's[2] relishing of Othello's damnation: he even finds that we are left with a "feeling of reconciliation" because the damnation is merited. His theology is surely unsound when he sees Othello as damned from the moment of his killing Desdemona. E. E. Stoll,[3] dealing with Othello's acceptance of Iago's slander, urges that we should witness the action with a child's alleged readiness to believe what it is told, the dramatist being allowed his *données* in the interest of theatrical surprise. He is of course right to insist on theatrical performance as the test, on the value of surprise, and on the ultimately greater importance of the general picture of human destiny rather than of the verisimilitude of character and action. But surprise is most acceptable when it coexists with an immediate realization of psychological congruence (as when Hamlet kills Polonius); the general picture offered can only assert its validity if first we have been persuaded to accept the particular instance; and in the theatre there seems no difficulty in Othello's deception. This last point is convincingly made by Marvin Rosenberg[4] in a reply to Stoll's earlier discussions of the play. Félix Carrère[5] notes the use of the monologue in this play to show the speaker's state of mind, and interestingly observes that Othello and Desdemona, when speaking together, seem often to use differing languages; he stresses also, like Elliott, the imperfection of Othello's love. In John Money's[6] analysis of "It is the cause", perhaps the most useful point is the hint of the comic that he sees underlying Shakespeare's presentation of the Moor.

The remaining plays have not been so persistently handled during the year. Thomas A. Perry[7] suggests a relationship between Proteus and the current view of the Italianate Englishman. Miss Thelma Nelson Greenfield[8] finds that Christopher Sly is more fully characterized in *The Shrew* than in *A Shrew*, becoming a representative of "the literal world" in contrast to the world of dramatic poetry. K. Wentersdorf[9] claims that a fair sprinkling of Shakespearian images is to

[1] *Flaming Minister. A Study of Othello as Tragedy of Love and Hate* (Durham, North Carolina: Duke University Press, 1953).

[2] 'The Damnation of Othello', *PMLA*, LXVIII (Decembe J1953), 1068–78.

[3] 'Slander in Drama', *Shakespeare Quarterly*, IV (October 1953), 433–50.

[4] 'A Sceptical Look at Sceptical Criticism', *Philological Quarterly*, XXXIII (January 1954), 66–77.

[5] 'Deux Motifs sur l'*Othello* de Shakespeare: le monologue,—l'amour et la jalousie', *Annales publiées par la Faculté des Lettres de Toulouse: Littératures*, II (November 1953), 15–30.

[6] 'Othello's "It is the cause…" An Analysis', *Shakespeare Survey*, 6 (1953), 94–105.

[7] 'Proteus, Wry-Transformed Traveller', *Shakespeare Quarterly*, V (January 1954), 33–40.

[8] 'The Transformation of Christopher Sly', *Philological Quarterly*, XXXIII (January 1954), 34–42.

[9] 'The Authenticity of *The Taming of the Shrew*', *Shakespeare Quarterly*, V (January 1954), 11–32.

be found throughout *The Shrew*, and deduces that the play is wholly Shakespeare's. Paul N. Siegel[1] shows the complex of meanings, especially in the last Act, that would suggest themselves when *A Midsummer Night's Dream* was acted at a wedding. Karl Hammerle[2] strains our belief in identifying Bottom and Quince as a composite picture of Spenser, and the "little western flower" as Elizabeth Carey, at whose marriage in 1596 the play was perhaps acted. Cary B. Graham[3] stresses the debate-element in *The Merchant of Venice* as leading to a variety of interpretations: this approach might, if more fully developed, suggest a relationship between the play and the 'dark' comedies. T. W. Craik[4] tries to smooth out awkward places in *Much Ado* by suggesting a resemblance to *A Midsummer Night's Dream*. He admits, however, that the good-humoured effect is not consistently maintained. Examining the comedies as a whole, Northrop Frye[5] relates their characters to the stock-types taken over by Renaissance writers from classical practice and to the four comic types referred to in the *Nichomachean Ethics*: there is some straining in the attempt to fit all the characters into the Aristotelian moulds.

Several writers have concerned themselves with the histories as a group. Robert Adger Law,[6] while drawing attention to the careful linking of plays one to another, is sceptical of the view that the 'tetralogies' were planned as wholes. In reply, E. M. W. Tillyard[7] agrees that the great plan may have developed during composition but insists still on a preconceived outline. Miss Josephine A. Pearce[8] draws attention to the modification of historical event in the interest of the underlying idea, the use of classical rhetoric in the early histories, and the gradual extension of the dramatic field to include the comic and non-historic. Wolfgang H. Clemen[9] shows how, from *Henry VI* to *Richard II* and *John*, Shakespeare's use of foreboding grows in variety and in refinement. Harold Jenkins,[10] in a judicious summary of changing views of the histories during this century, gives sufficient hint that the more popular interpretations cannot be considered as firmly established.

The characterization of the tragic hero is the concern of Huntington Brown.[11] He contrasts the more sympathetic figures with Titus, Coriolanus and Timon, seeing in the first group, often at their first appearance, evidence of a divided mind: each of them has an outer character, highly individualized, concerned in particular and strange actions, and an inner character, speaking to us in soliloquy, that belongs to the community. Brown surely exaggerates in seeing the inner character as an 'everyday fellow', almost a Chorus-figure, yet he usefully suggests how Shakespeare, by the use of often colloquial soliloquy, makes us see his heroes as of our kin.

[1] '*A Midsummer Night's Dream* and the Wedding Guests', *ibid.* IV (April 1953), 139–44.

[2] 'Das Laubenmotiv bei Shakespeare und die Frage: Wer waren Bottom und die Little Western Flower?', *Anglia*, LXXI (1953), 310–30.

[3] 'Standards of Value in *The Merchant of Venice*', *Shakespeare Quarterly*, IV (April 1953), 145–51.

[4] '*Much Ado About Nothing*', *Scrutiny*, XIX (October 1953), 297–316.

[5] 'Characterization in Shakespearian Comedy', *Shakespeare Quarterly*, IV (July 1953), 271–7.

[6] 'Links between Shakespeare's History Plays', *Studies in Philology*, L (April 1953), 168–87.

[7] 'Shakespeare's Historical Cycle: Organism or Compilation', *ibid.* II (January 1954), 34–9. In a rejoinder (*ibid.* 40–1), Law reiterates his belief that the two Parts of *Henry IV* are 'quite different' plays.

[8] 'Constituent Elements in Shakespeare's English History Plays', *Studies in Shakespeare*, pp. 145–52.

[9] 'Anticipation and Foreboding in Shakespeare's Early Histories', *Shakespeare Survey*, 6 (1953), 25–35.

[10] 'Shakespeare's History Plays: 1900–1951', *ibid.* pp. 1–15.

[11] 'Enter the Shakespearean Tragic Hero', *Essays in Criticism*, III (July 1953), 285–302.

Miss Carmen Rogers[1] is ingenuously content with seeing the tragedies as illustrating God's punishment of evil-doers. John Earle Uhler,[2] while interestingly observing a critical element in the presentation of Brutus and Portia, proceeds to interpret *Julius Caesar* in a way not recently uncommon with the English histories: Caesar is an enfeebled Respublica, with the politicians representing Principle-without-Practice and the army Practice-without-Principle: the soldiers must take over to redress the damage done by the politicians. Warren D. Smith[3] ingeniously and unconvincingly makes Brutus ask for news of Portia because he wondered if his earlier news was false, his denial that he had heard anything of her being due to his desire, as "an able general", to keep ill tidings from his followers. Irving Ribner[4] successfully challenges Miss Lily B. Campbell's[5] view that Shakespeare was echoing James I's ideas in *Macbeth*, IV, iii: he points out that Macduff, in deciding not to support a Malcolm apparently unfit to rule, goes counter to Stuart doctrine. Brents Stirling[6] shows how the themes of darkness, sleep, raptness and contradiction are almost continuously present in *Macbeth*, and hints that the play is consequently a more complex thing than 'historical criticism' would often suggest.

The last plays have attracted less attention than usual. John Arthos[7] shows how the scenes of *Pericles* have a remote quality fitting the tone of the Gower-narratives: one may feel, however, that the play is sometimes more disturbing than he suggests. Roger J. Trienens[8] manages to believe simultaneously that Leontes's jealousy is apparent from the beginning of I, ii and that Shakespeare is using in this scene 'the tragi-comic technique of surprise'. Bernard Baum,[9] in an engaging comparison of *The Tempest* and *Hairy Ape*, suggests that Shakespeare's play is a simple exposition of an antinomy in Caliban (pure nature) and Prospero (nature-controlled-by-reason).

Heinrich Straumann[10] sees *The Phoenix and the Turtle* as existing on three levels—as an occasional poem, as a literary exercise deriving from Courtly Love, Emblem-devices and Platonist ideas, and as a poem on the possibility of blending Truth and Beauty, through Love, in a single being which, however, can have no progeny. This is ingenious and sensible, though perhaps Shakespeare did not write with the full seriousness that Straumann implies. We may feel more doubt when it is argued that the poem represents a turning-point in Shakespeare's thought, the earlier plays implying no difficulty in the blending here described, the later plays doubting its possibility or being preoccupied with its vulnerability (as in Desdemona and Cordelia). Rufus Putney[11] excellently brings out the comedy in *Venus and Adonis*, especially in its presentation of Venus: he does not deny the didactic element in the poem, but sees this as coexisting with the comic.

[1] 'Heavenly Justice in the Tragedies of Shakespeare', *Studies in Shakespeare*, pp. 116–28.
[2] 'Julius Caesar—a Morality of Respublica', *ibid.* pp. 96–106.
[3] 'The Duplicate Revelation of Portia's Death', *Shakespeare Quarterly*, IV (April 1953), 153–61.
[4] 'Political Doctrine in *Macbeth*', *ibid.* pp. 202–5.　　　　　[5] Noted in *Shakespeare Survey*, 6.
[6] 'The Unity of *Macbeth*', *Shakespeare Quarterly*, IV (October 1953), 385–94.
[7] '*Pericles, Prince of Tyre*: A Study in the Dramatic Use of Romantic Narrative', *ibid.* IV (July 1953), 257–70.
[8] 'The Inception of Leontes' Jealousy in *The Winter's Tale*', *ibid.* 321–6.
[9] '*The Tempest* and *Hairy Ape*: The Literary Incarnation of Mythos', *Modern Language Quarterly*, XIV (September 1953), 258–73.
[10] *Phönix und Taube. Zur Interpretation von Shakespeares Gedankenwelt* (Zürich: Artemis-Verlag, 1953).
[11] '*Venus Agonistes*', *University of Colorado Studies*, Series in Language and Literature, July 1953, pp. 52–66.

Among studies of wider scope the most stimulating is Patrick Cruttwell's.[1] He is perceptive of the complexities in the major plays and the sonnets, and he sees that a situation came into being in the earliest years of the seventeenth century which was eminently suited to the writing of Shakespearian drama. He is inclined to see that brief time as more golden than perhaps it was: for Cruttwell it was the Rationalists and the Puritans who destroyed the 'moment', but among the poets themselves there were conflicts and tensions, with a rationalist strain evident in Chapman, the existence of 'Rival Traditions' in the theatre, and something of Puritanism reluctantly manifesting itself in some major plays. Too easy a contrast is made between Marlowe and the writers of "the Shakespearean moment", and Cruttwell is ill at ease when dealing with later seventeenth-century writers, in whom he misses the 'Anglo-catholic' strain. The forced liveliness which afflicts the writer's style and his occasional signs of partisanship should not blind us to his frequent acuteness. In John Erskine Hankins's[2] account of images which Shakespeare may have derived from well-known sources, a special indebtedness is suggested to Palingenius's *Zodiacus Vitae* and its translation by Barnabe Googe. The alleged derivations are by no means always convincing, but the book demonstrates the widespread occurrence of many ideas, themes and expressions in Renaissance literature. K. J. Spalding[3] presents a Dowdenesque view of Shakespeare's mind, complicated slightly by some recognition of recent work on the histories. The 'philosophy' that he claims to derive from the plays suggests no distinction of mind in the dramatist. Wolfgang J. Weilgart,[4] with the help of diagrams, strange outlines of the plays, and an altogether gnomic form of utterance, tells us how Shakespeare's characters achieve development and transformation. Wolfgang Clemen[5] has studied Shakespeare's use of messengers' speeches and the like: in the early plays such speeches merely extend the range of action, giving it a quasi-epic character; this, for particular effect, may also be used later, but Shakespeare develops a more complicated technique in the imparting of news, working it into dialogue, displaying the effect of the message on those who hear it, and making the messenger share in the emotional ambience which he brings about. Mrs Maria Wickert[6] surveys Shakespeare's uses of the word 'shadow' in sonnets and plays, and emphasizes a number of possibly Platonic implications. George Rylands[7] observes that a dominant idea in a drama may be looked at from many sides, praises the occasional set-speech, and notes how different characters may seem to speak in the accents of different poets, especially, it appears, romantic ones. John Holloway,[8] in illustrating Shakespeare's irony, wrenches some passages to suit his purpose. Miss Una Ellis-Fermor[9] indicates Shakespeare's skill in suggesting a turmoil of mind beneath the words and superficial behaviour that are directly presented. Rudolf Stamm[10] illustrates how Shakespeare, working

[1] *The Shakespearean Moment and its Place in the Poetry of the 17th Century* (Chatto and Windus, 1954).

[2] *Shakespeare's Derived Imagery* (Lawrence, Kansas: University of Kansas Press, 1953).

[3] *The Philosophy of Shakespeare* (Oxford: George Ronald, 1953).

[4] *Shakespeare Psychognostic. Character Evolution and Transformation* (Tokyo: The Hokuseido Press, 1952).

[5] *Wandlung des Botenberichts bei Shakespeare* (Munich: Verlag der Bayerischen Akademie der Wissenschaften, 1952).   [6] 'Das Schattenmotiv bei Shakespeare', *Anglia*, LXXI (1953), 274–309.

[7] *Shakespeare's Poetic Energy* (Cumberlege, 1953: British Academy Shakespeare Lecture for 1951).

[8] 'Dramatic Irony in Shakespeare', *Northern Miscellany of Literary Criticism*, no. 1 (Autumn 1953), 3–16.

[9] 'Shakespeare and the Dramatic Mode', *Neophilologus*, XXXVII (April 1953), 104–12.

[10] *Shakespeare's Word-Scenery with Some Remarks on Stage-History and the Interpretation of his Plays* (Zürich und St Gallen: Polygraphischer Verlag, 1954).

with his Globe stage, can evoke a picture through description or imagery or dramatic reference. G. Wilson Knight[1] has reiterated his view of the plays. Robert M. Adams[2] interestingly notes the device of "the overstepped or obliterated frame" in Shakespeare and Keats, but for a satisfactory treatment of induction-devices and the like much more reference to Shakespeare's predecessors and contemporaries is needed.

2. SHAKESPEARE'S LIFE, TIMES AND STAGE

reviewed by I. A. SHAPIRO

The aspect of Shakespeare's life and times which seems most interesting to researchers at present is the range of his reading and what this may indicate about his intellectual development. Foremost in this field is Virgil Whitaker's *Shakespeare's Use of Learning*,[3] which attempts to chart not only Shakespeare's reading and acquisition of knowledge, but also its effect upon his development as dramatist. As the book proceeds, it concerns itself less and less with the first and more and more with the second of these themes. This change-over is complete by the discussion of *Troilus and Cressida*, which Whitaker regards as "the keystone in the arch of Shakespeare's intellectual development" and "a philosophical poem expounding the ideas fundamental to his tragedies". The attempt made here to trace the extent of Shakespeare's knowledge involves three assumptions which seem to be fallacious and therefore to vitiate many conclusions drawn in the first part of the book. Whitaker first assumes that because we know some of the text-books used in some Elizabethan schools, we can safely infer what Shakespeare was taught at his grammar school. This will be quite unacceptable to anyone aware of the diversity of teaching in our grammar schools even as recently as forty years ago, when they were still staffed by learned individualists whose special interests were apparent in the curriculum as well as in their teaching, and unconfined by external examinations. The diversity must have been even greater in Elizabethan times. We can be certain of nothing about Shakespeare's schooling except that he learnt to read and write in English and Latin. A second assumption is implicit in Whitaker's first chapter: that Shakespeare's reading and knowledge as a schoolboy were limited to what he learnt in school. This may be true of some secondary schoolboys of today; it certainly was not true of English grammar schoolboys even two generations ago. There is no reason to suppose that Stratford was bookless in Shakespeare's youth. Can we be sure that he did not skim through Fabyan, Grafton, Halle, Hardyng or Holinshed while a schoolboy, or through other books found at home or in the homes of relatives and friends, or schoolmasters or parish priests, always well disposed towards a forward and promising schoolboy?

The third assumption is that we can infer from Shakespeare's allusions to the knowledge of his day the limits of his learning. Although Whitaker himself reminds us that we can seldom "conjecture with any safety what he did not know or did not think", this warning seems unfortunately to be forgotten as the argument is developed. Thus one cannot accept Whitaker's

[1] 'The New Interpretation', *Essays in Criticism*, III (October 1953), 382–95.

[2] '*Trompe-l'œil* in Shakespeare and Keats', *Sewanee Review*, LXI (Spring 1953), 238–55.

[3] Virgil K. Whitaker, *Shakespeare's Use of Learning. An Inquiry into the Growth of his Mind and Art* (San Marino, California, The Huntington Library, 1953).

inferences that Shakespeare commenced playwright with slight command of the learning of his day (p. 70), well versed in theology (p. 78) but knowing very little of natural science (p. 81). One must also question whether the early comedies "reflect a…growing familiarity with contemporary literature" (p. 82); their plots encouraged such allusions whereas those of the chronicle plays did not.

The best things in this book are concerned with Shakespeare's treatment of his sources and its significance. There are shrewd and illuminating remarks on *Romeo and Juliet*, for example, and to the discussion of many questions, such as the relations between Prince Henry and Falstaff or the nature of the tragic heroes, Whitaker brings a freshness and common sense which are stimulating. The latter part of his book abounds with excellent analyses of the significance of *Troilus and Cressida*, *Measure for Measure* and the tragedies. His strength is in criticism and interpretation, all the more effective because he sees Shakespeare's plays as full of significance for "our own sentimental and fuzzy-headed age".

Few of the source and parallel hunters present their findings with the caution and modesty which distinguish Arnold Davenport's article[1] on parallels between Nashe's *Pierce Penilesse* and *Hamlet* and *Macbeth*. In the same issue of the same journal G. Blakemore Evans also suggests[2] the same source for some of the *Hamlet* passages cited by Davenport, and both comment on its possible significance for elucidation of the "dram of eale" crux. Kenneth Muir has noted[3] further passages in *Othello* which may have been influenced by Holland's *Pliny*, and cites it to support the Second Folio reading of "feels" for "keeps" in II, iii, 456; Terence Spencer, on the other hand, discussing[4] the same passage, shows that the tideless flow of the waters of "the Propontic and the Hellespont" was widely known in Elizabethan times, and that Shakespeare's knowledge of it need not necessarily derive from Pliny or any other book. Spencer also traces further evidence of Shakespeare's reading of North's *Plutarch* in the reference to "that vile name" Demetrius in *Midsummer Night's Dream*, II, ii, 107, which he explains most satisfactorily. Arnold Davenport detects[5] a burlesque of Lyly's manner, and especially of a passage in *Campaspe*, in Falstaff's mock rebuke of Prince Hal in *1 Henry IV*, II, iv. Kenneth Muir[6] uses Ernst Honigmann's discovery of verbal parallels between Menenius's fable of the body and William Averell's *Mervailous Combat of Contrarieties* to support his views on Shakespeare's use of multiple sources. Peter Ure suggests[7] that Sylvester's translation of a passage from Du Bartas, rather than Eliot's translation in *Ortho-epia Gallica*,[8] may have been in Shakespeare's mind when he wrote *Richard II*, II, i, 40 *seq.*, but as he points out that in a later part of the translation Sylvester himself seems to have been influenced by Shakespeare's play, the correct interpretation of the parallels is obscure. Joseph Stull has found[9] additional support for the possibility that Shakespeare read Plutarch's

[1] A. Davenport, 'Shakespeare and Nashe's *Pierce Penilesse*', *Notes and Queries* (September 1953), pp. 371–4.

[2] G. Blakemore Evans, 'Thomas Nashe and the "Dram of Eale"', *Notes and Queries* (September 1953), pp. 377–8.

[3] Kenneth Muir, 'Holland's Pliny and *Othello*', *Notes and Queries* (December 1953), pp. 513–14.

[4] Terence Spencer, 'Three Shakespearian Notes', *Modern Language Review*, XLIX (January 1954), 48–51.

[5] A. Davenport, 'Notes on Lyly's *Campaspe* and Shakespeare', *Notes and Queries* (January 1954), pp. 19–20.

[6] Kenneth Muir, 'Menenius's Fable', *Notes and Queries* (June 1953), pp. 240–2.

[7] Peter Ure, 'Shakespeare's Play and the French Sources of Holinshed's and Stow's Account of Richard II', *Notes and Queries* (October 1953), pp. 374–7.

[8] See *Shakespeare Survey*, 6 (1953), 89.

[9] Joseph S. Stull, 'Shakespeare and Plutarch's *Life of Pelopidas*', *Notes and Queries* (December 1953), pp. 512–13.

Life of Pelopidas. John Draper has studied Shakespeare's references to the cities of the Lombardy plain, and concludes[1] that he certainly never went to northern Italy, "and to him the names of the famous cities of Lombardy were only names".

No addition to the little we know of Shakespeare's life was made in 1953–4, but speculation has been as rife as ever. Alan Keen has published[2] a more elaborate statement of his belief that annotations in a copy of Halle's *Chronicle* which he bought in 1940 are in Shakespeare's hand. All that seems certain is that an early owner of this book was the "Rychard Newport" who inscribed his initials in April 1565, when he was, judging by the facsimile on p. 124, probably still an adolescent. Keen identifies him with Sir Richard Newport of Ercall (d. 1570) but offers no supporting evidence. On this basis, and the faint possibility that about a hundred years later the book belonged to a Robert Worsley of Lancashire, Keen constructs an elaborate but illusory "connection" with Alexander Houghton of Lea Hall and his servant William Shakeshafte, snatching enthusiastically at every bit of "evidence" that would bring Shakespeare into his picture of the "annotator".

John Berryman has summarized[3] what is known, and much of what has been guessed, about Shakespeare around the age of thirty, adding some conjectures of his own, one of which is that Shakespeare began sonneteering about 1586–7. Judging by his documentation, which is slight and sporadic, his article is intended for very "general" readers, not for scholars.

H. A. Shield resuscitates[4] Grosart's identification of the author of *Love's Martyr* with Sir Robert Chester of Royston, Herts, and argues that it deserves further consideration because Sir Robert was at the Middle Temple with John Salisbury, to whom *Love's Martyr* was dedicated, and also "could not have been a stranger to Shakespeare and his associates", but his "evidence" is far from compelling.

Speculation of a different kind is Harold Grier McCurdy's[5] "venture in psychological method" derived from the "theory of personality projection". "Since the theory of projection is intimately bound up with the theory of dreams, and dreams are more like plays than any other form of literature", Shakespeare's plays seemed suitable material to work on. McCurdy's first three chapters explain "the method" and the theories it is based on. Since "it is scientifically desirable to be quantitative wherever possible...the twelve leading characters of each play...are assigned numerical values indicating their relative importance within the play..." based on the number of lines each speaks. This presumably exemplifies the methods by which psychologists "open the way to elegant description and mathematical ingenuity in the development of scientific hypotheses" (p. 48). Two later chapters study Shakespeare's principal characters and his themes on lines similar to introductions to school editions such as Verity's. Detailed recitals of the plot and situations are supplemented by magisterial interpretation of the characters and their motives, and of the themes of the plays. McCurdy's analysis is Freudian while Verity's of course was

---

[1] John Draper, 'Shakespeare and the Lombard Cities', *Rivista di Letterature Moderne*, IV (January–March 1953), 54–8.

[2] Alan Keen and Roger Lubbock, *The Annotator. The Pursuit of an Elizabethan Reader of Halle's Chronicle Involving some Surmises about the Early Life of Shakespeare* (Putnam, 1954).

[3] John Berryman, 'Shakespeare at Thirty', *Hudson Review*, VI (Summer 1953), 175–203.

[4] H. A. Shield, 'Links with Shakespeare, XI', *Notes and Queries* (July 1953), pp. 280–2.

[5] Harold Grier McCurdy, *The Personality of Shakespeare. A Venture in Psychological Method* (New Haven: Yale University Press; London: Cumberlege, 1953).

Victorian, but it is not otherwise clear, at least to this reviewer, how McCurdy's first three chapters are indispensable prolegomena to his last four. McCurdy believes "that literary criticism and the psychology of personality will eventually coalesce". If so, it would seem that future critics will approach literature much as the Victorians did, but with a Freudian scale of values.

Hector Bolitho has printed [1] an addition to Shakespeare mythology which he came across in Australia thirty years ago. It is a long letter written by an elderly woman (née Ford; we are not told if she married) who claimed to be a descendant of Shakespeare's schoolmaster Thomas Jenkins, and purports to give recollections that survived in her family of Shakespeare's childhood at Stratford. So much of it is demonstrably (indeed ludicrously) erroneous that we need not worry at the probable extinction of the source of these "recollections", but there is no need to suspect the woman's good faith. Probably she belonged to a family with some Stratford connexion and as she grew older confounded what a parent had told her about the town's greatest son with what she had learnt about her own family's history.

Shakespeare's literary 'background' has attracted lately much less attention than other aspects of his environment. That is by no means one's only reason for welcoming Madeleine Doran's very useful survey [2] of Renaissance assumptions about literary art. Her aim is to bring to Elizabethan drama "such a touchstone...as the poets themselves would have understood and used". She has therefore synthesized the numerous studies of bits of the Elizabethan heritage of literary conventions and ideas. Her approach is frankly guided by Wölfflin's argument, in *Principles of Art History*, that one age of art differs from another because its artists have different modes of imaginative beholding. She sees this principle as applying to literature just as to plastic and graphic art. Whether this approach gets her much nearer to the heart of the matter than she would have got without it may be disputable, but it certainly produces a stimulating review of Elizabethan critical theories, with numerous enlightening *obiter dicta* on the non-dramatic as well as the dramatic literature of the time. Nor does Miss Doran's learning weigh her down; she is obviously interested in more arts than literature, and not merely academically.

Other publications which relate Shakespeare's works to their time have not been numerous. Paul Siegel supports [3] Stoll's view that Shylock reminded Elizabethan audiences of pharisaical Puritan usurers, and cites evidence that in the popular mind Puritanism, usury and Judaism were associated. Cecil Roth notes [4] a parallel between Richmond's speech in *Richard III*, v, iii, 112-14, and passages in the Jewish liturgy, and wonders whether Shakespeare had had access to a translation. Hotson's theory that Shakespeare wrote his sonnets about 1588-9 continues to provoke dissent. Walter Stone has investigated [5] the origins and development of the "Prediction of Regiomontanus" which Hotson claimed was the "presage" that the "sad Augurs mock" in Sonnet CVII. Stone contends that Regiomontanus's and other "presages" were thoroughly

[1] Hector Bolitho, 'Shakespeare: A Fantastic Document', *John o' London's Weekly*, LXIII (23 April 1954), 405-6.
[2] Madeleine Doran, *Endeavors of Art: A Study of Form in Elizabethan Drama* (Madison: University of Wisconsin Press, 1954).
[3] Paul N. Siegel, 'Shylock and the Puritan Usurers', *Studies in Shakespeare*, ed. Arthur D. Matthews and Clark M. Emery (University of Miami Press, 1953), pp. 129-38.
[4] Cecil Roth, 'Shakespeare and the Jewish Liturgy', *The Times Literary Supplement* (15 May 1953), p. 317.
[5] Walter B. Stone, 'Shakespeare and the Sad Augurs', *Journal of English and Germanic Philology*, LII (October 1953), 457-77.

discredited by 1584, and that astronomically and astrologically 1588 was a very ordinary and unexceptionable year. His evidence is impressive and seems irrefutable, as does his conclusion that Sonnet CVII cannot refer to the events of 1588.

G. R. Waggoner discusses[1] the Elizabethan attitude to peace and war. He shows that many dramatists, like the nobility and gentry, thought that because a long peace encouraged luxury and idleness it was dangerous internally and externally, and that therefore a just foreign war was a normal and healthful activity. R. H. West argues[2] that nearly all Elizabethans *did* believe in witchcraft and demonology. He insists that Reginald Scot's views, which he details, were unique (at least in print) and remained so for some time afterwards, and argues that the Protestant distaste for speculative demonology has been mistaken by modern scholars for the rationalist attitude which developed only much later.

Gabriele Baldini has published[3] a comprehensive study of Webster's dramatic activity, paying rather more attention than is usual to Webster's collaboration. Baldini concludes that *Westward Ho!* and *Northward Ho!* far from being hack-work, represent a definite stage in Webster's dramatic development, although the sudden ascent to *The White Devil* remains inexplicable. Baldini's analysis of the plays and their characters is interesting even when it does not command assent. He suggests that *The White Devil* is musical rather than dramatic in conception and compares its technique with Maeterlinck's and its imagery with the painting of Bosch and Breughel. A briefer study of the poetry of another of Shakespeare's contemporaries is Ants Oras's article[4] on the importance of the vowel-sounds for verbal music in Marlowe's poetry, a quite convincing analysis which breaks new ground in Marlowe criticism.[5]

Research on the Elizabethan theatre and staging continues to demonstrate the uncertainty of our supposed knowledge, and includes some of the year's most valuable Shakespearian publications. The most important is Leslie Hotson's preliminary report[6] on his researches in the accounts of the Elizabethan Office of Works, where he found references to the setting up of a stage "in the middle of the Hall" for court entertainments at Whitehall. Hotson insists that this must mean exactly what it says, and that we have been wrong in supposing the stage was set up across the end of the hall. He argues that since the audience was seated all round the stage there was no possibility of scenic wall or background. Plays at court must have been presented on an un-curtained stage in the middle of the hall, "set with painted canvas-and-frame 'mansions' at both ends and surrounded by the audience as in a circus". He claims that there can have been no fundamental difference in production when plays written for a public theatre were played at court, and that therefore this circus-arena presentation must have characterized the public theatres too. He supports his view with a persuasive quotation from Thomas Platter and some

[1] G. R. Waggoner, 'An Elizabethan Attitude Toward Peace and War', *Philological Quarterly*, XXXIII (January 1954), 20–33.

[2] Robert H. West, 'Elizabethan Belief in Spirits and Witchcraft', *Studies in Shakespeare*, ed. Arthur D. Matthews and Clark M. Emery (University of Miami Press, 1953), pp. 65–73.

[3] Gabriele Baldini, *John Webster e il linguaggio della tragedia* (Rome: Edizioni dell' Ateneo, 1954).

[4] Ants Oras, 'Lyrical Instrumentation in Marlowe: A Step towards Shakespeare', *Studies in Shakespeare*, ed. Arthur D. Matthews and Clark M. Emery (University of Miami Press, 1953), pp. 74–87.

[5] Several articles in *Notes and Queries*—by T. C. Hoepfner, T. H. McNeal, C. A. Greer, and Abraham Feldman—seem to present no new material.

[6] Leslie Hotson, 'Shakespeare's Arena', *Sewanee Review*, LXI (Summer 1953), 347–61.

convincing criticism of certain modern theories that much acting took place on the "balcony", "upper stage", or "study", and claims that his theory is confirmed by the early illustrations of the pre-Restoration theatres which show spectators at the back of the stage, and also by the contemporary references to the "lords' room" over the stage. Much will turn on whether Hotson is right in supposing that "in the middle of the hall" is to be taken literally. To the present reviewer it seems possible that the entries mean that the stage was located in the middle of *one side* of the hall; this would bring court and public theatre presentation very close indeed. Such interpretation, however, would hardly modify the important implications of Hotson's article for our view on Elizabethan acting and staging. A full report of the entries in the Works Office accounts will be awaited with impatience.

Very strong (but unwitting) support for Hotson's views on staging is provided in Warren D. Smith's article[1] on the references to stage business in the dialogue of Shakespeare's plays. Smith argues that the practical stagecraft of such lines as "Look how she rubs her hands" (useless as a cue for an actor) readily emerges "if we picture the projecting platform"; these "directions" in the dialogue "are actually descriptions for those spectators who could not be expected to see clearly" because "some members of an audience that surrounded three sides of the stage must have been blocked from seeing stage business...either by the back of a player or by the intervening body of another". He points out in a footnote that the convention described is not limited to Shakespeare, but permeates the plays of the whole era. Smith's article is most convincing, and reinforces not only Hotson's views about the Elizabethan arena-stages but also John R. Brown's contention[2] that acting on the Shakespearian stage was naturalistic, not formal and declamatory as it is fashionable to assume. Brown re-examines the seventeenth-century references usually quoted and argues convincingly that they prove that by Shakespeare's time formal acting was fast dying out and that a new naturalism was developing, aimed at an illusion of real life, and that the best actors achieved it. Brown presents his case too diffidently; this reviewer found it conclusive. It may well turn out that formal and oratorical declamation characterized much university acting, but not that in the London theatres of Shakespeare's day. A less convincing study of stage-business is Warren Smith's[3] suggestion that announcements of a character's entrance by another already on the stage is a Shakespearian device "to give these characters the excuse necessary to shift their position in preparation for a graceful re-grouping with the newcomers".

The London theatres, especially The Globe, are the subject of a handsome illustrated study[4] by Walter Hodges, who brings an artist's imagination and a practical experience of stage-designing to bear on the data provided by recent scholarship. He makes acute comments on the implications of extant contracts for building pre-Restoration theatres, and some original suggestions about the height of the stage, its hangings, and the possibility of action in "the yard". He finds no clear evidence of an "inner stage" and argues that very little, if any, action need have taken place within the curtained recess. He agrees, however, that there must have been an

[1] Warren D. Smith, 'Stage Business in Shakespeare's Dialogue', *Shakespeare Quarterly*, IV (July 1953), 311–16.
[2] John Russell Brown, 'On the Acting of Shakespeare's Plays', *Quarterly Journal of Speech*, XXXIX (December 1953), 477–84.
[3] Warren D. Smith, 'The Elizabethan Stage and Shakespeare's Entrance Announcements', *Shakespeare Quarterly*, IV (October 1953), 405–10.
[4] C. Walter Hodges, *The Globe Restored* (Ernest Benn, 1953).

"upper stage" and suggests it was on some structure projecting forwards from the back wall. In addition to numerous line drawings and reproductions in the text his book has an unusually generous selection of plates. For the general reader and for undergraduates it is an admirable introduction to the latest knowledge about the Elizabethan theatre; scholars may jib at two or three slips, but few will read it without learning much from it. It should be consulted by all would-be constructors of Elizabethan stages, most of whom in recent years have accepted un-critically the theories of Cranford Adams. A more scholarly reconstruction is Richard Southern's model of an Elizabethan playhouse, of which he has published a brief illustrated account.[1]

A problem of stage business which greatly interests Hodges (pp. 58–60) and others is the hoisting of Antony into the monument in *Antony and Cleopatra*, IV, xv. Roy Walker,[2] *a propos* Joan Rees's suggestion that Daniel indirectly reports the original stage business,[3] refers to the way it was contrived at Stratford in 1898, when Antony was drawn up by strips of linen wound round him, and inquires whether Benson was adopting a traditional piece of business or got it from Daniel. The possibility that traditional stage business may help us to interpret or present the plays correctly makes detailed accounts of past performances especially interesting to Shake-spearian scholars; there is, moreover, always the possibility that a gifted and experienced actor or producer will have grasped the significance of 'directions' in Shakespeare's dialogue which have eluded scholars unfamiliar with the theatre. Arthur C. Sprague has therefore continued to note such accounts of stage business as escaped his attention in *Shakespeare and the Actors* (1944), and now adds a postscript which is entertaining as well as interesting.[4] Sprague has also pub-lished re-creations of a series of great Shakespearian performances from Betterton as Hamlet to Booth as Iago, with chapters on William Poel and later Shakespearian productions.[5] To read what he records of Kean and others is to realize that although great progress has been made in presenting Shakespeare's plays as intelligible wholes, our leading Shakespearian actors may yet not be able to work on us as did their greatest predecessors. The same thought is provoked by Gordon Crosse's recollections[6] of his Shakespearian playgoing. He writes simply as a playgoer with no professional interest in the theatre, and relies on a journal of his impressions written while they were fresh, but these are particularly valuable because they record how lines were spoken and what stage business was enacted. It is because any records of dramatic perform-ances may enable us to track down such information that they are to be welcomed.[7]

The importance of the theatre in Shakespeare's life is already gaining recognition in German-speaking countries. Saladin Schmitt[8] pleads that Shakespeare's plays be approached as the work

[1] Richard Southern, 'An Elizabethan Playhouse: A New Model Reconstruction', *Britain Today* (April 1954), pp. 28–31, and *The Listener* (29 April 1954), p. 727.

[2] Roy Walker, '*Antony and Cleopatra*', *The Times Literary Supplement* (29 May 1953), p. 349.

[3] *Shakespeare Survey*, 6 (1953), 91.

[4] Arthur Colby Sprague, *The Stage Business in Shakespeare's Plays: A Postscript* (Society for Theatre Research, Pamphlet No. 3, 1954: available only to members of the Society).

[5] Arthur Colby Sprague, *Shakespearian Players and Performances* (Cambridge, Mass.: Harvard University Press; London: A. and C. Black, 1954).

[6] Gordon Crosse, *Shakespearean Playgoing 1890–1952* (A. R. Mowbray, 1953).

[7] Thomas Barbour, 'Theatre Chronicle', *Hudson Review*, VI (Summer 1953), 278–86; Hennig Cohen, 'Shake-speare in Charleston on the Eve of the Revolution', *Shakespeare Quarterly*, IV (July 1953), 327–30.

[8] Saladin Schmitt, 'Shakespeare Drama und Bühne', *Shakespeare-Jahrbuch*, LXXXIX (1953), 18–34.

of an actor writing for the theatre, and Richard Flatter[1] argues that we have underestimated both Shakespeare's standing as an actor in his own day and its influence on his technique, especially his dialogue. John Long[2] appears to be concerned with a special defect of American productions of the plays, for in England it is not true that in "the usual productions of Shakespeare's plays the music receives scant consideration". Gerda Prange[3] has made a detailed survey of Shakespeare's allusions to dancing, conveniently grouping all which refer to the twelve dances he names. She indicates their role in his stage-craft and shows how they point, and occasionally clarify, passages of dialogue. She concludes that Shakespeare's knowledge of dancing was considerable.

3. TEXTUAL STUDIES

reviewed by JAMES G. McMANAWAY

How dependable is the First Folio? For the text of seventeen plays it is the only source. Until recently, editors and commentators have acted on the tacit assumption that all copies of F are alike and that not only in these seventeen plays but frequently in others the reading in a particular copy of F is authoritative and, for practical purposes, impeccable. In Shakespeare's 'King Lear', for example, as was pointed out in this space (Shakespeare Survey, 3, p. 148), the editor of this critical text made full use of W. W. Greg's collation of all twelve copies of the First Quarto but contented himself with the readings from one unidentified original or facsimile of the First Folio. Forewarned, the New Arden editor, whose "text...is based on F...consulted [he does not say collated] facsimiles of two different copies of the Folio as well as the two originals accessible in Leeds" without discovering any variants. And perhaps emboldened by these negative results, he states that "as no evidence has yet been produced that the Folio is made up of corrected and uncorrected sheets, [he is] sceptical of this theory". Just one year later Hinman announced the discovery of a page of proof of Lear[4] and published a photographic reproduction of it. But information about press corrections in p. 292 of Lear were already available, for the Staunton (1866), the Halliwell-Phillipps (1876), and the Methuen (1910) facsimiles have the corrected state, and the Lee (1902) the uncorrected state. And two other pages of proof of the First Folio had been published, one as early as 1932 by E. E. Willoughby in his monumental book, The Printing of the First Folio, and the second in 1942 by C. J. K. Hinman in The Library (4th ser., xxx, 101–7). The editorial problem is no longer as simple as once it was.

Charlton Hinman, who has already published descriptions of two pages of First Folio proof discovered in the course of collating with his machine the copies of F in the Folger Shakespeare Library, announces the discovery of yet another page.[5] It is possible that others may come to

---

[1] Richard Flatter, 'Shakespeare, der Schauspieler', Shakespeare-Jahrbuch, LXXXIX (1953), 35–50.

[2] John H. Long, 'Music for the Replica Staging of Shakespeare', Studies in Shakespeare, ed. Arthur D. Matthews and Clark M. Emery (University of Miami Press, 1953), pp. 88–95.

[3] Gerda Prange, 'Shakespeares Äusserungen über die Tänze seiner Zeit', Shakespeare-Jahrbuch, LXXXIV (1953), 132–61.

[4] 'Mark III: New Light on the Proof-reading for the First Folio of Shakespeare', Studies in Bibliography, III (1950–51), 145–53, Plates I and II, following p. 152.

[5] 'The Proof-Reading of the First Folio Text of Romeo and Juliet', Studies in Bibliography (1951–2), IV, 61–70.

light before he finishes collating the entire collection of Folger copies a year or two hence. Meanwhile, on the basis of the collation of a third of the plays in F in some twenty copies, he publishes some statistics that are startling in their implications and points to certain inferences that may be drawn from them and an examination of the four known examples of Jaggard's proofs.

First of all, there is the possibility that more than one man marked proof corrections; this should be neither unexpected nor surprising in the case of so large a volume. Second, proportionately more pages of *Romeo* contain stop-press corrections than in nearby plays—already twelve of the twenty-five sheets have been found in two states. Third, the corrections on each page of *Romeo* are relatively few in number and trifling in quality, with the result that the text is lamentably inferior. Fourth, when formes are known in two or more states, the proof-reading was tardy and the percentage of uncorrected copies is high. Hinman is led to conjecture that "to some extent the typesetting, but above all the proof-reading that went into the Folio text of *Romeo and Juliet*, is of a special order, clearly differentiating this play from most of the plays nearby. A particular *attitude* towards the *Romeo* text would seem to have prevailed in the printing-house...as if the compositor and the proof-reader alike...were but too well aware that they were here perpetuating only the reprint of a reprint of the play." This brings us to a fifth observation, that collation to date of the Folio texts adjacent to *Romeo* has produced "not a single variant [page] in *Coriolanus*, only four variant pages in *Titus*, no variants whatever in *Timon*, four variant pages in *Julius Caesar*, and one variant page in *Macbeth*: a total of nine variant pages in these five whole plays as compared with twelve in *Romeo and Juliet* alone". Of these five adjacent plays, only *Titus* appeared in an earlier edition. Do Hinman's statistics mean that special attention was given to the type-setting and proof-reading of plays set from manuscript and then being printed for the first time? And is it permissible to think that such plays as *Julius Caesar*, of which F is the only text, have been printed with a high degree of accuracy?

Two things have combined to usher in a new age of textual criticism in Shakespeare. The earlier in point of time was recognition of the fact, dimly and only reluctantly apprehended even yet, that copies of the First Folio differ among themselves in hundreds, probably thousands, of readings. The later, and even more important, is that two or more compositors set the type used in printing the First Folio; that they had different ideas about the typographical appearance of a page, as determined by the spacing of stage directions and the handling of lines of verse too long for the narrow columns of F; that each tended to impose his own preferential spelling and punctuation on the text he was setting; and that in consequence it is possible to identify the pages, columns, and with good fortune some shorter passages of text set by each compositor. Better yet, using the methods of Willoughby, Hinman, and Philip Williams (to name only three), it begins to be possible to discover the work habits of Jaggard's compositors and, in particular, to ascertain how accurately each man reproduced his copy in type. The First Folio is no longer a unit. It consists, as we are beginning to find out, of pages printed from type that may be marked off with some confidence into units of work done by men with certain known characteristics and habits of workmanship.

The leader in this most recent attack upon editorial problems is Miss Alice Walker, whose *Textual Problems of The First Folio* (noticed last year) will come to be regarded as equally significant for our generation as was Pollard's *Shakespeare Folios and Quartos* in 1909. In a review of primary importance, Philip Williams [1] pays generous tribute to the value of Miss Walker's book and the acuteness of her observations about the texts of *Richard III, Lear, Troilus, 2 Henry IV, Hamlet* and *Othello*. These six plays are all dependent upon quartos that preceded the Folio. There had been agreement about this dependence in the case of *Richard III, Lear* and *Troilus*; Williams accepts Miss Walker's proofs as almost mathematical for *2 Henry IV* and *Othello* and thinks she is probably right about *Hamlet*. But he urges that the dependence is with a difference. He also questions the adequacy of present spelling tests, suggests that at least three compositors may have worked on F, and rejects Miss Walker's conjecture that two boy actors of Shakespeare's company connived in preparing the manuscript from which the *Lear* Q was printed. He disagrees sharply with the supposition that a hurried compositor will perpetuate copy spellings with great fidelity and raises the question whether the King's Men may not have used annotated quartos as prompt-books to an extent hitherto uncontemplated.

Lacking space to present detailed evidence in his review, Williams gives this in an article in the same issue.[2] Here, by the use of new spelling tests and a study of the centring of stage directions, he demonstrates conclusively that compositor B did not work alone on the F text of *Troilus* and *Lear*, as had been supposed; in both, A had a hand, and in *Lear* there may have been a compositor C whose characteristics are still shadowy. What has been published recently about the contamination of *Lear* by compositor B must largely be done over. And what Williams has done with *Lear* must be tried with several other plays.

Of even greater importance is Williams's modification of Miss Walker's proposition that the six plays studied in her book were set directly from corrected copies of the quartos. The F compositors who set such plays as *A Midsummer Night's Dream* from Q tended to perpetuate the Quarto speech-headings with only such variations in spelling as might be needed to justify the line. In *Lear*, however, variations in the speech headings, in the spelling of Gloucester's name, and in the use of roman and italic type are such as to make it improbable that F was set directly from Q. Williams can be the more confident of the validity of his findings because for the first time he has noted and made use of the fact that Jaggard's compositors A and B worked on the 1619 quartos. By a comparison of their treatment of the 'Pide Bull' text of *Lear* in 1619 with what they did in setting the F text in 1623, he can make much shrewder conjectures than Miss Walker. Now Miss Walker, and before her P. A. Daniel and Greg, had demonstrated conclusively the dependence of F on Q. Williams rehearses the serious objections to the thesis that F was printed from an annotated copy of Q and argues that in 1622 the official prompt-book of *Lear* was composed of "good" pages of Q supplemented by inserted manuscript leaves to replace corrupt passages. A transcript of this prompt-book was, he thinks, used as copy for F. He suggests that the same condition probably existed in the case of the other five plays considered in Miss Walker's book. To me it seems more likely that the F copy for *Lear* was a transcript of Q corrected and amplified *currente calamo* by reference to an authoritative playhouse manuscript. Either process would perpetuate some of the textual and bibliographical peculiarities of Q while introducing the new readings, and particularly the aberrant spellings and the palaeographical details, that are otherwise inexplicable.

[1] *Shakespeare Quarterly*, IV (October 1953), 481–3.
[2] 'Two Problems in the Folio Text of *King Lear*', *Shakespeare Quarterly*, IV (1951–2), 451–60.

L *

In 'The Folio Text of *1 Henry IV*',[1] Miss Walker continues her efforts to determine what precise degree of reliance may be placed on the F text, with attention focused on a play of which only a fragment of Q1 has survived and which was reprinted from Q5. Greg remarks (*Editorial Problem*, p. 129) that "the stage directions have been slightly edited, but in a literary rather than a theatrical sense.... There is no evidence whatever of the use of a playhouse manuscript or of a copy of the quarto that had served as a prompt-book. The fact therefore that profanity has been very thoroughly removed once again suggests that this was sometimes at least done by the editor." The text in F is not, then, a simple reprint of Q5. What are the changes, who made them, and what authority do they have? Not so long ago, the answers to these questions would have been couched in aesthetic or theoretical terms. Miss Walker's answers contain hard bibliographical and textual facts. It is a fact, she says, that of the twenty-five and one-half pages of F text, compositor A set eleven, and B fourteen and one-half. It is a fact that about one hundred and seventy dialogue readings in F differ from Q5. Twenty-six of these are almost certainly correct, since they restore Q1 readings that had been corrupted at some point between Q2 and Q5; nine are in pages set by A, seventeen in those by B. Most of the other variants may be regarded as errors. Eighteen of them occur in A's eleven pages, but one hundred and thirteen are in B's fourteen and a half. Analysis reveals that B committed twelve times as many literal errors as A, omitted words or phrases fifteen times as often, had almost five times as many interpolations, and made more than three times as many substitutions, though he set only about one-third more pages than A. When we find one transposition in A and eight in B, it is not difficult to agree in Miss Walker's diagnosis that B had "a habit of following the matter with the mind rather than with the eye".

All this arouses respect in Miss Walker for A's normal accuracy and conservatism and inclines her to the opinion that the alterations in his sections of the text are intentional. Some of the changes in B's section likewise seem to fall outside the limits of his usual errors. Of one thing she is confident: too many of Q5's manifest errors remain uncorrected for there to have been a systematic comparison with a playhouse MS.[2] Instead there was, apparently, some casual correction "by someone familiar with the play", perhaps a person connected with the playhouse, for some speech-tags were altered; there may have been sporadic conjectural emendation in Jaggard's shop. After due allowance has been made for the corruption introduced by the compositors, this play contains a residuum of variants that probably had a different origin. Upon these the editor must fix his scrutiny, bearing in mind how little reason there is to consider them authoritative, for, as Miss Walker cautions, "If there was conjectural interference with the copy for one play there may have been tinkering with the copy for all, and the conjectural alterations of an erratic improver are as much a blemish on an edited text as the careless errors of a compositor."

For the second time in five years, Great Britain can boast the publication of an independent text of Shakespeare's complete works.[3] Like its predecessor, edited by Peter Alexander, it is a

---

[1] *Studies in Bibliography*, VI (1954), 45–59.

[2] If proof-reading had been as careful in Jaggard's shop as it usually is today, most of the Q5 errors would have been corrected, as well as most of the variant readings introduced by A and, especially, B. In this play a few corrections were made as a result of proofing, but for the most part the modern editor's work must begin with the clearing away of the errors overlooked by Jaggard's proof-reader(s).

[3] *William Shakespeare: The Complete Works*, ed. Charles Jasper Sisson (London: Odhams Press, 1954). The earlier was *The Tudor Shakespeare*, ed. Peter Alexander (1951)—see *Shakespeare Survey*, 5, p. 148.

one-volume edition, with clear type and reasonably opaque paper. Introductory material of a general nature is provided by five scholars associated with Sisson, one of whom, Harold Jenkins, has edited *Sir Thomas More*. All the other texts, with their prefaces, are the work of Sisson. Collation of passages in several plays with original editions and with other modern editions indicates that Sisson has produced a truly independent text. Certain of the readings he has introduced are noted in his prefaces. Since the plan of the work, however, necessarily denies him the space to state the textual problems, much less to defend the readings he has adopted, one is left with a feeling of frustration. It is profoundly to be hoped that both Sisson and Alexander will shortly publish their full critical apparatus, so that the fruits of their technical skill and ripe learning will not be hidden in one-volume editions but will be made available to others who are concerned with Shakespeare's text.

With the publication of *Richard III*,[1] John Dover Wilson moves one volume nearer to the completion of his edition. Accepting the textual theories of D. L. Patrick, Greg, and Miss Walker, he breaks with tradition even more extensively than did Alexander in 1951, whose *Tudor Shakespeare* contained in this one play more than a thousand differences from the old Cambridge text. In particular, Wilson has accepted the challenge to amend the readings common to Q1, Q6, and F, or to Q1, Q3, and F in the five hundred odd lines that were printed in F from pages of Q3. This is a move in the right direction. One important observation made by Wilson is that Q, though a reported text, runs to about 3400 lines. This means that the acting text on the London stage was certainly no shorter and acts as a strong deterrent from accepting the theory that the average acting version was 2400 lines in length. No longer must we believe that in the preparation of the prompt-book every Shakespearian play was given Procrustean treatment.

Three new volumes of the New Arden Shakespeare are now in circulation.[2] In the first, J. C. Maxwell inclines to a date of 1589–90 for *Titus Andronicus* and to exclusively Shakespearian authorship, but he is troubled by the close resemblances to *Venus* and *Lucrece* that indicate a later date, and by the style and diction and certain grammatical usages in Act I that suggest George Peele's participation. On the matter of structure, he agrees with H. T. Price that it is Shakespearian. Scene ii of Act III, which appears first in F, he dismisses casually as probably part of the play in 1594. In much of this he is directly at odds with Dover Wilson. There are still many unanswered questions about *Titus*.

In the second volume, M. R. Ridley retains as much as possible of the original edition of R. H. Case and concerns himself chiefly with the staging of certain scenes and with the problems of punctuation and mislineation in F, the only text of *Antony and Cleopatra*, a play printed apparently from Shakespeare's manuscript—see especially the Preface to the Revised Edition, pp. vii–xviii, and Appendixes III and II. Curiously enough, Appendix II has no reference to the studies by Miss Walker and others of the habits of the F compositors and the differences in their treatment of lineation.

Little remains of the original Arden edition of *Henry V*, the third play. The introduction, footnotes, and appendixes are by the new editor, J. H. Walter, who is thus able to restate his

[1] *Richard III* (Cambridge University Press, 1954).
[2] *Titus Andronicus*, ed. J. C. Maxwell; *Antony and Cleopatra*, ed. M. R. Ridley; and *Henry V*, ed. J. H. Walter (London: Methuen, 1953, 1954, 1954).

earlier arguments that Falstaff was originally a character in the play and that his enforced deletion is the cause of the disjointed state of the text. That the text is disjointed can hardly be denied, and the Brook family may safely be blamed for the enforced liquidation of Sir John Falstaff—just as it may for the change of Brook to Broome in *Merry Wives*. Walters might have cited documentary evidence that not only the public but even Shakespeare's own company called *1 Henry IV* "Oldcastle" long after the playwright's death.

Attention should also be directed to two other editions of Shakespeare. The first is a reprint in four volumes of the Nonesuch Edition.[1] While necessarily less sumptuous than the original edition, it is yet a beautiful work, with good paper and excellent typography. The text is as it left the hands of Herbert Farjeon many years ago. The second edition is the Penguin, edited by G. B. Harrison, of which two more titles are now available.[2] These nicely printed little books, one play to a volume, are provided with introductory material and an edited text and are admirably suited to the use of the general public.

Once more the authorship of *Pericles* is called in question, this time by Kenneth Muir's Introduction to a welcome reprint of George Wilkins's novel.[3] The editor rejects the explanation recently proposed by Philip Edwards,[4] namely that two individuals of differing capacities reconstituted the text of the play from memory, and returns to the older theory of divided authorship. He would like to think that Wilkins, or better yet Thomas Heywood, was the other dramatist. There has never been more than a minimum of internal evidence to support Heywood's candidacy, and Wilkins seems to disqualify himself by his entreaty that "the Reader...receiue this Historie as it was vnder the habite of ancient Gower...by the King's Maiesties Players excellently presented," or, as the title-page has it, "The true History of the Play of *Pericles*, as it was lately presented...", and by the fact that while he calls the History "a poore infant of my braine" he is careful to avoid laying any claim to the very popular play.

The posthumously published studies[5] by the late Albert Feuillerat of the authorship of six of Shakespeare's early plays rather detract from than add to the stature of this scholar, whose meticulously accurate publication of documents relating to the Queen's Office of the Revels is one of the dependable foundation stones of Elizabethan study. Though written with passionate conviction, they seem, at least to me, to be wrong in almost every respect.

Time was when a man might hope to be familiar with all that was known about Shakespeare, but the ramifications of Shakespearian studies are now so numerous that one must, alas, specialize. In consequence, research tends to become departmentalized. Few people, for example, who work on textual problems are expert philologists. Helge Kökeritz's fine book[6] on Shakespeare's pronunciation helps fill a great gap. It is written primarily for the expert, but any reader will find it profitable to glance at the discussion of rhymes, puns, and dialect; and editors will have

---

[1] *The Complete Works...to Which Are Added Pericles and the First Quartos of Six of the Plays, with Three Plays of Doubtful Authorship: Also the Poems...*, ed. Herbert Farjeon. (London: Nonesuch Press, 1953.)

[2] *Richard the Third; Love's Labour's Lost* (Penguin Shakespeare), ed. G. B. Harrison. (London, Melbourne, Baltimore: Penguin Books, 1953.)

[3] *The Painful Adventures of Pericles Prince of Tyre by George Wilkins* (Liverpool Repr. no. 8), ed. Kenneth Muir (University Press of Liverpool, 1953).

[4] *Shakespeare Survey*, 5, pp. 25–49.

[5] *The Composition of Shakespeare's Plays: Authorship, Chronology* (Yale University Press, 1953).

[6] *Shakespeare's Pronunciation* (Yale University Press, 1953).

to master it entire. It may be questioned whether the author does not rely too implicitly on exactness of identity in the pronunciation of rhyme-words and puns, when frequently a reasonable approximation was all Shakespeare intended—or needed. The author seems to have ignored the Folger facsimile of *Titus Andronicus* (1594) and Philip Edwards's study of *Pericles*.

Closely related to the subject of Shakespeare's pronunciation is that of his spelling, which has been discussed recently by A. C. Partridge.[1] Under the heading of orthography, Partridge includes all the accidentals "peculiar to author, scribe, editor or printing house"—"spelling, punctuation, elision, aphesis, syncope and contractions generally". He thinks Shakespeare preferred full spellings (sonne, proppe, woorde, heere, hee); final -ie rather than -y (dutie, laye); odd spellings (sacietie=satiety, ceaze, skorne); and visual rhyme. In this early period (of *Venus*, *Lucrece*, *Richard II*, *Romeo* Q2, *Hamlet* Q2), Partridge believes that Shakespeare did not use the apostrophe as a mark of elision or in the possessive genitive, and he inquires whether these usages changed after the influence of Ben Jonson became strong. The punctuation of *Venus* and *Lucrece* he attributes largely to the printers in Richard Field's shop. It is possible that Partridge has underestimated the extent to which the spelling and punctuation of the plays, too, represent compositorial usages rather than those of the author.

In a book[2] that concerns equally the biographer and the textual expert, E. B. Everitt proposes additions to the Shakespearian canon and a chronology of the "lost years" that stretch credulity to the cracking point. He believes, as I cannot, that *Edmund Ironside*, *The Second Maidens Tragedy*, W. P.'s letter to Ned Alleyn, Shakespeare's Will, and two other legal documents are in the handwriting of William Shakespeare. If he is right in these claims, and in others that await publication, a revolution has begun in Shakespeare studies.

---

[1] 'Shakespeare's Orthography in *Venus and Adonis* and Some Early Quartos', *Shakespeare Survey*, 7, pp. 35–47.

[2] *The Young Shakespeare, Studies in Documentary Evidence* (*Anglistica*, vol. II). (Copenhagen: Rosenkilde and Bagger, 1954).

L**

BOOKS RECEIVED

BALDINI, GABRIELE. *John Webster e il linguaggio della tragedia* (Rome: Edizioni dell' Ateneo, 1954).

CROSSE, GORDON. *Shakespearean Playgoing 1890–1952* (London: A. R. Mowbray, 1953).

CRUTTWELL, PATRICK. *The Shakespearean Moment and its Place in the Poetry of the Seventeenth Century* (London: Chatto and Windus, 1954).

DORAN, MADELEINE. *Endeavors of Art: A Study of Form in Elizabethan Drama* (Madison: University of Wisconsin Press, 1954).

ELLIOTT, G. R. *Flaming Minister. A Study of Othello as Tragedy of Love and Hate* (Durham, North Carolina: Duke University Press; London: Cambridge University Press, 1953).

EVERITT, E. B. *The Young Shakespeare. Studies in Documentary Evidence.* Anglistica, Volume II (Copenhagen: Rosenkilde and Bagger, 1954).

FEUILLERAT, ALBERT. *The Composition of Shakespeare's Plays* (New Haven: Yale University Press; London: Geoffrey Cumberlege, 1953).

HANKINS, JOHN E. *Shakespeare's Derived Imagery* (Lawrence, Kansas: University of Kansas Press, 1953).

HODGES, C. WALTER. *The Globe Restored* (London: Ernest Benn, 1953).

JOSEPH, BERTRAM. *Conscience and the King. A Study of Hamlet* (London: Chatto and Windus, 1953).

KEEN, ALAN and LUBBOCK, ROGER. *The Annotator. The Pursuit of an Elizabethan Reader of Halle's Chronicle Involving some Surmises About the Early Life of Shakespeare* (London: Putnam, 1954).

KÖKERITZ, HELGE. *Shakespeare's Pronunciation* (New Haven: Yale University Press; London: Geoffrey Cumberlege, 1953).

LASCELLES, MARY. *Shakespeare's Measure for Measure* (University of London, Athlone Press, 1953).

McCURDY, HAROLD GRIER. *The Personality of Shakespeare. A Venture in Psychological Method* (New Haven: Yale University Press; London: Geoffrey Cumberlege, 1953).

PARIS, JEAN. *Hamlet ou les personnages du fils* (Paris: Editions du Seuil, 1953).

PARTRIDGE, A. C. *The Accidence of Ben Jonson's Plays, Masques and Entertainments, with an Appendix of Comparable Uses in Shakespeare* (Cambridge: Bowes and Bowes, 1953).

PARTRIDGE, A. C. *Studies in the Syntax of Ben Jonson's Plays* (Cambridge: Bowes and Bowes, 1953).

RYLANDS, GEORGE. *Shakespeare's Poetic Energy.* Annual Shakespeare Lecture of the British Academy, 1951; from *Proceedings of the British Academy,* xxxvii (London: Geoffrey Cumberlege, 1953).

SECCHI, NICOLO. *Self-Interest.* Translated by William Reymes. Edited by Helen Andrews Kaufman (Seattle: University of Washington Press, 1953).

Shakespeare Newsletter, vol. III (Pembroke, North Carolina, 1953).

Shakespeare Quarterly, vol. IV (New York: Shakespeare Association of America, 1953).

SHAKESPEARE, WILLIAM. *Complete Works.* Edited by C. J. Sisson (London: Odhams Press, 1954).

SHAKESPEARE, WILLIAM. *Antony and Cleopatra.* New Arden Shakespeare. Edited by M. R. Ridley (London: Methuen, 1954).

SHAKESPEARE, WILLIAM. *Henry V.* New Arden Shakespeare. Edited by J. H. Walter (London: Methuen, 1954).

SHAKESPEARE, WILLIAM. *Love's Labour's Lost.* The Penguin Shakespeare. Edited by G. B. Harrison (London: Penguin Books, 1953).

BOOKS RECEIVED

SHAKESPEARE, WILLIAM. *Richard III.* The Penguin Shakespeare. Edited by G. B. Harrison (London: Penguin Books, 1953).

SHAKESPEARE, WILLIAM. *Richard III.* New Cambridge Shakespeare. Edited by J. Dover Wilson (Cambridge University Press, 1954).

SHAKESPEARE, WILLIAM. *Titus Andronicus.* New Arden Shakespeare. Edited by J. C. Maxwell (London: Methuen, 1953).

SPALDING, K. J. *The Philosophy of Shakespeare* (Oxford: George Ronald, 1953).

SPRAGUE, A. C. *Shakespearian Players and Performances* (Cambridge, Mass.: Harvard University Press; London: A. and C. Black, 1954).

STAMM, RUDOLF. *Shakespeare's Word-Scenery with Some Remarks on Stage-History and the Interpretation of His Plays.* Veröffentlichungen der Handels-Hochschule St Gallen. Reihe B, Heft 10 (Zürich and St Gallen: Polygraphischer Verlag, 1954).

STRAUMANN, HEINRICH. *Phönix und Taube* (Zürich: Artemis-Verlag, 1953).

Studies in Bibliography. Papers of the Bibliographical Society of the University of Virginia, vol. VI, 1954. Edited by Fredson Bowers (Charlottesville, Virginia).

Studies in Shakespeare. University of Miami Publications in English and American Literature, vol. I, March 1953. Edited by A. D. Matthews and Clark M. Emery (Miami, Florida).

WEILGART, WOLFGANG J. *Shakespeare Psychognostic. Character Evolution and Transformation* (Tokyo: Hokuseido Press, 1952).

WHITAKER, VIRGIL K. *Shakespeare's Use of Learning. An Inquiry into the Growth of his Mind and Art* (San Marino, California: The Huntington Library, 1953).

INDEX

INDEX

Cardozo, J. L., 4, 6
Carey, Denis, 123, 124, 125, 126
Carey, Elizabeth, 143
Carrère, Félix, 142
Case, R. H., 157
Caxton, William, 31
Cazamian, L., 9
Cellini, Benvenuto, 120
Cervantes Saavedra, Miguel de, *Don Quixote*, 67
Chambers, R. W., 10, 12, 16, 17, 68 n.
Chambers, Sir E. K., 4, 6, 7, 40, 107 n.
Chapman, George, 55, 56, 145
Charlton, H. B., 2, 3, 7, 8, 47
Chaucer, Geoffrey, 17, 109
    The Tale of Patient Griselda, 18–19
    The Friar's Tale, 24, 25
    Troilus and Criseyde, 31, 36
Chester, Sir Robert, *Loves Marytr*, 121; authorship of, 148
Chettle, Henry, 100
Clark, Cumberland, 7, 110, 111
Clarke, Helen A., 8
Claudel, Pierre, *Partage de Midi*, 109
Clemen, W. H., 8, 68 n., 112, 119, 143, 145
Coghill, Nevill, 4, 8
Coleridge, S. T., 26 n., 28, 110
Collins, J. Churton, 68 n.
Colt, Alvin, 122
Compton, Fay, 133, 134, 135
Condell, Henry, 90
Congreve, William, 68, 131
Conrad, H., 4
Copeau, Jacques, 118
Coulter, Cornelia, 2
Coventry Mystery Plays, 109
Craig, Gordon, 77, 80
Craig, Hardin, 5, 8, 111
Craik, T. W., 143
Crane, Milton, 68 n.
Cranfield, Lionel, Earl of Middlesex, 107
Creede, Thomas, 90, 95–6
Crosse, Gordon, *Shakespearian Playgoing 1890–1952* reviewed, 152
Cruttwell, Patrick, *The Shakespearean Moment and its Place in the Poetry of the 17th Century* reviewed, 145
Cunliffe, J. W., 3
Czechoslovakia, report on Shakespeare in, 119

Daly, Augustine, 76
Daniel, P. A., 98 n., 155
Daniel, Samuel, 152

Dante, Alighieri, 4; exposition of comedy, 17–18
    Convivio, 26 n.
    Divine Comedy, 17
    Paradiso, 17–18, 109
Davenport, Arnold, 147
David, Richard, 6
Davies, Godfrey, 105 n.
Davies, Sir John, *Epigrammes and Elegies*, 107 n.
Davies, W. Robertson, 5
de Beauvais, Vincent, 4
    definition of comedy, 17
De Boys family, 7
Declercq, Aimé, 118
Dekker, Thomas, 100
Demanez, Raoul, 118
Devine, George, 124, 125, 126, 132, 136–8
Dickens, Charles, 61
Dobrée, Bonamy, 39 n.
Dominique, Ivan, 118
Donne, John, 20, 32
Doran, Madeleine, 13 n.
    Endeavors of Art: A Study of Form in Elizabethan Drama reviewed, 149
Dowden, Edward, 1, 7, 10, 14, 145
Draper, J. W., 6, 148
Drummond, William, *Phoebus Arise*, 99 n.
Dryden, John, 28, 57, 66, 139
Du Bartas, Guillaume de Saluste, Seigneur, *see* Sylvester, Joshua
Dunn, Lionel, 123, 124, 126
Duthie, G. I., 81, 83, 97 n., 98 n.

Edinborough, A., 119
Edmund Ironside, conjectural Shakespearian autograph, 159
Edwards, Philip, 159
Eisner, Doris, 118
Eliaz, R., 120
Eliot, John, *Ortho-epia Gallica*, 147
Eliot, T. S.:
    The Cocktail Party, 109
    Marina, 121
    The Waste Land, 37
Elliott, G. R., *Flaming Minister. A Study of Othello as Tragedy of Love and Hate* reviewed, 142
Ellis-Fermor, Una, 12, 36, 145
Elton, W., 11
Emery, Douglas, 123
Emery, John, 122
Empson, W., 13, 141
England's Parnassus, 99 n.

INDEX

Enright, D. J., 139
Essex, Robert Devereux, second Earl of, 28
Etienne, Claude, 118
Evans, Dame Edith, 31, 130
Evans, G. Blakemore, 147
Everitt, E. B., *The Young Shakespeare, Studies in Documentary Evidence* reviewed, 159
Exodus, 17

Fabyan, Robert, 146
Farjeon, Herbert, edition of *Shakespeare, Complete Works* reviewed, 158
Farmer, J. S., 101, 104 n.
Feasey, E., 116 n.
Feasey, L., 116 n.
Fergusson, Francis, 140
Ferrer, José, 122
Feuillerat, Albert, *The Composition of Shakespeare's Plays: Authorship, Chronology* reviewed, 158
Ffarington, Sir William, 7
Field, Richard, 55, 159
Fink, Z. S., 5
Finland, report on Shakespeare in, 119
Fisher, A. Y., 8
Flatter, Richard, 118, 153
Fleay, F. G., 6
Fleg, Edmond, 118
Fleming, W. H., 7–8
Fletcher, John (*see also* Beaumont, Francis), 52, 55, 56, 66
Florentius, 116 n.
French, Leslie, 124
Freud, Sigmund, 148–9
Fripp, E. I., 7, 11
Fry, Christopher, *Venus Observed*, 109
Frye, Northrop, 2, 3, 8, 143
Furness, H. H., 52, 55

Gardiner, William, 6
Garrick, David, 69
Gassman, Vittorio, 120
Gaston, Robert, 125
Gay, John, *The Shepherd's Week*, 47
Gayley, C. M., 1
Gericke, Robert, 97 n., 98 n.
Germany, report on Shakespeare in, 119
Gielgud, Sir John, 130
Gilbert, Allan, 139
Gilder, Rosamond, 122
Gli Duoi Fratelli Rivali, 4
Globe Theatre, *see under* Theatre, Elizabethan

Goldie, Hugh, 125
Golding, Arthur, translation of Ovid's *Metamorphoses*, 94
Gollancz, Sir Israel, 3, 8
Googe, Barnabe, 145
Gordon, D. J., 4
Gordon, George, 1
Gosson, Stephen, 4
Grafton, Richard, 146
Graham, Cary B., 143
Granville-Barker, Harley, 5, 8, 52, 75, 80
Graves, Frank, 120
Gray, A., 6
Green, Andrew J., 141
Greene, Robert, 3, 56, 103
    Friar Bacon and Friar Bungay, 102–3
    Perimedes, Preface to, 102
Greenfield, Thelma Nelson, 142
Greenlaw, E., 2
Greg, Sir W. W., 2, 81, 82, 83–4, 89, 90, 97 n., 98 n., 104 n., 105 n., 106, 153, 155, 156, 157
Grimm, Brothers, *Fairy Tales*, 136
Grosart, A. B., 148
Guarini, Battista, 55
Guiness, Alec, 128, 129
Guthrie, Tyrone, 118, 124
Guttman, Selma, 4

Hall, Peter, 124, 125
Halle, Edward, 146
    Chronicle, 148
Halliwell-Phillipps, J. O., 153
Hambleton, T. Edward, 122
Hammerle, Karl, 143
Hankins, John Erskine, *Shakespeare's Derived Imagery* reviewed, 145
Hanmer, Sir Thomas, 52
Harbage, A., 9
Harding, D. P., 12
Hardy, Robert, 133
Hardy, Thomas, 24
Hardyng, John, 146
Harington, Sir John, 6
Harrison, G. B., Penguin editions of *Richard the Third* and *Love's Labour's Lost* reviewed, 158
Harrison, John, 123, 125
Harrison, John L., 140
Hart, H. C., 6
Hartley, William, 7
Harvey, Gabriel, 6
Hazlitt, William, 1, 28

INDEX

INDEX

Nagarajan, S., 140
Napoleon, 109
Nashe, Thomas, 6, 110
  Pierce Penilesse, 147
National Maritime Museum, Greenwich, 116 n.
Natwick, Mildred, 122
Neill, K., 5
Neville, John, 136
Newport, Rychard, possible identification with Sir Richard Newport of Ercall, 148
Newport, Sir Richard, *see* Newport, Rychard
Nicoll, Allardyce, 105 n., 116 n.
Noble, Richmond, 5
North, Sir Thomas:
  translation of Plutarch's *Lives*, 54, 147
  Life of Pelopidas, 148
Northward Ho!, 150
Norway, report on Shakespeare in, 120

Obertello, A., 120
Oenslager, Donald, 122
Office of the Revels, documents relating to, 158
Office of Works, Elizabethan, accounts, 150–1
Oldcastle, alternative title for *I Henry IV*, 158
Old Vic Theatre, 123–6, 127, 131, 132–6
Olivier, Sir Laurence, 130
Oras, Ants, 150
O'Riordan, Conal, 78
Oscarsson, Per, 121

Palingenius, Marcellus, *Zodiacus Vitae*, 145
Palmer, John, 1, 7, 28
Paris Garden, *see under* Theatre, Elizabethan
Paris, Jean, *Hamlet ou Les Personnages du Fils* reviewed, 140–1
Parrott, T. M., 1, 2, 4, 7
Partridge, A. C., 121, 159, 160
Pasinetti, P. M., 120
Patrick, D. L., 157
Patrick, J. Max, 141
Patterson, T., 127
Payne, Laurence, 124
Payne, R. J. G., 123
Pearce, Josephine A., 143
Peele, George, 56, 103, 157
Perry, Thomas A., 142
Pettet, E. C., 3, 11, 113
Pettigrew, H. P., 5
Piachaud, René-Louis, 121
Pinero, Sir Arthur W., 131
Plato, 145

Platter, Thomas, 150
Plowman, Max, 9
Plutarch, *see under* North, Sir Thomas
Poel, William, 152
  pioneer work for modern Shakespearian production, 77–8
Pollard, A. W., 3, 81, 82, 98 n., 100–1, 104 n., 105 n.
Pope, Alexander, 52
Pope, Elizabeth M., 12, 16
Porter, Charlotte, 8
Potter, Peter, 125
Powell, Peter, 124
Prange, Gerda, 153
Praz, Mario, 120
Presson, R. K., 11
Price, H. T., 8, 157
Productions of Shakespeare's plays:
  in England, 123–6, 128–9, 132–8
  abroad, 69–73, 118–22
  production of the comedies in England from 1856 discussed, 74–80
Promus and Cassandra, 16, 25, 27 n.
Prouty, C. T., 4–5, 8
Purcell, Henry, *Golden Sonata*, 71
Putney, Rufus, 144

Quayle, Anthony, 137
Quiller-Couch, Sir Arthur, 12, 41, 42, 44

Rabelais, 59
Rainsford family, 7
Raleigh, Sir Walter (1861–1922), 4, 7
Raleigh, Sir Walter (ob. 1618), 6
Raysor, T. M., 26 n.
Rea, J. D., 4
Rees, Joan, 152
Reinhardt, Max, 79, 80
Rey, Jean-Pierre, 118
Reynolds, G. F., 11
Ribner, Irving, 144
Riche, Barnabe, *Farewell to Military Profession*, 4
Ridley, M. R., 'New Arden' edition of *Antony and Cleopatra* reviewed, 157
Roberts, James, 95
Roesen, Bobbyann, 139–40
Rogers, Carmen, 144
Rollins, H. E., 10
Rosalinda, operatic version of *As You Like It*, 75
Rosenberg, Marvin, 142
Rossetti, Christina, 138
Rossiter, A. P., 34

168

INDEX

INDEX

INDEX

This book is to be retu

SHAKESPEARE   SURVEY

THE   COMEDIES

8   57946